Wakefield Press

The Hawke Legacy

The
HAWKE
LEGACY

Edited by Gerry Bloustien,
Barbara Comber and
Alison Mackinnon

Wakefield
Press

Wakefield Press
1 The Parade West
Kent Town
South Australia 5067
www.wakefieldpress.com.au

First published 2009

Cover design by Liz Nicholson, designBITE
Typeset by Wakefield Press
Printed and bound by Hyde Park Press, Adelaide

National Library of Australia Cataloguing-in-Publication entry

Title:	The Hawke legacy/editors Gerry Bloustien, Barbara Comber, Alison MacKinnon.
ISBN:	978 1 86254 864 0 (pbk.).
Notes:	Includes index.
	Bibliography.
	Hawke, Bob, 1929 – Career in politics.
	Australian Labor Party.
	Australia – Politics and government – 1976–1990.
Other Authors/	Bloustien, Gerry.
Contributors:	Comber, Barbara.
	Mackinnon, Alison, 1942- .
Dewey Number:	320.994

University of South Australia | **Hawke** Research Institute

Government of South Australia

Arts SA

fox creek wines

The Hawke Intersections series of books aims
to foster the social sustainability and social
justice goals of the Hawke Research Institute
at the University of South Australia.

Contents

Acknowledgements   vii

Introduction   viii
Gerry Bloustien, Alison Mackinnon and Barbara Comber

PART 1: *Consensus and governance*

1   The Hawke government and consensus   3
Carol Johnson

2   The politics of intimacy: a conversation with Bob Hawke   15
Pal Ahluwalia and Greg McCarthy

3   Legitimacy, governance and consensus:
a candid conversation with Graham Freudenberg   30
Gerry Bloustien

PART 2: *Equity, education and inclusion*

4   Towards gender equality: two steps forward, one step back?
Equal opportunity from Hawke to Rudd   45
Alison Mackinnon

5   Education, equity and the Hawke government   57
Marie Brennan and Alan Reid

6   Equity, globalisation and higher education   70
Ian Davey and Ianto Ware

7   Hawke and Ryan: an acceleration of Indigenous
education policy   83
Peter Buckskin

8   Delineating multicultural Australia   96
Alan Mayne

9   The Hawke legacy: social justice as a right not charity   112
Rosemary Crowley

PART 3: *Health, housing and the environment*

10 Medicare and Australian health policy   125
    Ron Donato

11 Work in progress: developing new directions for affordable
    housing policy in the Hawke/Keating governments   140
    Brian Howe

12 Environment: 'What was right was also popular'   152
    Joan Staples

PART 4: *The economy, work and industrial relations*

13 Economic policy of the Hawke years   167
    Martin Shanahan

14 The best of times, the worst of times: the Hawke and Rudd
    governments, employment and industrial relations   180
    Barbara Pocock

15 The super revolution   198
    Rhonda Sharp

16 Leading the unions:
    sexual politics and international alliances   212
    Suzanne Franzway

Postscript

17 The constant mediator: a tribute   223
    Elizabeth Ho

Contributors   231

Appendix:
Chronology of prime ministers of Australia and
election dates, 1972–2007   241

Index   243

Acknowledgements

The genesis and successful completion of *The Hawke Legacy* relies, as does every publication, on a wide number of colleagues and friends as well as various forms of institutional support. On a formal level we are very grateful to all of the members of the Hawke Research Institute and the Bob Hawke Prime Ministerial Centre for the opportunity to explore and realise this exciting collaborative project from the initial discussions and stimulating conversations and seminars to the final finished papers. Particular thanks must go to Kate Leeson, editor at the Hawke Research Institute, for her wonderful editorial expertise and endless patience. Thanks too for the additional administrative and research support from Laura Fuss, Ianto Ware, Catherine Daniel, Amy Morgan and to Margaret Goedhart and Helen Livingston at the Bob Hawke Prime Ministerial Library. We particularly want to thank Doug McEachern, University of Western Australia, Michael Bollen and Stephanie Johnson for their critical and supportive input and of course very special thanks are due to Graham Freudenberg for agreeing to an interview for this book.

Finally, of course, the greatest debt of gratitude must go to Bob Hawke himself for his leadership and legacy that inspired both this volume and the ongoing work of the Bob Hawke Prime Ministerial Centre and the Hawke Research Institute in their projects for social and economic justice and social inclusion.

Gerry Bloustien
Barbara Comber
Alison Mackinnon

Introduction

Gerry Bloustien, Alison Mackinnon
and Barbara Comber

This collection offers a timely look at the legacy of the Hawke era (1983–1991). As the Rudd Labor government considers its policies and directions, it is appropriate to consider the important lessons from history that might inform the present. The authors engage in a retrospective consideration of what was attempted and achieved by the Hawke government with the benefit of hindsight, considering 'what have we learned?', 'what we have gained?' and 'where are we now?' The collection represents the views of some of Australia's leading scholars who reflect on the legacy of the Hawke era from a variety of disciplinary and activist perspectives at this key junction in Australia's political history.

Bob Hawke, the man

Who is the man, Robert James Lee (Bob) Hawke, AC and whence comes such a legacy? Born 9 December 1929, Bob Hawke was Australia's twenty-third prime minister and he became the longest-serving Australian Labor Party prime minister. He led his party to four federal electoral victories in 1983, 1984, 1987 and 1990.

Born in Bordertown, South Australia, where his father was the Congregational minister, Hawke spent his early years in the country and suburban life in South Australia and then Perth. His uncle, Albert Hawke, an active member of the Labor Party during Bob's early life, became his political mentor and influenced his own attraction to and membership of the party at age seventeen.

He was by all accounts an excellent and popular student, achieving highly at the academically prestigious Perth Modern School and going on to graduate in economics and law at the University of Western Australia. In 1953 he was awarded a Rhodes Scholarship to Oxford University where he completed his studies, undertaking a thesis on wage fixing in Australia.

Back in Australia in 1956 he took on a research role for the Australian Council of Trade Unions, and he was elected president of the ACTU in 1969. Hawke was ACTU president for ten years, and he has been acknowledged as being integral to the transforming of wage fixing in Australia and as the system's best advocate. He developed good relations with unionists but also with his opponents, the employers and government representatives, and this power of negotiation and persuasion, together with his wide national and international networks, were to stand him in good stead in his later political career. Under his stewardship and by his example, the ACTU became heavily involved in international injustices, such as the plight of the 'refuseniks', Jewish people unable to get permission to leave the Soviet Union, and the anti-apartheid demonstrations against the tour of the South African Springboks rugby union team.

In 1971, elected to the federal executive of the Australian Labor Party, Bob Hawke's skills as an effective negotiator, working to resolve industrial disputes through consensus, quickly became his trademark quality. He continued to be active in international labour issues, and in Australia became the most prominent figure in the union movement. He was elected federal president of the Australian Labor Party in 1973, representing the labour movement and the Labor Party on governing and advisory bodies. His belief that trade unions were effective instruments of social reform led him to revitalise the ACTU and widen its scope. A 1975 poll declared him 'the man most wanted as prime minister'.

Hawke's move into federal politics occurred in 1980, when he was elected to the safe Labor seat of Wills. Two years later he challenged Bill Hayden's leadership of the parliamentary Labor Party. Although he lost that bid he had to be taken very seriously as the potential leader who would be most likely to lead the party to victory at the next election. In 1983 Hawke did lead the party to victory in the March elections, promising to bring about a centralised wage-fixing system and national reconciliation between employers and unions. These themes are clearly still evident in the discussions of his legacy below.

The Hawke legacy

In this collection, we bring together the views of scholars and contemporaries from a range of disciplines including politics, education, history, sociology and anthropology to give their analysis of the Hawke era. The majority of these writers are connected in various ways with the University of South Australia's Hawke Research Institute and the Bob Hawke Prime Ministerial Centre – two bodies established to recognise the Hawke era by educating the public and fostering new collaborative research based on his perspectives and concerns with social justice. The authors, including two former members of the Hawke government, have drawn on their personal knowledge of and access to Bob Hawke and to his papers in the Bob Hawke Prime Ministerial Library.

In 2003 Susan Ryan and Troy Bramston published a retrospective collection on the Hawke government (Ryan and Bramston 2003). They claimed that 'the period was and remains enormously significant for Australia' (p. 1). They hoped that through their work the Hawke legacy could 'form the building blocks for the next Labor government' (p. 3). Ryan and Bramston wrote during the Howard years, a period characterised by Hawke as 'not simply the most conservative in our history but, more alarmingly, the most dangerous' (Hawke 2003, p. vii). Now several years later the election of Kevin Rudd and his Labor government offers new scope to pursue policies akin to those espoused by the Hawke government. It also allows us to reconsider those 'building blocks' and revisit the notion that the Hawke era remains significant in the present. There are very differing ideas in our community about the nature of that legacy, as our writers attest. In the midst of global financial turmoil Hawke and Keating's economic reforms are seen as key to Australia's relative financial stability: these were reforms that a conservative, even neo-liberal, government could condone and build upon. On the other hand, some argue that the Hawke era reforms to women's rights have been consistently eroded by a conservative government, occasioning strong comment from critics and some of the authors in this book. It is not yet clear if those rights will be returned and built upon by the Rudd government, although the large number of progressive women in Cabinet offers hope.

This collection presents a challenge to the Rudd Labor government, and to a prime minister with an approval rate rivalling that of Hawke, to reconsider the Hawke era and to continue its legacy. As our authors note, while much was achieved in the Hawke terms of office there is still much unfinished business. While much of the Hawke legacy stands firm – significant economic reform, groundbreaking legislation in the area of health and equal opportunity, for example – other gains were seriously undermined under the Howard government. In some ways the sheer scope of the challenges facing the Rudd government rival those facing the new Hawke government in March 1983.

Hawke came into office facing formidable economic obstacles. Rudd faces even stronger economic challenges. Hawke confronted challenging foreign policy issues, as does Rudd, not least of which is calibrating relationships with countries such as the United States in accord with Australia's national interest. And while Hawke put in place major environmental policies, in relation to the Franklin Dam and Antarctica, for example, the Rudd government has to deal with the looming threat of climate change and the very real disaster of the destruction of the Murray-Darling Basin ecosystem.

The editors of this collection are all involved with the Hawke Research Institute at the University of South Australia, which is the research arm of the Hawke Prime Ministerial Centre. They sought to bring together key researchers in a volume that would reassess the period as outlined above. A workshop was held with many contributors, including two members of the Hawke government who have had continuing involvement with the Hawke Research Institute and the Hawke Library at the University of South Australia – and the rest, as they say, is history. The editors see it as history for not only a new government but for the next generation for whom the Hawke era, indeed anything before the Howard era, is the dim dusty past.

The collection is organised around four main areas for which the Hawke era is renowned in terms of policy action and change:

consensus and governance; equity, education and inclusion; health, housing and the environment; and the economy and work.

Consensus and governance

The first section deals with the way in which Hawke governed, his well-known emphasis on consensus, and his acknowledged ability to bring differing groups to the negotiating table. Carol Johnson, a widely published author on political matters, dissects Hawke's distinctive style and sees his ability to overcome the divisiveness of the previous years as a key element in achieving change. That success, she argues, was in combining social democracy with the emerging neo-liberalism and its support for market-driven economies. She makes a strong case for Labor's innovativeness, arguing that 'long before Blair's Third Way or Gerhard Schroeder's "Neue Mitte" in Germany, Australian Labor governments were trying to find a way between extreme neo-liberalism and old-style Keynesian welfare liberalism'. Johnson's claims are supported in the following chapter, an interview with Bob Hawke by Pal Ahluwalia and Greg McCarthy. Ahluwalia and McCarthy characterise Hawke's politics as 'the politics of intimacy', arguing that Hawke's 'particular form of political and populist sentimentality links intimacy to a shared narrative of equality … vital in producing … a national-popular collective will'.

The interview is striking as it allows Hawke, as he approaches his eightieth birthday, to reflect on his achievements and to canvass his current concerns. Hawke is proud of the 'new conceptual framework' his government produced linking social democracy with a new economic framework.

In the following chapter Gerry Bloustien talks with Graham Freudenberg, Labor historian and one-time speechwriter for Bob Hawke, who also reflects on Hawke's achievements. He claims that Hawke's major achievement was restoring the legitimacy of the Labor Party as a party of government in Australia. That legitimacy had been lost, he argues, through the Cold War and the split in the Labor party over the Vietnam War.

This opening section sets the scene for the chapters that follow, where authors from a wide range of perspectives examine particular policies in detail, testing the strength of the consensus approach –

and the new conceptual framework developed by Hawke and commented on by Johnson and Freudenberg. The reader can also assess the way in which the 'politics of intimacy' and the 'new conceptual framework' manifested themselves in various policy areas.

Equity, education and inclusion

The first five chapters in Section 2 examine particular policies that were concerned in various ways with equity, education and inclusion. These accounts are followed by a personal reminiscence from former Senator Rosemary Crowley, whose lively depictions of life 'in the corridors' reminds us that the final product of parliamentary deliberation was often fiercely contested behind the scenes.

Alison Mackinnon opens this section with an overview of equal opportunity from Hawke to Rudd. She argues that significant legislation was put in place under the Hawke government which, drawing on the strength of the 1970s women's movement and the determination of key ministers, notably Susan Ryan, moved the world forward for women. Many would argue, Mackinnon included, that that legislation was groundbreaking and continues to have a powerful effect: others such as Anne Summers have lamented 'the end of equality'. Brennan and Reid argue that under Hawke conditions were put in place to achieve legitimacy for a national role in school education, working from a strong 'needs-based' equity value position. After the first Hawke term this 'equity' position was firmly tied into the economic agenda and federal educational infrastructure, particularly under John Dawkins, which ironically put in place the means by which equity issues could be stripped out of education in the Howard decade.

Brennan and Reid distinguish between the regimes of education ministers Susan Ryan and John Dawkins – the first animated by notions of equity, the second by a more economically focused agenda. The following authors Davey and Ware, writing about a key moment of change in higher education, also make that distinction. They argue that higher education 'was transformed from small-scale, collegial institutions to a major force in the economic and social life of the country, with an immense increase in the emphasis on student access and equity coupled with a push to strengthen ties to business and industry'.

Both of these education chapters argue that attendance levels, at secondary school and at university, increased enormously during this period, endorsing Hawke's evident pride, manifest in his interview, in the increase in educational opportunities under his government. The access of women to education also rose significantly, an aspect noted in both education chapters.

Taking further the concern with equity at a time of economic reform was the Hawke government's approach to Aboriginal affairs 'progressing the notions of self-management and self-determination by Aboriginal peoples through practical, representative bodies that were able to influence government policy more significantly than Aboriginal voices had ever done before', as Peter Buckskin writes.

Buckskin claims that, while Hawke was not able to fulfil all his promises to Aboriginal people, he did open a vital new era of listening to Aboriginal representative groups and of taking seriously Aboriginal and Torres Strait Islander education.

The issue of equity for people of diverse cultural backgrounds is also spelled out by Alan Mayne in his chapter on multicultural Australia. Mayne argues that those responsible for framing the National Agenda for a Multicultural Australia in 1987–89 produced 'a document that would work, that could be a handbook for all governments and all Australians'. Mayne believes that the agenda endures as the cornerstone for social inclusiveness and tolerance in a culturally diverse nation, concluding: 'It is a credit to Bob Hawke that he initiated, championed and implemented the National Agenda for a Multicultural Australia.'

The chapters in this section all give credit to the Hawke government for much-needed social reform to further equity and diversity within late twentieth-century Australian society. It is these issues that help maintain the social fabric, which contributes to a sustainable society. Yet, as the chapters also document, there was much unfinished business, presenting challenges for a new twenty-first-century Labor government.

Health, housing and the environment

In Section 3 we also hear accounts of policy successes and a sense of unfinished business. Donato outlines the steps by which Medicare, a system of compulsory, national health insurance, came to be accepted on both sides of the Australian political divide, arguing that what was put in place by the Hawke government was eventually accepted by the Coalition in the 1996 election. Yet problems remain; there is business still to be attended to. Specifically Donato mentions 'the complex division of powers and patterns of joint involvement in the funding, provision and regulation of healthcare services between Commonwealth and state governments'.

Brian Howe, formerly Minister assisting the Prime Minister on Federal–State Relations and Minister for Social Security in the Hawke government, and later Housing Minister and Deputy Prime Minister in the Keating government, gives both an insider glimpse and an academic coverage of the problems faced by the Hawke government in its determination to improve housing affordability as part of the social wage. Howe notes the innovative formation of COAG and credits Hawke with providing the vehicle for making housing reform part of a national agenda. More, however, remains for the Rudd government to do to increase housing affordability.

While much more also remains to be done in environmental policy and practices, Joan Staples reminds us of the considerable progress made by the Hawke government, particularly during Environment Minister Graham Richardson's term of office. Staples, herself an Australian Conservation Foundation national liaison officer in that period, points out that most of the significant environmental decisions of the Hawke era were made during Richardson's three-year term. Indeed in 1989, Environment Minister Graham Richardson took a submission to Cabinet for a 20 per cent reduction in greenhouse gas emissions by 2005. This did not happen. It is interesting to speculate where Australia would be in international leadership on environmental matters had that submission been adopted.

The economy, work and industrial relations

In Section 4 we turn to the changes for which the Hawke government is most commonly invoked today: changes in the economy and industrial relations. Martin Shanahan's chapter provides 'a brief overview of the major economic policy changes initiated under the Hawke government, and emphasises the change in economic thinking that became accepted during this time'. As Shanahan remarks, changes that now seem inevitable were not so at the time and required considerable courage and negotiating skills such as those Hawke exhibited in the Accord. The shift to a more market-oriented economy through such mechanisms as floating the exchange rate, taxation reform, trade and financial reform, and restructuring key institutions did not come easily.

Barbara Pocock focuses on issues of employment and industrial change. She also looks closely at the Accord, that centrepiece of consensus, whose 'merits for different classes of interests are contested, [but] there can be no doubt of its political success in allowing the Hawke government to exercise considerable power in restraining wage growth and significantly reshape social policy, not least the health system'. Pocock outlines the transformation of employment during the Hawke years, including the growth of part-time and casual jobs, the increasing participation of women and ironically, given Hawke's background, the decline of unions.

Rhonda Sharp's chapter on the superannuation revolution argues that, 'during the thirteen-year era of the Hawke and Keating Labor governments, Australia's retirement incomes system was transformed through the establishment of a private occupational superannuation funds industry'. Sharp traces the development of superannuation within Labor's economic policy framework. She concludes that, while mandated occupation-based superannuation could be claimed as a policy revolution, 'its privatised, occupational nature makes it a mechanism ... for extending gender, class and race disparities to the aged population'.

Suzanne Franzway considers Hawke's role on the international stage as a union leader, claiming that his strong union leadership also paralleled a period when women gained a stronger place in unions. Hawke was a member of the ILO Governing Body (1972–80) during his time as ACTU president and worked to build Australia's links with the international trade union movement. Franzway argues that the increasingly important place of women in the trade union movement in Australia is aligned with the political legacy of Bob Hawke and his leadership at national and international levels of the labour movement.

In a final tribute Elizabeth Ho reviews the most recent activities of Bob Hawke both in the university centre that bears his name and in the wider community both national and international. She deliberates on his many activities and passions, bearing out the notion of 'the politics of intimacy' alluded to earlier and attesting to Bob Hawke's continuing desire for responsible economic and social reform.

References

Hawke, B. 2003, 'Foreword' in eds S. Ryan and T. Bramston, *The Hawke Government: A Critical Retrospective*, Pluto Press, Melbourne

Ryan, S. and Bramston, T. (eds) 2003, *The Hawke Government: A Critical Retrospective*, Pluto Press, Melbourne

Part 1

Consensus and governance

Chapter 1

The Hawke government and consensus

Carol Johnson

Bob Hawke, like Kevin Rudd, became a Labor prime minister in difficult times. The Rudd government was elected when there were signs of economic problems ahead but virtually nobody was expecting the severity of the global financial crisis. By contrast, the Hawke government came into office in what Hawke had acknowledged to be the worst economic crisis for fifty years (Hawke 1984a, p. 16). Both governments were well aware that they were coming into office at a time of heightened industrial tension. The Hawke government was elected following a period of severe industrial disputation during which unions had achieved some notable successes, resulting in a Liberal government-imposed wages pause. Rudd came into office promising to abolish the Howard government's controversial WorkChoices legislation, which unscrupulous employers had quickly used to reduce pay and conditions.

There are therefore some similarities between the circumstances in which the Rudd and the Hawke governments came into office. Indeed, Rudd's victory speech drew directly on the Hawke legacy by stating that he wished to move beyond the old battles between labour and business to establish a consensus (Rudd 2007, p. 12). I will argue in this chapter that the Hawke government's attempts to do these two things were among the defining features of his government. In the process, Hawke not only established principles that were to be drawn on nearly a quarter of a century later by another

Australian Labor prime minister facing difficult times. Hawke also anticipated developments in social democratic policy that were later to be associated with Tony Blair's 'Third Way' (and indeed, German social democratic and US Clintonite Democrat policies).

Hawke's conception of consensus not only drew on the skills he had developed as a negotiator during his many years with the ACTU; it was also designed to heal the damage that Hawke felt had been done by the Fraser years. In his 1983 election speech, Hawke argued that the period of the Fraser government had been marked by an extraordinary divisiveness that had damaged the Australian social and economic fabric. Consequently:

> We are asking ... for a decision from the Australian people which will declare to the world that the politics of division, the politics of confrontation – the deliberate setting of Australian against Australian – which have debased the national leadership and disfigured the national life for so long, have no part in the true Australian way. (Hawke 1984a, p. 11)

Hawke felt that the divisiveness had been so intense that there was a need for what he termed 'national reconciliation' – a process that would restore the Australian social fabric after the 'politics of division' and the 'vicious cycle of confrontation imposed by seven long years of the Fraser government' (1984a, pp. 13–14). Like Barack Obama's campaign at the end of the presidency of George W. Bush (albeit in a very different context), Hawke successfully mobilised positive emotions to heal what he depicted as a fractured nation.[1] As journalist Paul Kelly noted at the time,

> No other politician in recent years could have run a campaign on reconciliation because the concept refers essentially to the emotional condition of the nation. Only a leader like Hawke, whose relationship with the electorate was deeply emotional, could make such a pitch. (1984, p. 410)

It was a masterly election strategy given that recent research has emphasised the importance of emotion in influencing the opinion of the electorate (Neuman et al. 2007). It was also a strategy related to a particular program for government.

'Reconciliation' is a term that we are now more likely to associate with Indigenous issues but for Hawke the key need for reconciliation at this time was between business and labour. The answer lay in finding the common ground between competing sides: 'Essentially industrial relations is about the pursuit by the two sides of industry of the same objective, i.e. the maintenance, and through time, the improvement of real standards of living' (Hawke 1984a, p. 41). Common ground could exist because Hawke rejected more left-wing views, for example that relations between business and labour were inherently exploitative. By contrast, Hawke believed that business and labour had a shared interest in encouraging a healthy capitalist economy. Economic growth would eventually generate employment and the possibility of higher wages, as well as more revenue for government expenditure on welfare, health and education.

> So often in our affairs the emphasis has been put upon the competing struggle between wage and salary earners and business, and residually, welfare recipients.
>
> I believe we must come to put the emphasis upon the fact that they all have a common goal and therefore a common interest. They all seek the same thing – the maintenance, and through time, an improvement, of their standards of living. The indispensable condition for the achievement of this common legitimate goal is real economic growth – an increase in the per capita output of goods and services. (1984a, p. 66)

Reconciliation involved a process of negotiation and compromise. In order to achieve this, the Hawke government drew on a method that had also been used extensively under the Curtin, Chifley and Whitlam governments, namely the idea of tri-partite advisory bodies in which government, business and unions would be represented. Those previous Labor governments had also believed in the possibility of social harmony in a capitalist society although it was not as explicitly articulated as in Hawke's conception of consensus (Johnson 1989, p. 104 and passim). Such policy processes led to suggestions that the Hawke government was corporatist, in terms of vesting policy making in key interest groups outside of parliament – a concern noted even by some members of his government (Jones 2003, pp. 413, 421).

However, Hawke's views not only drew on previous Australian Labor precedent, they also had similarities with Tony Blair's argument that there are diverse, legitimate stakeholders in the economy.

Consequently, Hawke announced in his 1983 election policy speech that 'a Labor government will establish an economic planning advisory council, representing all governments, business, unions, farmers and consumers' (1984a, p. 17). This was 13 years before Tony Blair made his famous speech about the various 'stakeholders' who needed to work together to create a dynamic economy that would benefit everyone (Blair 1996). Like Blair, Hawke embraced a (watered down) form of market economics that resulted from a melding of social democracy and neo-liberalism.

Social democratic governments may now be re-embracing Keynesianism in the context of the global financial crisis and the perceived failure of neo-liberalism. However, Hawke was coming into office at a time when Keynesian economic policy, with its support for an expanding public and welfare sector, was in decline and neo-liberalism, with its support for market-oriented policies, was on the rise. Indeed, the Whitlam government had already begun to break with Keynesianism in its ill-fated final budget (Australia. House of Representatives 1975). The break with Keynesian economics marked a departure from the views of the Curtin and Chifley governments, although there were links with pre-Keynesian Labor governments such as Scullin's (see further Johnson 1989).

Hawke and his treasurer Paul Keating were therefore in the vanguard of moves by international social democratic parties to embrace aspects of neo-liberalism. The then conventional economic wisdom was that Keynesianism had failed to prevent problems such as stagflation, when stagnation combines with inflation. Excessive government activity was seen to constrain the private sector and lead to lower economic growth which was then detrimental to everyone. Consequently, long before Blair's 'Third Way' or Gerhard Schroeder's 'Neue Mitte' in Germany, Australian Labor governments were trying to find a way between extreme neo-liberalism and old-style Keynesian welfare liberalism (Blair and Schroeder 2000). As Kim Beazley, who had served under Hawke and Keating, wryly put it: what 'others call ... the "Third Way" – we used to call ... government policy' (2000, p. 9).[2]

Blair was quite open about the fact that he had learned from Australian Labor:

I think the positions adopted by the ALP are very good modern left-of-centre positions because they are pro-business, pro-enterprise, but also have a strong commitment to social justice ... There is a tendency for people on the British left to look at Europe and, of course, we have studied what is happening there, but in many ways the ALP has far greater similarities than a lot of the European parties and we share many of the same positions. (*The Australian*, 13 July 1995, p. 4)

Blair had longstanding personal links with Australian Labor figures such as Beazley. Blair visited Australia in the early 1980s; returning in 1990 (and in 1995 under Keating) to observe Australian Labor in office.

Importantly, Hawke never went as far in flirting with neo-liberalism as the Liberal Party did. The Hawke government did pursue strong public sector cutbacks but advocated partial rather than full privatisation (e.g. of Telecom and Qantas). Welfare policies were targeted to those most in need as a way of cutting costs – a compromise that moved beyond previous conceptions of more universal provision while retaining a significant welfare safety net (Castles et al. 1996). The government emphasised getting people off welfare and into work but funded education and training schemes to assist them (thereby rejecting Keynesian policies of direct job creation) (Kerr and Savelsberg 1999, p. 241). Australia's Jobs, Education and Training (JET) scheme, introduced in 1989, was particularly important with its emphasis on encouraging sole parents into the workforce by providing educational training, employment advice and access to child care. British Labour acknowledged its debt to JET policies when it developed a similar scheme (Brown 1997, p. 1). However, while such schemes aimed to cut welfare and public sector provision they still involved considerable activity by government.

Above all, the Hawke government remained on good terms with the union movement, seeing unions as a partner whose cooperation would assist in wage restraint rather than holding to a neo-liberal view that unions were a 'third party' illegitimately intervening in negotiations between workers and employers. Indeed, the Hawke government arguably saw unions as having far more of a role in politics than the Blair government did (see further Johnson and Tonkiss 2002). For Hawke, there was no contradiction between the economic and the social since 'the great goals of equity in the distribution of income and power, and of national reconciliation, will be unattainable in the absence of a strong national economy' (1984b, p. 16). The belief in the common interest in a healthy capitalist economy allowed a reconciliation not only between business and labour but also with all who would receive government benefits and entitlements. It also facilitated the reconciliation between social democracy and a watered down form of market-based neoliberalism.

Moreover, the Hawke government rejected a crucial aspect of neo-liberalism. Neo-liberalism as developed by conservative parties in the US, UK and Australia (under Howard), involved a belief that I have termed elsewhere the 'state-based' model of exploitation, namely that particular forms of special interests were incompatible with a healthy capitalist economy. In that view, 'special interests', often associated with the social movements around issues of race, ethnicity and gender, were 'ripping off' taxpayers by unfairly obtaining state largesse (see further Johnson 2007, p. 180). For Hawke (as for Keating after him), such so-called 'special' interests were legitimate. One reason was that 'in a free and democratic society, the legitimate conflict of interests, the open contests between competing claims, is not only inevitable, but intrinsically valuable' (1984b, p. 17). Nonetheless, if taken to extremes, this conflict of interests could become divisive and dysfunctional, as Hawke believed it had during the Fraser years. The Labor government therefore had a crucial role in helping to forge key areas of common interest, and this lay at the heart of Hawke's conception of consensus.

> As a government what we have tried to do is to seek to identify ourselves, and, by the dissemination of knowledge and information, to assist the community to identify, the areas of conflict which are essentially artificial and the areas of common interest and shared purpose in which agreement is achievable, without any section or group being required to sacrifice their real interests or legitimate goals. (Hawke 1984b, p. 17)

Consequently, Hawke painted a stark picture of the alternative to Labor. He warned that the Liberals, if elected, would introduce a divisive far right agenda (Australia. House of Representatives 1991). As early as 1987, he argued that the non-Labor strategy was to forge a coalition that combined conservative fears of difference and social change with economic self-interest.

> [T]he strategy behind it all is very clear: to use the individual and sectional interests inseparable from times as complex and difficult as these, to exploit the anxieties of the groups which make up the fabric of this society, and to stitch together a temporary coalition of fear and greed. (Hawke 1987b, p. 7)

Hawke would no doubt argue that those are precisely the emotions the Howard government subsequently encouraged in its policies towards Indigenous Australians, feminists, ethnic groups, Muslims and asylum seekers; as well as in its privileging of business interests, attacks on unions and its more general appeals to economic self-interest (see further Johnson 2007, pp. 39–49, 161–184).

By contrast (and the similarities with Obama have already been noted), Hawke aimed to evoke positive emotions such as hope. He had summed up his own position in his 1987 election speech:

> The whole basis of our call to the Australian people at the election in 1983 and again in 1984 was an appeal to this great truth about the Australian community – the truth that the legitimate aspirations of the diverse groups and interests which go to make up the nation can best be achieved not by fighting each other, not by setting group against group, Australians against Australians, but by working together, recognising and respecting each other's rights, fair expectations and fair hopes and aspirations. (1987a, p. 5)

Note that in this formulation Hawke both acknowledges that the national interest can incorporate diverse interests and constructs hopes and aspirations – two buzzwords of early twenty-first century politics – not just in terms of individual aspirations but also, quite legitimately in his view, as group aspirations. Similarly, he celebrated the 'rich diversity' of Australia 'in which there are people from something like 130 lands in our country – all capable of making their contribution to the common good – the future we can share'. He affirmed the 'deep underlying unity' underpinning that diversity (1987a, p. 11).

Rather than seeing arguments for equity by particular groups as reflecting self-serving special interests, Hawke repeatedly reaffirmed

a happy coincidence between the needs of the market and the need
for equity. For example, the Hawke government advocated affirmative action on the basis that the Australian economy could not afford
to lose the contribution and skills of women:

> The Government is determined that women should be able to enter and
> compete in the labour market on an equal footing with men and that
> outdated prejudices or conventions should not prevent them from fully
> participating. Neither individual employers nor the nation can afford
> to waste the valuable contributions which women can, and do, make to
> our economy. (Australia. House of Representatives 1986, p. 862)

Nonetheless, while Hawke normally saw a happy coincidence
between the interests of the market and the interests of diverse
groups in Australian society, he also acknowledged that the market
was not everything. The Labor government has 'never believed that
the only values in life – in the life of our nation, in the life of our
families – are the ones with the dollar tag upon them' (Hawke 1987a,
p. 11). This was particularly true of the environment, where 'the
matchless beauty of our land has a value beyond dollars and cents'
which is why the government would protect the Franklin, Kakadu
and the Daintree (ibid.). Hawke also accepted (as Nicholas Stern was
to emphasise 20 years later) that market failure to cost environmental
consequences adequately was contributing to environmental problems, including climate change (Hawke 1989, pp. 6, 28). Admittedly,
the Hawke government did not propose the major transformation of
the economy that the Rudd government subsequently argued for in
its Emissions Trading Scheme (ibid., pp. 28–37). However, Hawke
did promise that Australia 'will be taking a lead in developing international conventions on climate change' (ibid., p. vi). Unfortunately,
this promise was not pursued so enthusiastically by the Keating government and, in regard to the Kyoto Protocol at least, was positively
opposed by the Howard government.

Assessing the Hawke government

It has been argued in this chapter that Hawke was ahead of his
time in many respects, particularly in terms of an early 'Third Way'
attempt to find a middle ground between neo-liberalism and previous forms of social democracy. However, at a time when main-

stream western governments are re-regulating, partially owning or effectively nationalising major financial institutions as well as funding huge stimulus packages that send their budgets massively into deficit, the Hawke government's economic policies seem problematic. Rudd's claims to be a fiscal conservative at the time of the 2007 election had more in common with Hawke's economic rationalism than his current policies do. Similarly, it would no longer be so acceptable for Hawke to jeer at ALP opponents of privatisation that: 'I hope we are not going to have a troika of Australia, Albania and Cuba' (*The Age*, 25 September 1990). International paradigms are shifting as neo-liberalism is under increasing challenge. Admittedly, one could argue that the Hawke government's deregulation of banking still retained some safeguards that other, more extreme neo-liberal countries such as the US did not, and that those safeguards have helped protect the Australian economy in the current global financial crisis. One could also argue that the Hawke government's industry plans did help to make Australian manufacturing industry more internationally competitive. Nonetheless, one should not join Kevin Rudd in trying to obfuscate the fact that both the Hawke and Keating governments did embrace major aspects of neo-liberalism such as deregulation, privatisation and corporatisation, albeit in a watered down, and arguably more humane form, than the Howard government did (Rudd 2009; see further Johnson 1989, pp. 92–108).

However, I have suggested here that the Hawke government provided a particularly interesting example of the merging of neo-liberalism and social democracy. Hawke's conception of consensus retained a role for social groups, which were meant to work together to achieve common goals. Consequently, the Hawke (and Keating) governments were more prepared to acknowledge the disadvantaged position of gendered, racial and ethnic groups in society than even the Blair government did and completely opposed Howard's view that they were illegitimate special interests (see further Johnson and Tonkiss 2002, p. 13). Hawke was also, incidentally, more likely to recognise the role of social groups than Rudd. At Hawke's economic summit, for example, many participants represented business, labour and welfare organisations. At Rudd's 2020 Summit people were there as individuals – and individuals who were constructed in meritocratic terms as the best and the brightest. Arguably, the post-Howard government ALP is still cautious of arguments that it supports 'special interests'. The Hawke government also involved the union movement far more in decision making than Blair did or Rudd does today. Rudd may be calling on workers to show wage restraint in difficult economic times, as Hawke did before him. However, the Hawke government engaged in a formal Accord process to negotiate social wage compensations.

Nonetheless, it proved less easy to reconcile interests, and achieve consensus, than Hawke had hoped. Sections of business felt that, despite years of wage restraint (and indeed real wage cuts), the Hawke and Keating governments had not gone far enough in cutting wages and conditions or reducing the influence of unions. Indeed, by the time of the Howard government's WorkChoices legislation, some sections of business seemed to feel that they no longer needed the cooperation of unions at all. Social movements were also critical. Feminists complained that the Hawke government's economic rationalism had resulted in detrimental outcomes for women, both in terms of the impact of particular economic policies and public sector cutbacks to women's services (see e.g. Sharp and Broomhill 1989; Sawer 1990; Johnson 1990). Welfare advocates also pointed out the tensions between the direction of economic policy and the need to secure the social safety net (Disney 2003, p. 227).

There are therefore significant criticisms that can be made of the Hawke government. Admittedly, Hawke was merely engaging with the economic orthodoxy of his day (as Scullin had earlier with market-driven economics and as Curtin and Chifley had subsequently with Keynesianism). The government also hoped that it was developing a more humane melding of social democracy and neo-liberalism that would avoid what Hawke saw as the excesses of 'contemporary versions of laissez-faire'. Hawke argued that his 'stress on national cohesion, co-operation, equity and consultation – all great principles of social democracy – are the antithesis to the economically libertarian approach which has flourished in the stagnant, divided industrial world in recent years' (1984b, p. 23). He singled out John Howard as exemplifying that approach as, indeed, Howard's WorkChoices policies arguably did. Above all, in attempting to forge a compromise between social democracy and neo-liberalism, Hawke was a pioneer of the approach that was later to be known as the 'Third Way'. Whatever criticisms can be made retrospectively, Hawke's was a highly innovative government that deserves both more national, and international, study.

Notes

1   See e.g. Obama's speech offering hope and 'unity over division' (Obama 2008).

2   Beazley also acknowledged the innovative role of New Zealand Labour governments.

References

Australia. House of Representatives 1975, *Debates*, B. Hayden, 'Budget Speech', 19 August, pp. 52–53

Australia. House of Representatives 1986, *Debates*, B. Hawke, 19 February, p. 862

Australia. House of Representatives 1991, *Debates*, B. Hawke, 19 December, p. 3775

Beazley, K. 2000, 'Foreword' to J. Claven, *The Centre is Mine: Tony Blair, New Labour and the Future of Electoral Politics*, Pluto Australia, Annandale

Brown, C. 1997, 'Blair plans to call lone parents to the jobcentre', *Independent*, 24 January, p. 1

Blair, T. 1996, 'The stakeholder economy', speech to the Singapore Business Community, January, in T. Blair, *New Britain: My Vision of a Young Country*, Fourth Estate, London

Blair, T. and Schroeder, G. 2000, 'The Third Way/die Neue Mitte', *Dissent*, Spring, pp. 51–65.

Castles, F. et al. (eds) 1996, *The Great Experiment: Labour Parties and Public Policy Transformation in Australia and New Zealand*, Allen and Unwin, Sydney

Disney, J. 2003, 'Social impacts of the Hawke years', in eds S. Ryan and T. Bramston, *The Hawke Government: A Critical Retrospective*, Pluto Press, North Melbourne

Hawke, B. 1984a, *National Reconciliation: The Speeches of Bob Hawke*, Fontana Collins, Sydney

Hawke, B. 1984b, *Principles in Practice: The First Two Years*, Australian Fabian Society Pamphlet, 43, Australian Fabian Society, Melbourne

Hawke, B. 1987a, Election Campaign Policy Launch, Sydney Opera House, 23 June, typescript

Hawke B. 1987b, 'Our fourth anniversary', Bathurst, 8 March, typescript

Hawke, B. 1989, *Our Country, Our Future: Statement on the Environment*, Australian Government Publishing Service, Canberra

Johnson, C. 1989, *The Labor Legacy: Curtin, Chifley, Whitlam, Hawke*, Allen and Unwin, Sydney

Johnson, C. 1990, 'Whose consensus? Women and the ALP', *Arena*, no. 93, pp. 97–104

Johnson, C. 2007, *Governing Change: From Keating to Howard*, Network Books, Perth

Johnson, C. and Tonkiss, F. 2002, 'The third influence: the Blair government and Australian Labor', *Policy and Politics*, vol. 30, no. 1, pp. 5–18

Jones, B. 2003, 'The Hawke government: an assessment from the inside' in eds S. Ryan and T. Bramston, *The Hawke Government: A Critical Retrospective*, Pluto Press, North Melbourne

Kelly, P. 1984, *The Hawke Ascendancy: A Definitive Account of its Origins and Climax 1975–83*, Angus and Robertson, Sydney

Kerr, L. and Savelsberg, H. 1999, 'Unemployment and civic responsibility in Australia: towards a new social contract', *Critical Social Policy*, vol. 19, no 2, pp. 233–255

Neuman, W.R. et al. (eds) 2007, *The Affect Effect: Dynamics of Emotion in Political Thinking and Behavior*, University of Chicago Press, Chicago

Obama, B. 2008, 'Iowa caucus night', Des Moines, 3 January, http://www.barackobama.com/2008/01/03/remarks_of_senator_barack_obam_39.php, accessed 5 May 2009.

Rudd, K. 2007, 'Time to roll up sleeves for the future', *The Australian*, 26 November, p. 12

Rudd, K. 2009, 'The global financial crisis', *The Monthly*, February, p. 25

Sawer, M. 1990, *Sisters in Suits: Women and Public Policy in Australia*, Allen and Unwin, St Leonards, NSW

Sharp, R and Broomhill, R. 1989, *Short-Changed: Women and Economic Policies*, Allen and Unwin, St Leonards, NSW

Chapter 2

The politics of intimacy: a conversation with Bob Hawke

Pal Ahluwalia and Greg McCarthy

The following is a transcription of an interview that was conducted in the Sydney office of former Prime Minister Bob Hawke on 6 April 2009.

In this interview, Mr Hawke traverses considerable ground, reflecting upon his days as a student, his time with the trade union movement including his leadership of the ACTU, his period in government and his life after a highly successful political career. The interview reflects his international character, his vast intellectual concerns and his far-reaching influence. Above all, these myriad experiences were underpinned by a particular politics of intimacy that has marked both his public and private life.

The very nature of the politics of intimacy is that it is located not only in the public domain but also manifested within the private realm. His recollection of inviting visiting Asian students to the privacy of his home at a time when the White Australia Policy was in force is testament to Bob Hawke's generosity and friendship.

Bob Hawke often came across as a leader with whom the population could identify, the leader who could weep with the nation as the tragedy of Tiananmen Square unfolded or share in the joy of Australia's America's Cup win in the early hours of the day, declaring at a press conference that 'Any boss who sacks a worker for not turning up today is a bum'. It is this form of political and populist sentimentality that links intimacy to a shared narrative of equality, which is so vital in producing, in Gramscian terms, a national-popular collective will (Berlant 1997). It is this intimacy that drove Bob Hawke's political engagement with perhaps the most expansive social democratic reform agenda that the nation has ever faced. The ramifications of that reform agenda continue to reverberate today as we continue to evaluate the full impact of the Hawke legacy.

PA/GM: Let us begin by saying that you have been on a remarkable journey and that you will be turning 80 soon. Is there anything that you would have done differently?

Hawke: Inevitably the answer to that question is coloured by the fact that you know what's happened subsequently. Without wanting to leave the impression that I don't think I've made mistakes, there's nothing significant that I would have done differently.

What was, I think, in a sense unique about my experience was that I spent a lot of time living another life before going into parliament, and it's one of the things I say to young people now when I talk to them. A lot of kids want to get into parliament very early, and my advice to them is to make a life, make a contribution, before trying to rush into parliament. I was extraordinarily fortunate having had what many people regard as the second most important job in Australia, running the trade union movement, which was a very powerful force in those days, and it was a marvellous training ground for the next job.

PA/GM: Kevin Rudd recently published his most ideological piece in *The Monthly* critiquing neo-liberalism. How much of this do you think can be traced to your own ideological predilection, or is this a major departure from the past?

Hawke: No, I think I laid down a new direction for the social democrats. The best way of looking at that is that after I'd been prime minister for a while I had a visit from two young British MPs from the Labour Party. They came out to see me and said they'd been impressed by the things I'd done, the new directions I'd taken over the movement, and they asked me to explain a little to them. I spent two or three hours with them going through it, and they were taking furious notes, and went off. The two blokes were Tony Blair and Gordon Brown. I always had a bit of a laugh when I heard about Blair's Third Way. I mean essentially they drew very much upon what we'd done.

PA/GM: It seems to us that you set the benchmark for modern social democracy in Australia.

Hawke: We did set a new conceptual framework. I mean we were different from anything gone before. I had the view that the basic economic driving force in the world today is private enterprise, the way in which people harness capital and labour through the incentive of growing richer and building their enterprises. That thrust was necessary. But it had to be harnessed in a way that recognised the social obligations of industry and of government, and so that was the whole point of the summit,[1] which was underpinned by a sense of reconciliation of interests, and all the success, as I said, brought them together. Essentially I said in the summit to business, 'Your aspirations are absolutely legitimate to grow your businesses and prosper.' I said to the unions, 'Your aspiration is to improve, through time, the wages and conditions of employees and this is absolutely legitimate.' I said to the welfare sector, 'Your aspiration is to see that people who depend on social welfare gradually, through time, get a share of it. Absolutely legitimate. All your aspirations are much more likely to be achieved if we cooperate rather than brawl.' And then I laid out my plan to them, because the Australian economy was an absolute bloody mess.

What Lee Kuan Yew had said in 1980 was right. 'The way Australia is going it's going to end up as the white trash of Asia.' He was right, so we had to make fundamental changes, but we could only do that with an understanding of all the parties. So I instructed Treasury at the start of the summer, I said, 'Look, every delegate has got to have all the information, economic information, about the state of the Australian economy and where we're going.'

So at the summit they had all the information and I said, 'Now, if the Australian economy is going to recover we must work together.' What I went to the election with was the three Rs: reconciliation, recovery and reconstruction. So the summit was reconciliation and then we laid down the plans for recovery, because we were at 11 per cent unemployment and 11 per cent inflation, and things had to be reconsidered through reconciliation, and then reconstruction followed. The basic thing that had to be done to get this to happen was genuine consensus, and they cooperated. We got a unanimous communiqué out of it, so this was all new. No-one had done this before.

PA/GM: And it was a very different politics of consensus in terms of the Accord. You built up respect and trust through your ACTU period. A lot of business people really trusted you.

Hawke: The employers trusted me, they knew that I was a reasonable man, and the trade unions obviously trusted me, so I had a good basis from which to do it. I probably came to the prime ministership better prepared in an economic sense than anyone before me, because I not only had academic qualifications as an economist, but all that period as advocate and president of the ACTU. I was in a very detailed sense involved in what was happening in the Australian economy. I was a member of both the Jackson and Crawford inquiries into the Australian economy set up by Whitlam and Fraser. I was appointed by each of those prime ministers, so by the time I came to the prime ministership I really knew the Australian economy as well as anyone in the country, in a sense.

PA/GM: We want to raise with you the three Rs. Why were they necessary, at that particular moment in Australian politics?

Hawke: Well if you look at Australia in 1983 as we came to that election, people tend to forget just how riven the Australian society was. So it just seemed to me, as I thought through it logically, the first thing before you started talking about the actual policies, you actually had to have a reconciliation, a bringing together of people, a creation of the understanding that I talked about before. They all had legitimate aspirations but they had to see those aspirations in the light of others' equally legitimate aspirations. Once they understood that you could then explain to them the steps that had to be taken in terms of immediate recovery, and then reconstruction, so it was a perfectly logical exercise as far as I was concerned.

PA/GM: We would like to turn to foreign policy and Australia's engagement with Asia.

Hawke: From a very early stage at the University of Western Australia (my first year at university was 1947), there were a lot of overseas students there, and I became very close to them. I founded the International Club because I was terribly worried that they were just living in little enclaves and they were not getting the best out of us, and we weren't getting the best out of them. So I used to go to their homes, their digs, and I'd eat with them, and I'd have them home to me, and I developed a genuinely close affection towards these people. I could see that Asia was growing in importance. I continued to have that view right through.

And then the first press conference I had as prime minister, the first press conference for international correspondents, I said Australia's future depended very much on the extent and the way it became enmeshed in Asia. That would determine more than anything else what the quality and standard of life in Australia would be into the future. So I had developed consistently over quite a period of time this conviction about the importance for Australia of Asia, and moved then very rapidly. I had the opportunity to move very quickly because Fraser had actually invited the premier of China, Zhao Ziyang, while he was still premier, and so I entertained Zhao Ziyang within just a couple of weeks of becoming prime minister; the new parliament hadn't been brought together. We established an extremely cordial and close relationship, and so much so that in that period of the 80s it was recognised that I had a closer relationship to the Chinese leadership than any other western leader, and I actually acted as a go-between on some things between the United States and China.

So it was, for me, something that was not just a spur of the moment thing in '83. It had risen out of my intellectual and emotional conviction about the importance of Asia, and I'd been very much involved within the party in throwing out the White Australia Policy. That was Dunstan's legacy and I more than anyone extended the legacy to Asia and so I saw Australia's future with Asia.

PA/GM: On China, we wonder how much engagement with China is constantly hampered by domestic politics in Australia.

Hawke: I think more and more Australian people do realise that whatever historical prejudices they may have had, and vestigially may still retain, that objectively what I said in '83 is right, that our economic welfare, the well-being of each individual Australian, is going to depend very much upon us having an effective relationship with Asia. It tends to be talked about mostly in economic terms, which is important. I mean now Asia is far and away our major trading destination: 70 per cent of our exports go there. China is our single most important trading partner. But you know there is more than this. One of the things that tends to be overlooked and which is very important is education. Of all the foreign students in Australia, 23 per cent of them are Chinese, the biggest single component, and people don't realise the economics that go with education. Education earns export income for us more than the combined income of wheat, wool and meat.

This is important not only in strict, immediate economic terms but these kids are going to go back and occupy positions of importance in industry and government and so on, and it's impossible to measure the importance. The continuing sense of this relationship is why it's very important that we treat these people well when they're here, and make them feel at home.

PA/GM: One of the points you make in your memoirs is that you see a link between economic development and democracy.

Do you think that this intertwined path is where China is heading?

Hawke: I went to China first in 1978, so my period with China coincides exactly with the opening up, the move towards a market economy. And if you compare the China of today with that China, it's almost unrecognisable.

An article that's very well worth reading is by a man called Henry Rowan. I think it's called 'The short march: China's road to democracy', and it was written in about 1996, and he writes about the way in which China has moved to a more democratic society. He uses three criteria, as I recall. One was the rule of law; one was the freedom of the press; and one was the elections, village elections and so on. And he makes the point that what's happened is remarkable, and he made a pretty good attack upon the America media. He compared the number of positive stories about these sorts of things with all the negative stories in the five major media outlets at the time, *Newsweek, New York Times, Wall Street Journal* and the *Washington Post*. Over a period of time the ratio was 100:1 negative to positive stories. He said, 'If you're objective about it and look at it, you can see this is happening.' It's going on. It will continue to go on.

PA/GM: When you came into office you stressed reconciliation. This takes me to the Indigenous question in the country, and I guess what's always fascinated us is Keating's Redfern speech. It is seen as a kind of inauguration of a different engagement with Indigenous Australians, but we have always wondered how much of that road was paved by your own conviction and your agenda of reconciliation.

Hawke: Paul [Keating] had to do a job and it was a great speech, but he did have the advantage of the *Mabo* decision. Before the *Mabo* decision, politically we had the problem of some state governments who were less than cooperative with reconciliation and very difficult, particularly the Western Australian government of [Brian] Burke, and it did frustrate me. I would have liked to have done more. But I established personally a very close working relationship with the Aboriginal people. I had a good relationship with them, and I think that, really, the concept of reconciliation did lay the basis upon which they were able to move subsequently on that.

Moreover, on the intervention, I have mixed feelings about it. You've got the foundational facts that there's an awful situation up there of abuse, of kids in particular, by Aboriginal men, and abuse of Aboriginal women, and it's awful. I think that experience has shown that there have been some pluses with the concept, but there have certainly been minuses. I think it's the sort of thing that I'd like to see the government sit down and do more work on, in consultation with the Aboriginal people, starting on the premise that we are not laying down, that we are concerned about the fact that your people are being abused by your own people, and we want to create the framework within which we can do the utmost we can to eliminate that. So I think there's more work to be done.

PA/GM: What about the dismantling of ATSIC and Aboriginal sovereignty?

Hawke: One of the unfortunate facts of life was that within the framework of ATSIC there was some abuse of power by some of the Indigenous people, and that was unfortunate. But I think my overall point now would be that the most important issue is the one of disadvantage in education, housing and health, and the issue of abuse, that the concentration of efforts should be on those things rather than structures of government. That's something that can follow. I mean, in terms of priority, that's what I'd be concentrating on.

PA/GM: Moving on to multiculturalism, when you came into office you must have been conscious of UK race riots, and the way race always plays a huge role in US politics, so was there something you were concerned about in introducing your policies that really allowed John Howard to pick on multiculturalism, and the Howard/Hanson factor which drove that particular ethnic/race wedge?

Hawke: Let's go back. That question, in a sense, is based upon a negative, a quasi-negative, view about Australian attitudes. I think to be fair we've got to look at the history of it. At the end of the Second World War, we were 98.5 per cent Anglo-Celt of a 7 million population. Now in that period after the end of this war, and this was one of the things that brought me into the Labor Party, I was just absolutely supportive of a massive immigration program, and getting rid of the White Australia Policy. And when you think about it, there's probably been no other country in history that has undergone such a massive transformation in its ethnicity and cultural bases as Australia has done in such a short time, and so peaceably, genuinely peaceably. So my point is that I defend Australia's achievement and attitudes, while recognising that within that there are still some obvious and latent rednecks, but I think the emphasis should be upon the enormous achievement there has been. I was absolutely committed when I became prime minister that we should draw upon the strength of this infusion from so many different sources. We are economically and culturally enriched as a nation by what's happened, and we've got to build upon this. We become stronger as people that have come from different countries are able to express their own culture, and so on, in the framework of commitment to Australia.

PA/GM: We want to ask you about the two Iraq wars and the differences between them.

Hawke: Well the fundamental difference was that in the first case you'd had a sovereign independent country invaded, without provocation, by another country, which was threatening not only the lives and welfare of the citizens of that country, but posing an associated threat in the region. If you'd allowed that then the whole basic system in those relations was going to fall away, and you can't tolerate that sort of situation. And I was close to George Bush and made it clear that we'd be in there supporting it, on the basis that he had a United Nations mandate, and of course he had. He had an enormously broad coalition, including a significant number of Arab states, Islamic states, and so we were there supporting him on that basis.

It was very interesting in the latter part of it when it was very quickly over, and I thought it would finish quickly, and we had an interesting discussion with our military people. They thought it was going to take a long time and I said, 'I don't think you know your own business. It's going to finish much quicker.' They laughed and they offered me a generalship, you know. But the most interesting moment of course was when Bush rang me up and said he was under a lot of pressure to go on to Baghdad and what did I think about that. I said it would be absolutely improper and immoral. I said, 'You've got to justify the action and the gathering of the coalition on a very clear basis, a United Nations mandate to get them out of Kuwait. You have no mandate to go on', and he said 'Thanks Hawke.' He said, 'That's exactly what I think.'

PA/GM: You've had a longstanding interest in the Middle East, and it does seem to be such a fraught area of the world. How do you see the Middle East in terms of your larger belief in reconciliation? Do you think you've changed some of your views on the region over time?

Hawke: I have, you know, a specific proposition about the whole question of the Middle East in particular, but it's related to the broader question of the Muslim world and terrorism. I mean, I've had the proposition about how to resolve the Palestinian–Israeli thing and put it in writing. My ideas are now being pushed before Obama. I presented it first to Colin Powell, when he was still the Secretary of State, and I called it the Power Plan for Palestine. It's based on the concept of the Marshall Plan. I've said that if you look at the whole history of Palestine/Israel since the creation of Israel, all the talking about how to settle it has been erroneously based. It's all been politics: where are the dividing lines, what do you do with Jerusalem, and so on. The basic issue is you've got to create a viable Palestinian economy. So my proposal was that the United States should take the lead in pouring in hundreds of billions of dollars in there, to create an economy, education system, give the kids education, jobs and hope. I said, 'You'd change the whole mindset, the whole mindset of the Islamic world about the United States and what the relationship is.' And that still remains my fundamental view. If that were done you would, as I say, change the mindset of the whole thing. But the Islamic world thinks of the United States as just the handmaiden of Israel, anti-Islamic. Whereas if the US went in and said 'We are going to create a Palestine, a viable Palestine for you', the whole thing would change. The political considerations about the divide would be much easier, and the people are going to be much more receptive to compromise in that situation than if it's just drawing a line. In fact in many ways creating a State of Palestine and not doing anything about creating a viable economy would make it worse.

I have the view that the greatest threat to a peaceable world is religious fanaticism. That threat of terrorism is real, and it's a greater threat now than it's ever been. I just think that doing everything we can to increase dialogue between the Muslim and non-Muslim world to get practical measures of cooperation going, the more likely we are to create a situation at least minimising the risk of these things.

One of the issues, it's not really talked about, is that within the Muslim world the Shiah–Sunni conflict is real and it's been going on for centuries and centuries, but it's getting more significant. Muslim economies generally are underdeveloped, and if you look at it historically, the condition of Europe moving towards economic growth was bringing to an end the religious wars. Until religious wars came to an end, and that was out of the way, Europe wasn't ready to grow economically. And within the Muslim world they've got to get a basis of cooperation and understanding, rather than conflict. There's no reason why the state of the Muslim economies should be so abysmal, but they are.

PA/GM: It's interesting just reflecting on your own life, being the son of a clergyman, how you've been able to have such a balanced view of religion.

Hawke: Well, my father was the most tolerant man I've ever met and he saw good in everyone, and he taught me tolerance. He said, 'If you believe in the fatherhood of God then you must necessarily believe in the brotherhood of man.'

PA/GM: The last thing we want to ask you is your reflections on education.

Hawke: When I came to power under 33 per cent of our kids finished secondary school, which was pathetic by international standards in developed countries, and we pushed it up to 75 per cent by targeted financial incentives, which were means tested. I've had certain fundamental beliefs, I've talked about them, the equality of human beings is one, and the other is education, the importance of education, and the creation of equality of opportunity in education. These are, to me, the most fundamental things about a decent society.

I was fortunate. I had a mother who was passionate about education. She was a school teacher herself, and I remember her saying to me, she said, 'Bobby, you've been blessed, you've got brains', she said, 'but you've got to use them and work with them', and so on. So she instilled into me the importance of developing whatever talents you're blessed with. One of the first things that struck me overwhelmingly when I went to the ACTU in 1958, all the blokes – and they were all men; there were no women officials then – there were fellows there that could have been doctors, lawyers, architects, but they'd come from a generation where they hadn't been able to finish their education. Some hadn't finished primary, most of them hadn't finished secondary, and I saw these blokes of dedication, commitment and talent, who could have been anything, giving themselves to helping other people. That reinforced with me just how important it is to have educational opportunities. You know, there's nothing more objectionable to me than that because a kid comes from a rich family they're more likely to get their talents developed than if they come from a poor family.

PA/GM: One of the things about global reconstruction is that there would obviously be winners and losers in globalisation. Do you think the balance was right?

Hawke: Well we've got to recognise that there have been a lot of winners out of globalisation. Not just business, but a lot of people in the developing countries have been helped by the process. It's not just the difference between developed and undeveloped countries. One of the most staggering things is, if you look at what's happened within the United States, one of the most fascinating statistics is that three decades ago the ratio between the income of a CEO and his average employee was about 35:1. Before the onset of globalisation and neo-liberalism it was about 350:1. And real wages had actually gone down in the United States, so one hopes that out of this, and there is obvious evidence of it, that there's going to be moves to contain executive salaries in the finance and business sector. But the most basic thing that can be done in an immediate sense is to give access to the markets of the developed countries to the developing countries for their agricultural projects.

PA/GM: Well really it goes back to your setting of APEC and the whole Cairns Group agenda, because you've had a long-held notion of opening up trade links.

Hawke: Well the Cairns meeting was all about strengthening our negotiating position to move towards a liberalised international trading system.

APEC is still doing good things. There are two aspects to it. One is the undramatic and unadvertised work that the subcommittees do, and officials working on things like trying to get some uniformity in customs regulations machinery, not the actual mechanics of moving goods and services across borders. These officials are continuing to do important work in those sorts of areas. That's one thing.

The second thing is that the leaders' meeting is still important. It's the only venue regularly once a year where they come together and can talk about the issues of the region, so it's still relevant.

PA/GM: What do you think is happening with the climate change agenda?

Hawke: Obama seems to be serious about it. So I hope that Copenhagen produces something, and I think the pressures and the increasing evidence that's coming out, there's hardly a week goes by where you don't get another bit of pretty damning evidence, I hope they'll have enough sense to start to move in Copenhagen.

PA/GM: Is there anything you want to add as a final remark?

Hawke: Well, one point I'd like to make is that I think our experience has shown that while we're a small country, we can have, if we're intelligent, hardworking and imaginative in our approach to issues, that we can have an effect far beyond our numbers. I'd just like to mention two things that happened on my watch, and I'm not saying this in a boastful way but I think this objectively demonstrates the validity of the observation.

Not necessarily in the order of importance, but apartheid, you know, I took the lead in the Commonwealth on that. We started off with trade embargoes and sanctions. They didn't work so I went to the Commonwealth Heads of Government meeting in Canada and said 'Look, these are not working', and I said, 'It seems to me the only possibility where we may be able to bring these bastards down is if we can have an effective investment sanction.' It was the investment ban that brought apartheid to an end. Now that was something that was Australian.

Secondly, the Antarctic Treaty, banning mining in Antarctica. My Cabinet said 'No, there's nothing you can do about it', and I said, 'We can.' We did. We went over and worked with the French and now we've got bans on mining in Antarctica. Thirdly, bringing peace to Cambodia. That was us.

PA/GM: Thank you very much.

Hawke: It's my pleasure.

Notes

1   National Economic Summit, April 1983.

References

Berlant, L. 1997, 'The subject of true feeling: pain, privacy and politics' in ed. A. Sarat, *Cultural Pluralism, Identity Politics and the Law*, University of Michigan Press, Ann Arbor

Rowan, H. 1996, 'The short march: China's road to democracy', *National Interest*, no. 57, pp. 61–70

Rudd, K. 2009, 'The global financial crisis', *The Monthly*, February, p. 25

Chapter 3

Legitimacy, governance and consensus: a candid conversation with Graham Freudenberg

Gerry Bloustien

Graham Freudenberg – noted Labor historian, journalist, speech-writer, press secretary, author and former member of the Council of the National Library of Australia – is arguably best known for his roles as press secretary, speechwriter and political adviser to three federal Labor leaders and three New South Wales Labor premiers. He advised Arthur Calwell (federal opposition leader) from 1961 and Gough Whitlam (federal opposition leader) from 1967.

He has written speeches for several leaders of the Australian Labor Party at both the state and federal level including Arthur Calwell, Gough Whitlam, Bob Hawke, Neville Wran, Barrie Unsworth, Bob Carr and Simon Crean. He was inducted as a life member of the NSW ALP in June 2005.

Graham Freudenberg's own books include: A Certain Grandeur: Gough Whitlam in Politics *(1977);* Cause for Power: the Centenary History of the NSW Labor Party *(1991);* A Figure of Speech *(2006); and most recently* Churchill and Australia *(2008).*

Born in Brisbane in 1934 to parents who took an active interest in politics, Freudenberg says he was inspired to consider a career in journalism at the tender age of 12, after reading a biography of Disraeli. He believed that journalism would be a means to entering politics. In 1952 he was offered a cadetship with the Brisbane Telegraph, a job that soon was followed by several other newspaper appointments before he left for London in 1953. In England he became more politically radicalised due to his close proximity to the unfolding international events at this time. In many interviews and particularly in his autobiography, A Figure of Speech, Freudenberg speaks of his reasons for returning to Australia in the 1950s including gaining the position of Deputy News Editor of Channel 9 television station. There he finetuned his skills of writing speedily and effectively which were to serve him so well in future years as speechwriter and policy advisor.

This chapter is drawn from a candid discussion recorded specifically for this book, with Gerry Bloustien from the Hawke Research Institute.[1] Here Graham talks about what he sees as Bob Hawke's personal legacy to politics, the nation and above all to the Labor Party itself.

Restoring the legitimacy of the Labor Party

The first thing I must say is I'm not really an authoritative source on the inner workings of the Hawke government. This was because I was being shared between the Wran government and the Hawke government, and as I say in my book, *A Figure of Speech*, this was not really fair to either of them, but suited me down to the ground. No one knew where I was, you see, or where I was supposed to be. But having said that, of course I've watched with varieties of joy, frustration and exasperation the rise of Bob Hawke. And overwhelmingly it was with joy and pride that I was able to be part of it.

In terms of Hawke's legacy I want to emphasise not so much his policy and policy achievements, though they were very considerable, of course, but rather the legacy for the Australian Labor Party. What Hawke did was to restore and establish for all time, I believe, the legitimacy of the Australian Labor Party as a party of government in Australia. Now this is something of an obsession or preoccupation of mine, because I see that as the crucial question for the Labor Party for the whole of the last half of the twentieth century, from the postwar period to the twenty-first century. I've always maintained that the denial of Labor's legitimacy as the party of government was the root cause of the dismissal [of the Whitlam government].

You might ask how a party founded in 1891, with the extraordinary record of success more than failure, such as the Australian Labor Party, how could its legitimacy ever be denied? But in fact that is what happened. You would have wondered, for instance, that having the great wartime governments of Curtin and Chifley after the abysmal failure of the Menzies and Fadden governments in 1941, how could such a party that had led Australia triumphantly through the war, and so successfully in the postwar reconstruction period, have its legitimacy denied? But so it happened, and I believed it happened through the baleful politics of the Cold War. This led to the split in the party and the loss for a time of the very substantial element of the Labor Party's Catholic support, which was always crucial to its success.

In later years this was epitomised by the opposition to the war in Vietnam. I'm talking here about the 1960s, and it's always forgotten how very popular the Vietnam War was, and, until at least the middle of 1968, how difficult and resented by the establishment the opposition to the Vietnam War really was. It was a popular war because it was an American war. And it was inconceivable to most of the Australian public that the United States might be wrong again in Vietnam, and inconceivable that they wouldn't win that war. When Arthur Calwell said 'America will be humiliated if this war goes on', it was regarded as a quite absurd and unpatriotic statement, because our stances of patriotism were measured by our loyalty to the American alliance. The combination of the Cold War and the split over Vietnam led to a very serious loss of Labor's legitimacy and electability.

That of course was Whitlam's task: to make the party electable again. Well, he succeeded in that, but as we can now see, and it's been put on the record, the Liberal Party, the Coalition, never accepted that the 1972 election was a legitimate act. It was just the act of a few. Senator Withers, the architect of the strategy that led to the dismissal, dismissed the success of the election as just an aberration from a few people in the western suburbs of Sydney and Melbourne. This denial of the legitimacy of that election persisted, and it wasn't altered even by the 1974 double dissolution. We won the election, but they continued their strategy just as they did before, and that strategy was based on the concept that an elected Labor government was not really legitimate because the people didn't know what they were doing. And because the people *shouldn't* have elected a Labor government, in effect they *hadn't* elected a Labor government. That was the pervasive attitude,

My own contention, and I think I argue it conclusively, is that the dismissal itself could only occur – the blocking of supply, and Kerr's intervention, every event that happened in the breach of convention by which the Senate was rigged – all these happened because of the denial of Labor's legitimacy to govern, and the legitimacy of those elections. So we ended in 1975 with a crushing denial of Labor's legitimacy, and it was miraculous that we survived that.

So Whitlam had talked up the Labor Party, had restored the sense of hunger for government. That was another thing about the Labor Party before 1972, and it was encouraged again by the events of 1975, that in large sections of the party there was this belief that government really didn't matter. That it was better to be a principled opposition and stand up for grand principles, than actually to be in that squalid business of government. It was a pervading thing, particularly in Victoria, but Whitlam restored the sense of hunger for office and the need for government. We realised that if we were going to achieve anything it had to be through government in a democracy. There was just no alternative.

But of course he had not restored that sense of legitimacy. I suppose the easiest way to define this is we were not seen as a natural government of Australia. For all those years we were denied that role as a natural government. In fact by definition a Labor government was unnatural, an aberration, and that's what I mean by the denial of our legitimacy.

Now Bob Hawke, both by winning four elections, and by the achievements of the Hawke government did, I believe, permanently restore that legitimacy. Of course the significant thing is that by the tenth anniversary of the dismissal we were in government in the nation and every mainland state.

Up to the Western Australian election we were even better: we had every state and territory and the national government. So from 1983 to the present you can see the absolute transformation. For a period around 1969 we had no governments anywhere in Australia, and never looked like having any governments anywhere in Australia, even in New South Wales. New South Wales had been devastated after 1965. In 1969 our biggest government was the Brisbane City Council, but by 1985 we had four of the mainland governments and the national government. And so it's continued. No-one would ever question Labor's legitimacy now.

You don't hear the expression 'being born to rule' now, but in fact that was a very real factor pre-1975. They [the Liberal Party] were the men born to rule and we [the Labor Party] were the aberration, you see. Hawke, more than anybody, has changed that, and I believe changed it absolutely. You can't talk about the denial of legitimacy to a party that has every government in the country, and there is no doubt that Hawke achieved that in a way that Whitlam absolutely failed. Hawke absolutely succeeded, as I say not simply because he won the elections in 1983, 1984, 1987 and 1990, but because of the way the government conducted itself. It conducted itself very much as *the* legitimate government, and that was never thereafter brought into question.

Hawke's traditional style of governance

Partly this was achieved in a very traditional way, in that Hawke, more than any postwar prime minister, restored the notion of government by the Cabinet. This was the real hallmark of the Hawke government, as very distinct from the Whitlam government, and distinct from the Keating government. This was government by the Cabinet in a quite traditional manner, that is, the traditions of consultation in Cabinet, consensus in Cabinet, and solidarity once the decision was made. These are the essence of Cabinet government, and Cabinet government is the distinctive mark of the Westminster system. This is what differentiates us from the presidential system, and it's the difference between a president and a prime minister. It's true these days that the attention is on the prime minister, and the prime minister is immensely powerful. He always has been, ever since William Pitt the Younger. But the traditional system of government is government by the Cabinet.

Whitlam's Cabinet didn't work, and that was our main problem, because you had these separate chieftains all doing their own thing, all with their old schools, all with their old scores to settle. We'd been out of power for so long that everybody had their hobby horse. Whitlam said, 'I don't care who's the prima donna of this Cabinet as long as I'm the prima donna absolute'. He was, but we paid a dreadful price for the disorganisation of the Cabinet government. Whitlam didn't run it as a proper Cabinet government, nor did Keating. Fraser tried to but in fact he just ran his Cabinet by exhaustion. He'd keep them in session hour after hour. He certainly talked to his Cabinet and ran his Cabinet, but it wasn't decision making by Cabinet; it was decision making by exhaustion.

But Hawke did, and I can't emphasise the traditional nature of this enough. He was upholding the great Westminster tradition, and the whole basis really of parliamentary government. The thing that distinguishes parliamentary government from the presidential system – and, if I may say so, makes the government in Australia immensely superior – is the process of government in Australia. The Cabinet system doesn't always operate in practice – but Hawke made it operate in practice as well as theory. It's that system, I believe, that makes parliamentary government and Cabinet government immensely superior to presidential government.

Hawke as an effective, consultative leader

Hawke was a superb chairman of committees and that's the essence. There was a happy 'coincide-ence'. I put it that way to distinguish it from 'coincidence'. There was a coinciding of Hawke's natural style and the theory of the Cabinet system: Cabinet solidarity, Cabinet responsibilities, stability and answerability. The Cabinet can only be *answerable* if people believe it is solid, united, and has been consulted about the decisions made in its name. There was this happy combination of Hawke's style, his temperament, and the theory of the Cabinet system. The prime minister is the chairman of Cabinet, Cabinet is a committee, and Hawke was a superb chairman of committees. It was a very able Cabinet, but in fact it was the way that Hawke ran it as its chairman that led to its success. I'm talking specifically about how the Cabinet operates, not about the public persona of the celebrity prime minister and all that. That's a different thing. I'm talking about the nitty gritty of how government works, and how effective governments can be.

The Cabinet system is so fundamental to our parliamentary system, and it worked, almost uniquely in postwar Australia, as operated by Hawke. Because it's so basic to establishing the legitimacy of government in our system, Hawke did restore the legitimacy, and restored the idea that the Labor Party was a natural, effective, worthy government of Australia. I think it was clearly established.

I think Kevin Rudd is probably following Hawke in his relations with his Cabinet because it seems to me that one of the indications of whether the Cabinet system is working properly or not is whether there are frequent rows or resignations involving ministers, and so far there haven't been any. In theory, this can either be because of the absolute dominance of the prime minister, or it can be because the Cabinet system – its processes of consultation and common responsibility – is working properly, and I suspect it's the latter with the Rudd government. I don't know for sure. But certainly Hawke established the model and by establishing the model has restored and guaranteed the legitimacy of Labor as a party of government in Australia. That is an outstanding success compared with Whitlam. Whitlam didn't create the circumstances in which our legitimacy was so vehemently denied, but he inherited it and he was unable to overcome it.

The media did recognise this was the most competent government we had had, as a Cabinet. They always spoke about the Cabinet or the ministry, you know. People like Laurie Oates did in fact acknowledge that the Hawke Cabinet was the ablest, as a group, that we had ever had. It is the ablest government since Federation. You know, if there were sort of a Cabinet equivalent of the intelligent quotient test, it would have rated the highest IQ in history, I'm sure, and this was recognised. You ask people like Oates about it.

Bob Hawke didn't enjoy the freedom [of selecting his own ministry] that Rudd has achieved for himself. The caucus still selected the ministry. Hawke's advantage over Whitlam was that, because of the extraordinary circumstances in which he became leader, he insisted on establishing the inner ministry and the outer ministry. Caucus would never allow Whitlam to do that, and he had to deal with every minister, the whole twenty-eight of them, in the Cabinet. So it was, to start off with, a terribly unwieldy Cabinet, even if they hadn't been such an unruly, independent mob themselves. But Hawke had that advantage: he had to make do with the material that he'd been given, but he was able to select from that material the ones he wanted, and then he went further. They had an inner committee within the inner ministry, which I think was just an inner committee of about 3 or 4. It was an inner core within the inner ministry, which I think was 8 or 10.

So Hawke operated his government on three levels, that inner committee, the inner ministry, and the Cabinet as a whole, but at each of those he used his chairmanship skills, and he was superb as chairman of a small committee or of a large committee. I'm talking more in terms of his style rather than of any specific occasion. He created a *style* of government where these things were operating automatically all the time. They permeated the conduct of the government.

For the first five years certainly [of Hawke's ministry], apart from the Cabinet, there was an atmosphere of inclusiveness. I don't want to get into the organisation of the factions that occurred, the institutionalisation of the factions, which is a different matter altogether. The factions did become more institutionalised and more predictable, I suppose, under Hawke, than they had been previously. Traditionally they'd been just on the left, and the rows were between the hard right and the hard left. In the Hawke years, Hayden organised the Centre Left faction, and I think there was a Centre Right faction. I think Hawke's was the Centre Right faction, and then there was the New South Wales Right, and then there was the Left. I'm not sure what the Left called itself, and how many subfactions they were divided into, but it certainly was more institutionalised than it had been, and this led to a certain stability, I suppose. But I think Hawke personally did create a sort of inclusiveness.

Consultation not confrontation

I tell in my book, *A Figure of Speech*, how I predicted that Hawke would be prime minister and I'd be his speechwriter. When he was elevated into the leadership at the Brisbane executive, the policies had been well prepared and the slogan was going to be 'Recovery and Reconstruction'. Hawke personally added the first word 'Reconciliation', so it became 'Reconciliation, Recovery and Reconstruction'. He preached consensus not confrontation, and these were the broad lines of the campaign. Against Fraser's confrontation policy, we established consensus. I remember Neville Wran saying, 'We'll find the limits of the consensus. This consensus is bullshit. It won't work.' Everyone thought the summit[2] would be just window dressing, but it was in fact a very effective operation. It established the lines on which the government conducted its economic policy for the next three years. Hawke achieved consensus to a remarkable degree. He actually believed his own rhetoric, and he made it work despite all the doubts, including those held by this speechwriter, because I'm not myself a natural consensus man.

I'm an oppositionist; I like opposition, that's why my happiest days were in the Whitlam opposition. Well I liked the fact of being in opposition – I'm like the old Victorian Socialist Left – but faith has dealt me a cruel blow by putting me in government for many more years than opposition. I'm glad to say this for Australia's sake.

The role of the trade unions

The second thing I want to emphasise, and it's also related to Hawke's consensus politics, is the role of the trade unions. The supreme example of consensus-style politics that was first articulated at the summit in 1983 worked not necessarily to the advantage of the unions in the long run. Because the benefits were shared by every worker, they couldn't see the value of unionism. I think that in fact indirectly contributed to the decline of union membership.

But the important thing in terms of the legacy, the long-term legacy, was to refurbish the idea of the unions and the union movement in the public mind. People could see the unions, represented of course by Crean and Kelty, as being extremely responsible and respectable. They were taking a part in the affairs of the nation at the centre, and accepting wage restraint when called upon by the government. This of course was the notable difference between the union movement under Hawke, during the Whitlam government, and the union movement with Hawke as prime minister. Our economic woes were home grown in the Whitlam government. The wage push of 1974–75 was a major cause of our problems. The oil crisis of 1973 may have been the real cause of the economic problems but the wage push was terribly inflationary and rendered us incapable of responding well to the oil shock. This was really an example of how the trade union movement didn't help a Labor government at all, even though Hawke was its president, but certainly it was a very different story after 1983.

The idea of legitimacy was at work here again, and people saw the unions in a much better light than ever before. It was the new role and new perceptions about the trade union movement, I believe, that led the Howard government, some twenty years later, into its disastrous industrial relations policy. Howard really believed that the people's attitude towards unions in the last years of the twentieth and first years of the twenty-first century was exactly the same as his attitudes in the 1950s when the union movement was terrifically on the nose, and it remained on the nose for a long time. But Hawke rehabilitated the union movement, both as president but even more as prime minister. As president he'd taken the union movement into enterprises and insurance and superannuation, and all those sort of things, broadening the basis, the nature really, of unionism. As prime minister in the way he dealt with the unions, indeed coopted the unions, he gave people a completely new perception. Certainly by the 2007 election, you can see that the whole [Liberal] campaign was based on a dud because people weren't responding to the idea that, you know, every member of the Rudd Cabinet will be a trade unionist. The Howard government tried to produce images of these bully boys, but the trade unionist that counted in the public mind was Bob Hawke.

Hawke's Labor government and Australia the lucky country

The third point I want to make is about Bob Hawke's legacy and Australia itself. In his own book (Hawke 1994), Bob talked about how lucky the Labor government was to be in power after the 1983 election so that it could adapt to the great changes that were occurring in the 1980s. I said that it wasn't just the Labor Party that was lucky. It was Australia that was lucky.

It wasn't just the political changes. There was immense change in the economy and in the economic attitude. There was a return to Keynesian fiscal theories. It was a time of high unemployment so it was felt that we needed a fiscal stimulus to end privatisation, which reflected the long influence of Thatcherism and Reaganomics. So there were immense changes in the world economy.

In Hawke's autobiography he wrote that the Labor Party was lucky to be in government. In opposition they would have had to stick with the same hobby horses, the same ideological baggage about nationalism, regulating economic control and taking command and so on. We were ill equipped to face the vastly new era. The Soviet Union and communism had not yet collapsed. The Labor attitude and cast of mind were totally ill-adapted to cope with the new economic and political realities. But the fact that we were in government and that we had Hawke and Keating meant that they were able to convince the party to take an open-ended approach. They were one of the most successful governments in the world in doing so.

The British Labour Party in the mid 1980s was led by Michael Foot who was the nadir of British Labour. By the mid 1980s in

Britain there was a real chance that Labour would stick to the third party role. All they could do was to denounce Margaret Thatcher. Their philosophy was still rooted in the 1930s and 1950s. The [British] Liberals would have become the second party. The Hawke/ Keating duo became a model for Tony Blair until George Bush arrived on the scene.

Conclusion

One week after Whitlam's 'It's time' victory of December 1972 a group of us went to dinner to celebrate at the Four Seas restaurant in Redfern. The party included Bob and Hazel Hawke, Mick Young and John Ducker. There was a great sense of euphoria that Labor had come into power after 23 years in the wilderness. Despite Whitlam's win, I said to Bob then, 'There will come a time when you will be prime minister and I will be your speechwriter'. In 1983 – ten years later – Bob Hawke replaced Bill Hayden. A few hours after this occurred Bob Hawke rang me and reminded me of my prophecy. 'Does the offer still hold?' he asked me. I said yes.

On 7 March I moved into my small office to start working with Bob Hawke. That night back in Sydney at dinner I made a speech to follow on from my predictions at the Four Seas in 1972: 'For you it is a new beginning. For me it is a resurrection. Neither of us doubts the difficulties and the size of the challenges ahead. I have no doubts of your capacity to meet them.'

But it was arranged that I would work for both Bob Hawke and Neville Wran. Until 1988 I commuted between Sydney and Canberra which I felt was unfair to both men but neither complained. The double role was tested at the economic summit when I drafted the opening and closing speeches for both Neville Wran and Bob Hawke. The summit allowed Bob Hawke to express his long-held views about the resolution of conflict through consensus. As I say in my book A Figure of Speech (2006, p. 214), Bob Hawke was as much a 'conviction politician' as Margaret Thatcher but he had the passion and ability to persuade people to his point of view, to reach a consensus based on his own convictions. In the three days of the summit Hawke successfully set an ineffaceable stamp on his government.

At the opening of the Sydney entertainment centre in 1983 Gough Whitlam asked me, 'Comrade, how are you getting on doing what Our Lord said was impossible – serving two masters?'

'Oh fine', I replied. 'Neville sticks to the script more or less. But Bob is a bit different. He tends to ad lib a bit. I think Bob is convinced he can write a better speech that I can.'

Whitlam replied, ever modest, 'Oh Comrade, I understand your problem. Hawke has such an ego.'

Overall though, the success and popularity of the Hawke government was Cabinet and caucus solidarity. Two factors led to Hawke's success. First of all Hawke was a superb chairman, as I said before. Secondly, the solidarity was due to the effectiveness of Hawke's inner staff. As Hawke says in his memoirs, 'they were not into deference'. People like Peter Barron, Geoff Walsh, Bob Hogg, Sandy Hollway and Graeme Evans, his principal private secretary, kept him balanced. They 'took the micky' out of him, deflating him when necessary.

Notes

1   The interview took place in Sydney on 3 April 2009.

2   Freudenberg is referring here to the National Economic Summit sponsored by the Hawke government in April 1983. Representatives of the Commonwealth and state governments, unions, several large corporations and organisations representing industry, farmers, miners, Aborigines, welfare agencies, conservationists and ethnic communities met in the House of Representatives chamber.

References

Freudenberg, G. 1977, *A Certain Grandeur: Gough Whitlam in Politics*, Macmillan, South Melbourne

Freudenberg, G. 1991, *Cause for Power: the Official History of the New South Wales Branch of the Australian Labor Party*, Pluto Press and NSW ALP, Leichhardt, NSW

Freudenberg, G. 2006, *A Figure of Speech: A Political Memoir*, John Wiley & Sons Australia, Milton, Qld

Freudenberg, G. 2008, *Churchill and Australia*, Pan Macmillan, Sydney

Hawke, B. 1994, *The Hawke Memoirs*, William Heinemann Australia, Port Melbourne, Vic

Part 2

Equity, education and inclusion

Chapter 4

Towards gender equality: two steps forward, one step back? Equal opportunity from Hawke to Rudd[1]

Alison Mackinnon

Introduction

In 2003 Anne Summers, Head of the Office of the Status of Women from 1983 to 1986, wrote a book titled *The End of Equality*. How could someone who had played such a significant role just twenty years before come to reflect that 'women are facing the end of equality' (Summers 2003, p. 16)? Summers wrote that thirty years ago women had had 'to reinvent the world and their place in it' in such a way that they felt on track 'to achieve ... justice for women' (p. 17). Now she claimed we had to face 'the end of equality'. In this chapter I look at the heady days that Summers recalls when the Hawke government passed groundbreaking legislation to advance women's rights in education and employment. I also briefly track what followed in the Howard years and the dismantling of agencies and services that led to Summers' despair. In concluding I suggest an urgent agenda for the Rudd government, a government with unprecedented numbers of women parliamentarians, with a female Deputy (and, frequently, Acting) Prime Minister, a female Governor-General and a female Deputy Opposition Leader. And, indeed, a reformist mandate. This chapter might usefully be read in association with that of Barbara Pocock on employment and industrial relations, Suzanne Franzway on sexual politics and unions, and Brennan and Reid on education, all of which have a bearing on the issues discussed here.

The roaring eighties: they can sometimes get what they want ...

The vast surge of activity that constituted the feminism of the 1970s and 1980s resulted in some momentous legislation during the Hawke years. This was a turning point, as Susan Ryan (2003) points out in her assessment of the era. Spurred on by women parliamentarians such as Ryan and Senator Rosemary Crowley, the Hawke government passed the historic *Sex Discrimination Act 1984* and the *Affirmative Action (Equal Opportunity for Women) Act 1986* (see also Crowley, this volume). Those pioneering women legislators, later followed by Margaret Reynolds and Wendy Fatin and others, had much to be proud of. The groundbreaking legislative initiatives shaped the way forward for years to come and gave women the tools to argue against discrimination on the grounds of sex, marital status, pregnancy, potential pregnancy or family responsibilities or involving sexual harassment. It also mandated the agencies to put the ideas into practice. They promised a new world where women would be equal players in education and the workforce. Those Acts have been considerably amended over the ensuing years but still remain centrepieces of gender equality. In 1992 a parliamentary review of the *Sex Discrimination Act* and the *Affirmative Action Act* by the House of Representatives Standing Committee on Legal and Constitutional Affairs brought out the report *Half Way to Equal* and strengthened the sex discrimination and equal opportunity legislation.[2]

What made it happen?

Those players close to the action have strong views on the genesis of that early legislation. Susan Ryan gives much credit to Bill Hayden who when in opposition in the late 1970s and early 1980s undertook an extensive policy review of his party. This review led to 'the first ever policy agenda for women' and to a sense that gender equity mattered to the ALP (Ryan 2003, p. 207). This found expression in the document *Towards Equality* (ALP 1983) which was widely endorsed across the party and led women to believe that change was on the way. Thus on coming into government the Hawke administration had a solid platform to work from.

We must acknowledge too the importance of timing, of the combination of the election of a reformist government and a strong social movement of women. At a time when the women's movement is relatively quiescent it is important, but sometimes difficult, to remember the excitement and activity of the 1970s and 80s when Australian women, inspired by the writings of Anne Summers, Germaine Greer, Gloria Steinem, Simone de Beauvoir, Kate Millet and many more who analysed the disadvantages of women, took it upon themselves to change the world. This activity underpinned the policy achievements.[3] Most notably the Women's Electoral Lobby, a feminist lobby group formed in 1972, interrogated parliamentarians on a range of key questions vital to women and publicised the results widely. This story has been told in a recent history (see Sawer 2008b), and Susan Ryan has written widely on the period from her perspective as the only women in the Hawke Labor Cabinet from 1983 to 1988 and as a founding member of WEL (Ryan 1999; 2003). Ryan was appointed Minister for Education and Minister assisting the Prime Minister on the Status of Women. Hawke symbolically acknowledged the significance of the issue by returning the Office for the Status of Women to his own department of Prime Minister and Cabinet. This not only signalled his commitment but gave the office the opportunity to have input into all Cabinet submissions, thus securing support from the top levels of leadership. It also ensured a vital whole-of-government approach.

Bob Hawke's high level of commitment to women's issues has also been commented on by the women closely involved in the battles of the 1970s and 80s (see Crowley in this volume). The judgement of academic commentators on Hawke's commitment has not always been so positive (see, for instance, Sharp and Broomhill 1989; Johnson 1990). Hawke's popularity in the business community, his leadership and his strategic thinking were vital to the passing of the legislation in Summers' and Ryan's views. It put the issue squarely on the national agenda. Faced with possible resistance to the *Affirmative Action (Equal Opportunity for Women) Act 1986* Hawke personally wrote letters to the CEOs of twenty big companies and to university vice-chancellors inviting them to oversee a pilot program testing different approaches to the legislation. Such personal touches were vital to gaining cooperation and preventing resistance.

Two other aspects of the Hawke government are critical here: the focus on consensus or social harmony and the place of the social wage in the Accord, the agreements reached with the trade union

movement. Hawke's concern with consensus and his negotiating
style (see Johnson, this volume) led to what Valerie Braithwaite
referred to as the 'gentleness, looseness and weakness' of the affirmative action legislation (Braithwaite 1998, p. 116). The fact that
the legislation did not prescribe outcomes, but processes aligning
closely with standard business practices (its 'gentleness'), that the
mechanisms for correcting discrimination were left to the employers
and employees (its 'looseness'), and the lack of sanctions for non-
compliers (its 'weakness') were central to its success, she believed.
Braithwaite argued that such a mechanism can be more successful
in producing 'the psychological surrender that is a necessary part
of changing culture' (p. 108). She demonstrated that these qualities underpinned 'the building of consensus among politicians from
opposing parties, a left-right alliance that was crucial to getting the
legislation passed by both houses of parliament' (p. 108). In the long
term, she argued, taking issue with other analysts in the area, loose
and gentle legislation can be more productive as long as its implementation is properly planned, resourced and monitored. In the
event, she claims, it was not.[4]

Equal opportunity and affirmative action were clearly linked
in Hawke's thinking with the economy, with developing the workforce, which was vital at the time, as Pocock (this volume) points
out. His approach might be characterised as 'equality as good business sense'.[5] He declared: 'the government firmly believes that all
jobs should be awarded on merit … and that affirmative action
programs will only achieve long term benefits, for women and the
economy, if they are regarded as employment policies designed to
improve the skill, efficiency and mobility of the work force' (cited
in Braithwaite 1998, p. 118). At the time Johnson questioned the
emphasis on the workforce, claiming that the notion that a healthy
capitalist economy that benefitted all men would necessarily benefit
women was erroneous and would lead to the neglect of other issues
vital to women (Johnson 1990, p. 98), presaging Eisenstein's recent
comments below.

Integral to the Accord was the notion of the need for 'social
wage improvements in return for wage restraint' (Ryan 2003, p. 203;
see also Pocock on the Accord). Many of the ensuing developments
favoured women rather than men, in Ryan's estimation, particularly universal health insurance, cash payments to families, child

support, and growth in TAFE and higher education. The centrality of education to Hawke's platform and the rapid increase in school retention are outlined in Brennan and Reid (this volume). Girls and young women were major beneficiaries of educational reform and Ryan has shown that 'between 1981 and 2001, the retention of girls to Year 12 increased from 38 per cent to over 79 per cent' (Ryan 2003, p. 212). A concomitant increase in university attendance saw women increasingly accessing faculties such as medicine and law and totalling over half of the undergraduate numbers by the late 1990s. This was indeed an education revolution for women and girls (Mackinnon 2006).

Aboriginal women too 'regained their voices' (Sawer 1990, pp. 128–139). In 1984 the Department of Aboriginal Affairs established an Aboriginal Women's Unit, later made permanent and in 1986 upgraded to the Office of Aboriginal Women. In 1986 the Aboriginal Task Force produced the groundbreaking report *Women's Business* (Daylight and Johnstone 1986), a benchmark publication, although the response to it was disappointing, and its recommendations were delayed and overlooked.

In all arenas during the early 1980s, inspired by the women's movement, women fought for better conditions. I too experienced those early successes. I was a tutor at the University of Adelaide, the lowest position in the staff hierarchy. Yet with a courageous professor, the late Fay Gale, and another staff member, Jill Thomas, we challenged that university's academic board to improve conditions for women. We were heard, and the ensuing committees set up structures for part-time work for women at the university with small children, for maternity leave and for the establishment of a Research Centre for Women's Studies at the university. They were heady days indeed.

How did it unravel?

An unprecedented rollback of women's rights was underway.
(Summers 2003, p. 141)

Summers argued that the Howard government stifled the voices of women within the federal bureaucracy by the end of his first year in office. There was to be no Sex Discrimination Commissioner, although Pru Goward was appointed to this position in 2001. The

Women's Bureau in the Department of Employment, Education, Training and Youth Affairs (a strong advocate for equal pay) was abolished. There was a serious effort to shut down the Affirmative Action Agency (Summers 2003, p. 130). The Human Rights and Equal Opportunity Commission's budget was cut by 40 per cent. The Women's Statistics Unit in the Australian Bureau of Statistics was abolished in 1996: it had done vital work ensuring disaggregation of statistics to track women's progress. The federal Office of the Status of Women (OSW) was moved in 2004 from the Department of Prime Minister and Cabinet to the Department of Family and Community Services. This not only eroded the possibility of direct input into Cabinet but was symbolic of the government's view of women as family members first and foremost rather than as individuals in their own right. OSW was further weakened through the appointment of Pru Goward, who was not known to be sympathetic to its aims, and by slashing the budget. Women's Budget Statements were abandoned in 1996. Australia refused to ratify the Optional Protocol to the Convention on the Elimination of all Forms of Discrimination against Women. The Aboriginal and Torres Strait Islander Commission was abolished. In 1999 the Howard government introduced a new *Equal Opportunity for Women in the Workplace Act*, reducing the reporting requirements for industry that had existed under the previous *Affirmative Action (EEO for Women) Act 1986*. The new Act was depicted as 'more business friendly', as moving towards a more 'business-regulated approach' (Bacchi and Eveline 2003, p. 105).

The concern for business signalled a major change in the political discourse which positioned women differently in the political stakes. With the neo-liberalism of the 1990s and the market dominant, terms such as social justice and affirmative action lost their purchase. Marion Sawer argues that with the rebirth of market populism groups seeking equality were depicted as elites, or 'special interests', whose aims were inimical or irrelevant to the rest of the population (Sawer 2004, p. 10). Thus women, and feminists in particular, were disenfranchised. The removal or disempowerment of agencies staffed by femocrats, women trained and motivated to speak on gender, ensured a further silencing of women's voices.

The speed with which women's concerns can be dismissed should not surprise us. History teaches us to put key legislation in place that cannot easily be reversed such as women's suffrage and equal opportunities in education. Looking to the future then, we need to consider what legislation might be achieved during the Rudd government's time in office that will be a fitting part of their legacy. A national system of mandatory parental leave appears to be a key candidate. This would complete a major item of unfinished business from the Hawke era. In the 2009 budget Labor signalled its intention to introduce such a scheme from January 2011. Should this go forward as planned a key plank for women's equality will be in place. Another plank is equal pay for women, an ever more elusive goal in the deregulated marketplace of the twenty-first century. Female earnings as a proportion of male earnings reached their highest point in 1994 but have declined thereafter.

Fightback: what do we need to do now?

The context in the early twenty-first century for a new leap forward is very different from that of the 1980s, as several chapters in this book clarify. Ryan points out that the 'equitable treatment now generally available to women in finance, goods and services, education and employment is taken for granted' (2003, p. 209). So much so, we might argue, that many young women do not see any reason to ally themselves with the notion of feminism. Some young women feel that their feminist mothers and teachers told them that they could 'have it all', but they are not finding this to be true. They feel let down, even angry. On the other hand they also dissociate themselves from what they consider 'victim feminism'. While feminists of an earlier generation dispute these constructions of their message, and point to unforeseen changing circumstances in the deregulating workplace and global economy, nevertheless the perception is troubling. Fortunately, most recently, a few young women writers have come forward, recuperating feminism and arguing for its continuing relevance (see, for instance, Dux and Simic 2008; Bulbeck, forthcoming).

This dissension in itself is a major difference in the current context. There is no united women's movement ready to take new initiatives further – although many of the old guard stand ready and willing to reclaim what was lost and to demand new changes.

The changing employment and industrial climate, described by Pocock, has raised a new series of challenges for women in employment. The deregulated marketplace, the endless focus on productivity and the diminished role of trade unions have not favoured women. While they have increased their place in the workforce (see Pocock) it has often been in part-time, non-unionised, casual jobs. Professional women who have gained from the educational revolution of the 1980s and 90s find themselves working ever longer hours in a tightly competitive workplace with little state assistance in the form of maternity leave and child care. It is in this context that some commentators have argued that the 1970s feminists' emphasis on the importance of paid work and economic independence for women has been coopted by neo-liberal governments who have used it against 'welfare mothers', for example, urging them into the workplace and undermining their benefits (see for instance Eisenstein 2009a; 2009b). Hester Eisenstein, for example, argues that the US 'bourgeois revolution' defined women as workers rather than as homemakers, with work viewed as liberation, thus preparing the way for the individualism required by capitalism, where women can be viewed separately from their role as wives or mothers. This repositions women with caring responsibilities disadvantageously.

Yet perhaps all of this is to change – the pendulum to swing again. Now too the state is central again, not only in discourse but in a very real sense as the financial bedrock of a troubled economy where the excesses of neo-liberalism have all too clearly failed. The language of neo-liberalism and of New Public Management is being roundly challenged and the fact that individual effort, or enterprise, is not enough is becoming obvious. The days of the collective, however, appear to have gone forever and feminism in word and deed is slow to make a comeback.

Can the type of consensus reached during the 1980s be found again? The current Prime Minister Kevin Rudd does not have the long history with trade unions that Bob Hawke claimed, nor does he enjoy the close involvement with the big end of town. His commitment to issues concerning women is yet to be fully tested, although the presence of his female Deputy, Julia Gillard, and a female leader of the Australian Council of Trade Unions, Sharan Burrow, gives cause for hope. Burrow has thrown the weight of the trade union movement behind the push for a mandatory national scheme of maternity leave, although, disappointingly, she has accepted the delayed time frame proposed.

The global financial crisis and growing budget deficits of the early twenty-first century provide government with an excuse not to fund immediately new and much delayed initiatives such as a national mandatory parental leave system, an initiative that has seemed tantalisingly close. The arguments that continue to have purchase in this environment are those that focus on productivity, on the need to build a workforce that can withstand the perceived pressures of an ageing population. On both of these counts assisting women to remain in the workforce will make a difference. So we are back to economic arguments, rather than those that focus solely on women's 'rights' or issues of equality, if we wish to move forward. Pragmatism seems essential here. This might involve, as Marion Sawer has argued, a form of 'ideological bilingualism, that is speaking one language while thinking another' (Bulbeck 2005, p. 486).

The issue of women's equality, however, both economic and otherwise, must be placed back on the agenda (HREOC 2008). Pleasingly this has been signalled by the new Minister for the Status of Women, Tanya Plibersek (Plibersek 2008). Decades of change in employment and industrial relations have left the pay gap between women and men wider than ever, in part a function of women's increasing part-time and casual work, in part attributable to the Howard government's WorkChoices policies (Pocock, this volume). It is also, however, a reflection of the fact that Australian women still struggle with issues of maternity leave and work breaks for child rearing, with their impacts on career progression, and the constant search for good child care. The recent collapse of large profit-based childcare empires offers the opportunity for a restructuring of the provision of publicly funded child care and a return to high standards (see Brennan 2008).

We need to revisit the question of flexible working hours in a way that facilitates work for mothers of young children or carers of the elderly or disabled, rather than responding to the needs of employers. We must demand reasonable entitlements for all, particularly those with young children, and end the trading off of entitlements for pay, part of the now discredited WorkChoices policy of the Howard government. Equal opportunities in education and work also require an equal chance to secure economic independence in retirement (see Sharp, this volume). There is a huge gender gap in retirement savings.

We do need to resume the language of equality, of social justice, of women's rights, and to speak of women as individuals in their own right rather than only as mothers and potential contributors to the birthrate or to the labour force. Women are not a special interest group or indeed an elite, to be dismissed as one of many voices lobbying for change. They constitute over half of the population. Indigenous women's rights are central to this agenda. Much of the *Women's Business* reported on in 1984 such as inadequate housing and issues of violence remains to be addressed.

Domestic violence, bullying and harassment still cause untold misery for both Aboriginal and non-Aboriginal women, in spite of the existence now of well-codified guidelines and legislation and greater understanding of what constitutes unacceptable behaviour (see also HREOC 2008; Plibersek 2008). Exposing the anti-female agenda behind some 'men's' groups, given a prominent voice during the Howard era, is also important (Sawer 2008a, pp. 6–7).

Above all a new agenda must engage young women, using their language, their technologies and addressing their issues. Young Australian women take for granted many of the gains of the recent past and their concerns, in common with those of young men, prioritise broad issues such as global human rights, the need for a treaty with Indigenous Australians and the hope that Australia will lead the world in addressing climate change. Yet interestingly the first of the 'Top Ten Ideas' to emerge from a 2008 nationwide youth summit was a paid parental leave program for 'both working men and women' which would *inter alia* 'help to address gender imbalances in the workplace' (Australia 2020 Youth Summit 2008). If this desire of the younger generation could be met, and it appears that it might be, the Rudd government might truly usher in a new era of gender justice and equal relations between women and men.

In 1990 Marion Sawer, concluding her account of Australian women's remarkable achievements during the 1980s, noted that the whole political spectrum had moved to the right and that there had been a loss of confidence in the state. 'This means', she wrote, 'that the territory won over the last twenty years may be lost' (Sawer 1990, p. 253). Almost two decades later we can see that, while much has been lost, the gains for women enshrined in legislation, enacted in educational reform and in self-confidence for women have, in the main, stood firm. The Hawke era did move the agenda forward for women. The challenge for the Rudd government is to do likewise.

Notes

1   I am grateful to Chilla Bulbeck for helpful comments on an earlier version of this chapter.

2   For a much fuller account see Sawer (1990).

3   Sawer (1990) gives a comprehensive account of the development of the machinery for women's policy in this period.

4   For the full complexity of this interesting argument see Braithwaite (1998). Braithwaite also details the major features of the *Affirmative Action Act*.

5   With thanks to Chilla Bulbeck for this notion.

References

Australia 2020 Youth Summit 2008, *Communiqué*, http://www.australia2020. gov.au/docs/youth_summit_communique.pdf, accessed 22 April 2009

Australian Labor Party 1983, *The ALP and Women: Towards Equality*, ALP, Canberra

Bacchi, C. and Eveline, J. 2003, 'Mainstreaming and neoliberalism: a contested relationship', *Policy & Society*, vol. 22, no. 2, pp. 98–118

Braithwaite, V. 1998, 'Designing the process of workplace change through the *Affirmative Action Act*' in eds M. Gatens and A. Mackinnon, *Gender and Institutions: Welfare, Work and Citizenship*, Cambridge University Press, Cambridge

Brennan, D. 2008, 'Reassembling the child care business', *Inside Story*, 19 November, http://inside.org.au/reassembling-the-child-care-business/, accessed 26 March 2009

Bulbeck, C. 2005, 'Gender policies: hers to his' in eds P. Saunders and J. Walter, *Ideas and Influence: Social Science and Public Policy in Australia*, University of New South Wales Press, Sydney

Bulbeck, C. forthcoming, 'Unpopularizing feminism: blaming feminism in the population debate and the mother wars with a focus on popular Australian books', under review.

Daylight, P. and Johnstone, M. 1986, *Women's Business: Report of the Aboriginal Women's Task Force*, Australian Government Publishing Service, Canberra

Dux, M. and Simic, Z. 2008, *The Great Feminist Denial*, Melbourne University Press, Melbourne

Eisenstein, H. 2009a, 'Feminism seduced: globalization and the use of gender', keynote address presented at Two Decades of Gender and Difference: A Celebration of the Work of Chilla Bulbeck, University of Adelaide, Adelaide, 18–19 February

Eisenstein, H. 2009b, *Feminism Seduced: How Global Elites Used Women's Labor and Ideas to Exploit the World*, Paradigm, Boulder, CO

House of Representatives Standing Committee on Legal and Constitutional Affairs 1992, *Half Way to Equal: Report of the Inquiry into Equal Opportunity and Equal Status for Women in Australia*, Australian Government Publishing Service, Canberra

Human Rights and Equal Opportunity Commission 2008, *Gender Equality: What Matters to Australian Men and Women*, the Listening Tour Community Report, HREOC, Canberra

Johnson, C. 1990, 'Whose consensus? Women and the ALP', *Arena*, no. 93, pp. 85–104

Mackinnon, A. 2006, 'Girls schools and societies: a generation of change?', *Australian Feminist Studies*, vol. 21, no. 50, pp. 275–288

Plibersek, T. 2008, 'Women and men: a new conversation about equality', speech to the Sydney Institute, Sydney, 7 November.

Ryan, S. 1999, *Catching the Waves: Life in and out of Politics*, HarperCollins, Sydney

Ryan, S. 2003, 'Women's policy' in eds S. Ryan and T. Bramston, *The Hawke Government: A Critical Retrospective*, Pluto Press, Melbourne

Sawer, M. 1990, *Sisters in Suits: Women and Public Policy in Australia*, Allen and Unwin, Sydney

Sawer, M. 2004, 'Gender equality in the age of governing for the mainstream', paper presented to United Nations Division for the Advancement of Women (DAW) Expert Group Meeting on National Machinery, Rome, 29 November – 2 December

Sawer, M. 2008a, 'Disappearing tricks', *Dialogue*, vol. 27, no. 3, pp. 4–9

Sawer, M. 2008b, *Making Women Count: A History of the Women's Electoral Lobby in Australia*, UNSW Press, Sydney

Sharp, R. and Broomhill, R. 1989, *Short Changed: Women and Economic Policies*, Allen and Unwin, Sydney

Summers, A. 2003, *The End of Equality: Work, Babies and Women's Choices in 21st Century Australia*, Random House, Sydney

Chapter 5

Education, equity and the Hawke government

Marie Brennan and Alan Reid

Introduction: the education context of the Hawke government

In the Australian federal system, according to the federal Constitution, responsibility for activities remains with the states unless power is formally referred to the federal government. Education has remained a state responsibility. However, federal government presence in school education began to be established under the Menzies government in the 1960s, with the provision of libraries and science blocks to all schools regardless of affiliation. The rationale for federal funding of school education – and one that was reinforced by the Whitlam and Fraser governments that followed – was the issue of equity, albeit differently constructed in each of these periods. Thus, following the recommendations of the Karmel report (1973), Whitlam used equity as the basis of the policy for introducing systematic 'needs-based' funding to non-government schools and established a number of federally funded equity programs designed to address disadvantage and inequality of opportunity. Under Fraser, as the proportion of federal funds shifted to private schools, so too did the concept of equity begin to move to one based more on individual choice.

When Hawke led the successful election bid in 1983, he made education a central plank of the ALP platform; most particularly he argued for education as central to the economy and for improving social cohesion in a democratic society, as an important means for

moving out of poverty in a time of recession, inflation and unemployment (the latter stood at 10.5% in 1983: Hawke 1983). These
themes of economic development, social cohesion and enhancing
Australia's role in the world were also prominent in Hawke's 1987
bid for a third term in government (Hawke 1987). Indeed Hawke
could claim to be the last leader to place social issues equally on the
agenda with economic ones, even though this was gradually watered
down by the strong links made between education and the economy.
This approach once again reconstructed the links between equity
and education.

In this chapter we re-examine school education in the four
Hawke terms of government, covering the education ministerial
years of Susan Ryan (1983–87) and John Dawkins (1987–91). We
consider three main areas of achievement: 1) policy development for
national educational matters; 2) the establishment of a 'needs-based'
funding model for government and non-government schools; and 3)
approaches to national curriculum development. Our argument is
that under Hawke conditions were put in place to achieve legitimacy
for a national role in education, working from a strong 'needs-based'
equity value position. After the first term this 'equity' position was
firmly tied into the economic agenda, such that federal educational
infrastructure, particularly that instituted under John Dawkins,
ironically put in place the means by which equity issues were able to
be stripped out of education in the decade of the Howard governments – just as, before Hawke, the Fraser government had stripped
the schools funding of its equity rationale and operations.

Policy development for national education matters

There were three dominant themes informing education policy
during the period of the Hawke government: the contribution of
education to the economy, equity and national approaches to education. By the late 1980s all three were closely integrated in educational
policy discourse and practice, with each theme influencing the other
two. Although uneven in development and contested in implementation, the integration of these themes from 1983 to 1991 resulted in
a new role for the Commonwealth in schooling policy, one which
resonates with the contemporary period.

The first Hawke term (1983–1985) started out with a traditional Labor view of equity and education. For example, the gov-

ernment retained the Disadvantaged Schools Program (DSP) which began during the time of the Whitlam government and involved Commonwealth funding of programs designed to address educational disadvantage; and it introduced a new program, the Participation and Equity Program (PEP), with a special focus on access and participation. Based on an old-style Labor aspiration for universal participation in senior secondary education, PEP programs targeted the 40 per cent of schools with the lowest retention rates by placing a focus on curriculum and school culture with the aim of making school more attractive to disinclined students. PEP lasted until 1987, and is credited with making a significant contribution to the rapid increase in retention rates from just over 30 per cent in 1981 to almost 80 per cent by 1991. However it was not to be long before this approach to equity was to be transformed.

During the second Hawke term (1985–1987) the economic changes brought about by globalisation and described elsewhere in this volume – the deregulation of banks and other financial institutions, the abolition of tariff protection, the strong embrace of market ideology and so on – began to place education in the spotlight. The federal government argued that, since education played the key role in the development of human capital, it was central to a productive and internationally competitive economy. Associated with this policy emphasis was a growing commitment to budget surpluses, which meant that the federal government was looking for cost efficiencies and greater accountability for federal expenditure. It established the Quality of Education Review Committee (QERC) which reported in April 1985 and based its recommendations on these two emphases. The report argued that the input model upon which programs such as PEP had been based was inappropriate in the new environment and needed to be replaced by output models with a strong emphasis on goal setting, targeted programs and greater accountability for outcomes and expenditure (Dudley and Vidovich 1995).

By the beginning of the third Hawke term in 1987, and with John Dawkins as the new Minister of Education, the idea that education was a major tool of microeconomic reform was now a centrepiece of government policy (see Marginson 1993, esp. chapters 4, 5). This was never more strongly represented than by the release of Minister Dawkin's major policy statement *Strengthening Australia's Schools* (1988). This statement, and the policy developments that flowed from it, drew together the three major themes of the economy, equity and national approaches, in ways that produced the most dramatic change in the role of the Commonwealth in schooling policy since Federation.

Prior to 1988, the Commonwealth's influence on schooling policy in the states and territories was indirect, consisting of funding state-based programs, materials development and teacher support activities. However Dawkins argued that if education were to serve the needs of the economy, then education policy must be steered by the federal government, with state and territory support through the Australian Education Council (AEC), a body comprising state/territory and federal ministers of education. The first step was to abolish those statutory bodies that were not sufficiently under government direction. The Schools Commission, established by the Whitlam government, was dismantled and replaced by the large federal Department of Employment, Education and Training (DEET). This conjoining of education and employment with a focus on skills training, vocational education and user pays represented a more instrumentalist view of education than had been the case in the earlier period. It was accompanied by managerialist models of corporate planning which were introduced in an effort to reform the public service, and to place it under greater ministerial control (Lingard, Knight and Porter 1993; Dudley and Vidovich 1995; Knight and Lingard 1997).

Lingard, O'Brien and Knight (1993) describe the new approach to commonwealth–state relations in education as 'corporate federalism', involving the cooption/incorporation of key private sector groups (unions and industry) into a strategy to increase commonwealth influence over education through direct policy intervention and through greater control over the way Commonwealth funds were spent.

As well as the broad approach of tying equity to economic objectives, the third and fourth periods of the Hawke government saw the development and release of a number of policies and initiatives that focused on the needs of special groups. Here effort was directed to setting *national* equity objectives and targets to assist with planning at the local level to improve educational opportunities for girls and Indigenous students, through such polices as the National Policy for the Education of Girls in Australian Schools

(Commonwealth Schools Commission 1987; Mackinnon, this volume), and the National Aboriginal and Torres Strait Islander Education Policy (DEET 1989). While such policies were variously assessed on the basis of their content and effects (e.g. Daws 1997; McConaghy 1997; see also Buckskin, this volume), it is possible from the vantage point of nearly twenty years after the end of the Hawke government to recognise the ways in which they broke new ground in assessing progress across the country and seeking to connect the disparate policies and strategies that existed in the states and territories.

Federal funding of schools

McMorrow (2003) argues that gaining a level of consensus on federal funding of private schools was a major achievement of the Hawke government. Whitlam had instituted a needs-based funding model paid as block funding to states and the Catholic systems, with per capita funding to the poorest six categories of independent schools. Under Fraser, the equity basis for schools funding instituted under Whitlam was significantly eroded, with significant growth of funding for a growing number of independent schools. The education platform of resource agreements with the states led to a return to the sectarianism of the postwar era. Groups of private school parents became politically vocal and concomitantly public school groups such as DOGS (Defence of Government Schools) joined with teacher unions to provide alternative views. Under Fraser's version of small Commonwealth government roles, the idea of support for parental 'choice' had started to enter the public and media discussions as an entitlement, while the teacher unions were strongly opposed to funding of private schools.

In the first Hawke term, when Minister Ryan announced a reduction of 25 per cent of funding for the wealthiest private schools – what became known as the 'hit list' – major political unrest emerged from the total private school lobby, particularly the Catholics (Smart and Dudley 1990). These threats to Hawke's commitment to consensus building, and the Accord between government, industry and unions, had the potential not only for bad press in education but also to undermine the legitimacy of the government's approach. Ryan was able to avert significant dissension on this issue by referring the touchy issues of resource agreements with the states and the development of community standards to the Commonwealth Schools Commission for advice. The multiple group representation on the Schools Commission was to ensure that non-government schools would continue to be funded, but the recommendations carefully ensured that continued funding was to be based on need. Indeed, the commission's report went further and pointed to the dangers to the sustainability of public education if funding for non-government schools were not carefully monitored and managed:

> A continuing significant decline in the government school sector's share of overall enrolment is likely to change substantially the social composition of the student population in government schools, with potentially significant negative consequences for the general comprehensiveness of public school systems. The cumulative effect of these financial, educational and social consequences could, in the long term, threaten the role and standing of the public school as a central institution in Australian society. Such a development would be unwelcome to most citizens and is inconsistent with the stated policies of governments, as well as the major school interest groups, government and nongovernment. (Commonwealth Schools Commission 1985, para 20)

Yet despite such statements, public school groups put in a minority report, concerned with the longer-term effect on the public sector. This fear was to be realised under the Howard government, which effectively returned to policies based on choice and the movement of students into private schooling. However, the acceptance of the commission's majority report, which recommended needs-based support for all schools, reduced conflict for the duration of the Hawke government and helped to entrench the issue of equity and needs-based funding in public discourse for a significant period of time.

McMorrow's more recent analyses suggest that the hard-won agreement hamstrung further options for changes to education policy and funding (McMorrow 2008; Preston 2007; Smart and Dudley 1990) by entrenching funding for all levels of private schools – an effect that is politically almost impossible to reverse, as the Rudd government has found. From Whitlam on, the existence of subsidies to non-government schools has ensured their growth, such that there are now over half a million more students in Australian schools than in 1976 and all of this increase is in non-government schools. Hawke's capacity to work with Ryan to dampen the political unrest around schools funding was essential to achieving longer-term cooperation in the Accord across many government policy domains.

Approaches to national curriculum development

The first two periods of the Hawke government (1983–1987) saw a continuation of the approach to national curriculum efforts through state-based cooperation. In this period, the Curriculum Development Centre (CDC), established under the Whitlam government and abolished by the Fraser government, was revived as an arm of the Schools Commission. In conjunction with the states, CDC developed a number of curriculum resources and materials for use by teachers (Piper 1997). This was consistent with the approach in the 1970s where curriculum development was viewed largely as the concern of teachers working in partnership with their school communities.

As the economic context changed, however, so too did it strengthen the government's belief that curriculum decision making could not be left in the hands of professional educators. It was government business and the curriculum needed to serve the needs of the economy, not only individual needs, as part of education's contribution to microeconomic reform to make Australia internationally competitive. This change needed to be orchestrated at a national level in order to remove duplication and smooth out the anomalies that were apparent across the various state education systems. But rather than indirectly influence curricula through the development of materials, as had occurred in the previous twenty years of federal government involvement in curriculum, the strategy shifted to pushing for a single national curriculum for the compulsory years of schooling:

> What is required is the development of a common framework that sets out the major areas of knowledge and the most appropriate mix of skills and experience for students in all the years of schooling, but accommodates the different or specific needs of different parts of Australia. There is a need for regular assessment of the effectiveness and standards of our schools. A common curriculum framework should be complemented by a common national approach to assessment. We

need to examine how schools can report to parents on their aims and
achievements; how school systems can report to the nation on how well
our schools are performing against established goals. (Dawkins 1988,
pp. 4–5)

The mainly Labor-dominated state governments leant cautious support to the Dawkins initiative. Thus, in April 1989, the
Australian Education Council announced the Hobart Declaration
which set out an agreement on a set of national goals for schooling,
and an intention to establish a national curriculum agency, the
Curriculum Corporation of Australia. It also commenced a process
of national collaborative curriculum development, and introduced
an annual national report on schooling. The AEC also turned its
attention to the post-compulsory years of schooling, and in 1990
announced a national review of post-compulsory education and
training under the chairmanship of Brian Finn, then CEO of IBM.
The Finn Review argued for a convergence of vocational and general
education, and recommended that a number of generic work-related
key competencies should be developed.

However the states were wary about ceding too much control
over curriculum policy to the federal government. They used the
results of a mapping exercise of existing curricula in all states and
territories to make the case that since curriculum similarities already
existed across the state systems radical change at the national level
was unnecessary (Piper 1997, p. 18).

And yet, as the project unfolded, the momentum for a national
curriculum gathered pace. After the mapping exercise, in 1991 the
curriculum was organised into eight 'learning areas' and work commenced on describing these in terms of what became known as
statements and profiles. In the early months of the new Keating
government, the state-based writing teams continued to write and
then consult within very short timelines, and the new curriculum
was ready to be submitted to the June meeting of the AEC held in
Perth in 1993. At the same time, the Mayer Committee established
by the AEC to follow up on the Finn Report proposed seven across-
curriculum key competencies.

By mid 1993 the political complexions of the states had changed,
and some states were starting to get cold feet, fearing loss of control
over the curriculum. The national statements and profiles were

not endorsed at the June meeting, and were referred instead to the
Hobart meeting of the council in December 1993. At that meeting
they again failed to receive endorsement and were then referred
back to the states to do with as they pleased. As it happened, much
of the development work was adopted as the official curriculum
of a number of states and territories and in this way operated as a
surrogate national curriculum for the next fifteen years.

Although this bold attempt to achieve a national curriculum
had fallen at the last hurdle, it undoubtedly altered irrevocably
the curriculum field in Australia. It had consolidated the idea of a
national approach to curriculum and the central role of the federal
government in that process. The specific approach led by Minister
Dawkins had enlisted curriculum work in the name of national economic goals. And yet, running through the development phase was
a continuing concern about equity and the educational outcomes of
traditionally disadvantaged groups.

Conclusion

Whilst it is not new to point to Hawke's focus on consensus building
as a key feature underpinning his approach to government, it cannot
be denied that the efforts to build consensus among both the education community and the broader community were certainly key
to the work of both Susan Ryan and John Dawkins as ministers of
education. However, there were quite distinctive differences under
the two ministers.

Susan Ryan worked from a tradition of following educational
equity rationales, and this was the hallmark of her ministry.
The sponsorship of needs-based funding, her institution of the
Participation and Equity Program, support for the growth of retention among low socioeconomic status students, sponsorship of the
work that led to the National Policy on the Education of Girls, and
support for the development of the National Aboriginal Education
Policy are all testament to her commitments to consultation and
working for the most marginalised in schooling. Issues of states'
rights in a federal system remained largely undisturbed as a result of
both the consultative work and the placement of equity as a central
plank in ALP policy. The Schools Commission advisory role, with
its multiple and diverse educational community and parent group
membership, was able to work well with Ryan's interests in educa-

tion policy directions that furthered a strong social justice rationale. Her ministry concluded in parallel with the Wall Street crash of 1987, which then helped to feed a renewed concern with Australia's economic position in the globalising economy. Under John Dawkins, who succeeded Ryan as minister after the 1987 election, education was subsumed by economic concerns, linked to policy concerns for productivity, skills development and vocational reorientation of the workforce into new directions (see Dawkins 1988).

It is important to understand that the new focus on the economy and on efficiency and effectiveness did not displace a concern for equity – it altered the ways in which equity was understood. Rather than being based on a liberal progressive view of the individual, the new approach to equity was reconstructed around the belief that the effects of the new global economic circumstances on unemployment and poverty could be ameliorated through investment in human capital. That is, increasing the access to and participation of young people in the labour market was claimed to be as much an equity strategy as it was a necessity for the economy (Kennedy 1988, p. 360).

The linking of equity and efficiency altered the style of educational policy and programs that had a social justice focus. Fitzclarence and Kenway (1993, p. 94) point to the shift in policy language from the early years of the Hawke government (and the Whitlam years) where words and concepts such as diversity, equality of access and provision, social justice and socioeconomic disadvantage were used, to the years of the third and fourth Hawke terms where efficiency, effectiveness, productivity, performance indicators and equity became the *lingua franca*. Rather than focusing on inputs through increased resources and programs such as PEP, schools were enjoined to do more with less in an effort to improve educational *outcomes*, particularly for disadvantaged groups. Johnston (1993), for example, describes how the DSP shifted during the later years of the Hawke government from being an innovative program based on grassroots democratic decision making promoting a 'plurality of school-level responses to the problem of educational inequality' (p. 110), to one that was more top-down, outcomes-based and centrally determined. At the same time, in the light of the Howard years from 1996 to 2007, which stripped equity and social justice from the public agenda, it can be argued that the efforts to maintain a focus on equity can be seen as a continuation of the Labor tradition in changing economic and social circumstances.

In turning public debate about education towards its links with economic productivity, Dawkins and others in Hawke's government helped to forge a focus on 'human capital', treating workers as a third arm of capitalism alongside real estate and finance, ushering in versions of neo-liberal economics that, with hindsight, ought to have been better framed. Nevertheless, the focus of concern remained on those workers without qualifications and credentials, and how they might parlay their knowledge and skills into greater access to education and training as part of restructuring the workforce from the bottom up. Equity in these terms was still part of a structural understanding of the problems of labour under capitalism, and a commitment to ensuring policies that would address deep-seated inequalities through their links with education and training.

During the Dawkins years there were some significant changes in approaches to cooperation and decision making in education between the federal government and the states. Federal government departmental policy development and cooperative federalism initiatives through the AEC were put in place in the late 1980s, despite disagreements such as those noted above in the discussions of national curriculum. Growing globalisation has put significant pressures on federated systems (whether in Australia, in Europe or elsewhere) as federal governments seek to position their countries in a range of alliances, supra-national bodies and economic partnerships. It appears that countries that operate on federal lines, where education remains constitutionally a state/province/local responsibility, are less able to deal with international movements such as benchmarking, indicators and testing league tables. Thus, to appear internationally competitive, a movement that increases cooperation to create a 'national interest' and national infrastructure would be a major achievement.

Hindsight is, of course, the safest place from which to make judgements: we can point to the achievements and to the paradoxes by which those achievements were also pathways that could – and would – be used to undo equity commitments in favour of individualist and privatised forms of education that marked the conservative government under Howard. The challenge now for the Rudd Labor government is to take up the equity baton for these new times. The wider economic crisis is not a promising context in which to operate. However, it may well give a rationale for rethinking the residualisation of public sector schooling and the disproportionate subsidies that now accrue even to the most elite and well-resourced private schools. The reductive emphasis on 'human capital' as the rationale for the Rudd government's 'education revolution' undercuts any commitment to schooling that might contribute to the development of a cohesive, diverse society, let alone an interest in education for its own sake. Rudd's interest in cooperative federalism, demonstrated in new work through the Council of Australian Governments on a range of measures including health and education, can move Hawke's agenda into the twenty-first century – whether around national curriculum or education funding. Whether school education contributes to greater equity in the Australian society will continue to be a hugely relevant question for Rudd, as much as for Hawke.

References

Commonwealth Schools Commission 1985, *Planning and Funding Policies for New Non-Government Schools*, Australian Government Publishing Service, Canberra

Commonwealth Schools Commission 1987, *The National Policy for the Education of Girls*, Australian Government Publishing Service, Canberra

Dawkins, J. 1988, *Strengthening Australia's Schools*, AGPS, Canberra

Daws, L. 1997, 'The national policy for the education of girls' in eds R. Lingard and P. Porter, *A National Approach to Schooling in Australia? Essays on the Development of National Policies in Schools Education*, Australian College of Education, Canberra

DEET 1989, *National Aboriginal and Torres Strait Islander Education Policy*, Australian Government Publishing Service, Canberra

Dudley, J. and Vidovich, L. 1995, *The Politics of Education: Commonwealth Schools Policy 1973–1995*, ACER, Melbourne

Fitzclarence, L. and Kenway, J. 1993, 'Education and social justice in the postmodern age' in eds R. Lingard, J. Knight and P. Porter, *Schooling Reform in Hard Times*, Falmer Press, London

Hawke, B. 1983 'The way ahead', John Curtin Memorial Lecture, Perth, 28 September, http://john.curtin.edu.au/jcmemlect/hawke1983.html, accessed 7 May 2009

Hawke, B. 1987, Policy Statement, 23 June 1987, http://www.australianpolitics.com/elections/1987/87-06-23_alp-policy-statement.pdf, accessed 3 February 2009

Johnston, K. 1993, 'Inequality and educational reform: lessons from the disadvantaged schools project' in eds R. Lingard, J. Knight and P. Porter, *Schooling Reform in Hard Times*, Falmer Press, London

Karmel, P. 1973, Interim Committee for the Australian Schools Commission (Karmel Committee), *Schools in Australia*, Commonwealth of Australia, Canberra

Kennedy, K. 1988, 'The policy context of curriculum reform in Australia in the 1980s', *Australian Journal of Education*, vol. 32, no. 3, pp. 357–374.

Knight, J. and Lingard, R. 1997, 'Ministerialisation and politicisation' in eds R. Lingard and P. Porter, *A National Approach to Schooling in Australia? Essays on the Development of National Policies in Schools Education*, Australian College of Education, Canberra

Lingard, R., Knight, J. and Porter, P. (eds) 1993, *Schooling Reform in Hard Times*, Falmer Press, London

Lingard, R., O'Brien, P. and Knight, J. 1993, 'Strengthening Australia's schools through corporate federalism?', *Australian Journal of Education*, vol. 37, no. 3, pp. 231–247.

Marginson, S. 1993, *Education and Public Policy in Australia*, Cambridge University Press, Melbourne

McConaghy, C. 1997, 'The national Aboriginal and Torres Strait Islander Education Policy' in eds R. Lingard and P. Porter, *A National Approach to Schooling in Australia? Essays on the Development of National Policies in Schools Education*, Australian College of Education, Canberra

McMorrow, J. 2003, 'Education policy' in eds S. Ryan and T. Bramston, *The Hawke Government: A Critical Retrospective*, Pluto Press, North Melbourne

McMorrow, J. 2008, 'If I had a hammer: the tools of schools funding in Australia', paper presented to the Schooling Education 2020 Summit, Sydney, June, http://thestupidcountry.com/wp-content/uploads/2008/07/jim-mcmorrow.pdf, accessed 31 January 2009

Piper, K. 1997, *Riders in the Chariot: Curriculum Reform and the National Interest, 1965–1995*, ACER, Melbourne

Preston, B. 2007, *The Social Make-Up of Schools: Family Income, Religion, Indigenous Status, and Family Type in Government, Catholic and Other Nongovernment Schools*, Australian Education Union, Melbourne, http://www.aeufederal.org.au/Publications/Bprestonrep2007.pdf, accessed 27 March 2009

Smart, D. and Dudley, J. 1990, 'Education Policy' in eds C. Jennett and R. Stewart, *Hawke and Australian Public Policy: Consensus and Restructuring*, Macmillan, Melbourne

Chapter 6

Equity, globalisation and higher education

Ian Davey and Ianto Ware

Introduction

The Hawke era saw a fundamental shift in the function and perception of higher education in Australia. Building on the momentum of Whitlam, the sector was transformed from small-scale, collegial institutions to a major force in the economic and social life of the country, with an immense increase in the emphasis on student access and equity coupled with a push to strengthen ties to business and industry. The implementation of these changes can be divided into two periods, reflecting the priorities of Hawke's two ministers for education. Senator Susan Ryan, the minister during the first two Hawke ministries from 1983 to mid 1987, built on the legacy of the Whitlam government, which abolished university fees to open higher education to a broader spectrum of the community. John Dawkins, the Minister For Employment, Education and Training in the third and fourth Hawke ministries from mid 1987 to December 1991, drove a much broader agenda, as the inclusion of 'employment' in his title would suggest. It was his mission to reposition higher education, and the training system more broadly, to play a central role in the development of human capital and ensure the successful transition of Australia from a relatively protected and insular economy to a more internationally competitive one.

Both ministers left a lasting legacy. Susan Ryan, with strong support from the prime minister, successfully pursued an agenda of equity in higher education, opening the doors to a much wider demographic. Particularly, the number of female students increased significantly. When John Dawkins became Minister for Education in 1987 he thus inherited a system that had outgrown its traditional boundaries and was ready to adopt a new role within the life of the nation. Accordingly, he began a major shake-up of the higher education system, abolishing the binary divide between universities and colleges of advanced education as well as promoting links between universities and industry partners to help modernise the economy. He also oversaw the development of new funding mechanisms to help pay for his reform program, most notably the Committee on Higher Education Funding, led by Neville Wran, which introduced the Higher Education Contribution Scheme.

The reform agendas of Ryan and Dawkins are still influential twenty years on. Women are now much more likely to go to university than men – a reversal of the position prior to the Hawke government reforms. At the same time, as the recent Bradley review indicates (Bradley et al. 2008), class and race remain intractable determinants of access to higher education and the job market. The 'unified national system' established by Dawkins continues to define higher education but from the early 1990s there has been a balkanisation of the system with the establishment of sub-groups such as the Group of Eight and the Australian Technology Network which pursue different policy agendas, most notably around research funding. There has also been the proliferation of private providers catering primarily to the international student market. And, despite the efforts of the Hawke government and its successors, Australian industry still spends a relatively small amount on research and development compared to similar nations. Nonetheless, at the end of the first decade of the twenty-first century, the Rudd Labor government's positive response to the Bradley Review indicates that it will build on the Hawke legacy and begin to invest again in higher education.

The Ryan years

While the Whitlam government's removal of student fees had broadened access and changed the perception of the role of universities, it was Susan Ryan, as Minister for Education in the first two Hawke ministries, who tackled the issue of transforming the gendered structure of the Australian labour market through legislation. As Ryan has pointed out, when Hawke was elected in 1983

> the Australian labour market was the most gender segregated in the OECD. Fewer females participated in higher education, and female postgraduates were clustered in a narrow range of courses. Women made up only a small minority of those taking up postgraduate work. There was no female Vice Chancellor, few female professors, and very few females were awarded research grants. (Ryan 2003, p. 211)

As Prime Minister, Hawke immediately re-established the Office for the Status of Women inside the Department of Prime Minister and Cabinet, appointing Ryan as the minister assisting in the portfolio to develop legislation on sex discrimination and affirmative action (see Mackinnon this volume). In an age when public attitudes to these issues remained largely conservative, such changes cannot be understated. In the traditionally male-dominated higher education sector Ryan's policies resulted in a huge increase in the participation of women at all levels, increasing the number of female undergraduates, postgraduates, lecturers, researchers, professors and senior managers, including vice-chancellors. Similarly, to ensure that Aboriginal and Torres Strait Islander peoples' educational outcomes became part of the mainstream education and training agenda, Hawke immediately transferred Aboriginal education programs from the Department of Aboriginal Affairs to the Department of Education overseen by Minister Ryan (see Buckskin this volume).

The rapid modernisation of the Australian economy in the early years of the Hawke government provided opportunities to expand the reach of universities to include not only broader access for Australian students but also to cater for the education of international students. The impetus for this expansion of international education was provided by the *Report of the Committee to Review the Australian Overseas Aid Program* (1984). This report, chaired by R. Gordon Jackson, recognised the potential benefit to Australia of full-fee-paying places for overseas students and opened the door to developing Australian higher education as an export industry, geared heavily towards the Asian market. Whilst primarily concerned with the traditional use of education as a source of foreign aid, the committee recommended that

A liberal policy towards accepting foreign students should be adopted taking academic performance, cost effectiveness and available places into consideration. The overseas student charge should be gradually increased to full cost levels. The fees levied should accrue to the institutions that the students attend in order to build up appropriate courses for such students, increase the number of places available without cost to the taxpayer and encourage the development of education as an 'export' sector. (1984, p. 9)

As a result, in 1986, full-feeing-paying places for overseas students became an option for the higher education sector, which enrolled 2000 full-fee-paying overseas students that year. Since these modest beginnings, Australia has rapidly capitalised on a primarily Asian market for English language higher education and the numbers have grown to over 500,000 international students in 2009, making education the nation's third largest export industry. Australia's achievements in this new export industry have led to a major shift in perception about the place of Australian universities in a global environment, earning them a reputation as successful innovators in the thriving education market of the rapidly developing Asia-Pacific region.

The negotiation of these changes created considerable turbulence for Senator Ryan, who expressed discomfort at the push to subject the higher education system to market forces, especially when that involved risking the equity agenda by raising student fees. In the *Guidelines to the Commonwealth Tertiary Education Commission for 1987* she attempted to refocus policy on the provision of equitable, accessible higher education, writing that, as minister, she had 'committed the Government to a return to growth in the tertiary education sector' in terms of student numbers, favouring a $250 Higher Education Administration Charge over the more costly tutorial fees or student loans (Ryan 1986, p. 1). At the same time, Ryan knew the system was growing beyond the limitations of collegiality and was acutely aware of the need to increase its connections to industry, arguing: 'I have continually stressed the Government's objective of fostering closer links between tertiary education and industry' (1986, p. 7). Yet, without an active financial incentive, building those links seemed extremely difficult.

As the Commonwealth Minister for Education in the first years of the Hawke government, Ryan grappled with the reconciliation of two polar opposites. On the one hand, the collegial system of education in operation since the sixties had succeeded in opening higher education to more Australian students, reacting to the drive for access and equity. On the other, the rapid increase in student numbers and the global trend towards economic rationalism meant it was no longer feasible for universities to remain relatively small-scale, publicly funded institutions devoted to undergraduate teaching, pure research and the training of research students. Ryan saw the debate about full-fee-paying overseas students as emblematic of the gap between these two positions, writing in her autobiography that things had changed by the mid-eighties:

> The ideology of the market place had infected thinking about universities. The Jackson Report ... advocated student places as our new export product. Instead of being the beneficiaries of aid, Asian students were to become the new financial salvation for our cash-strapped universities ... I was alarmed at the proposals from the marketeers that the problems of under capitalized and overcrowded universities could be solved easily and profitably if I gave the go ahead to private universities. (Ryan 1999, p. 257)

These were times for a more radical approach to higher education reform, which would transform universities from collegial, relatively aloof, institutions into major drivers of the new economy. They suited the new Minister for Education admirably.

The Dawkins years

When John Dawkins took over the education portfolio in 1987 it was with the express goal of finding a compromise between higher education as equitable and as economically productive. Dawkins' aim was to turn Australian universities into large-scale, professional organisations designed to lead Australia into the new century and thrive in an environment characterised by neo-liberalism and globalisation. In this respect, the reforms reflected a wider Hawke government interest in adopting the economic rationalist agenda of Thatcher and Reagan whilst retaining strong themes of equitable and accessible education. Partly this was a reflection of changing attitudes about the role of universities in the wider Australian society. Partly, it had a grander objective, attempting to develop a university system that would help the nation become more internationally competitive. Accordingly, when Dawkins released *Higher Education: A Policy Discussion Paper* in 1987 he opened with a specification that his reforms aimed to recognise that higher education had a new role to play as the Australian nation faced changing social and economic conditions. In response to those changes, he argued, the 'education sector, and our higher education system in particular, must play a leading role in promoting these changes' (Dawkins 1987, p. iii).

The most obvious initial change was the abolition of the binary system in favour of a unified one, bringing together technical institutes, colleges of advanced education and universities. The binary system had been cemented in the 1960s by Sir Leslie Martin to support the position of universities as unique, superior institutions occupied with research and the knowledge industry, feeding down to technological institutes and colleges of advanced education which held a distinctly different, and lower, position. As Susan Davies notes, 'he took it that the role of the technological institution would be to translate the research findings of the academic university – the senior institution – into a form that could be applied in industry' (1989, p. 47). Dawkins abolished this distinction, insisting that existing universities, colleges and institutes should merge to create a new style of higher education provider with a background in technical and vocational education. The immediate result was that the number of universities in Australia more than doubled to thirty-eight by 1991, including Bond, the first private university, ushering in the era of mass higher education.

The removal of the binary system was the centre point of Dawkins' reforms, reflecting his aim of creating a stronger link between higher education and the society it purported to serve. To help achieve this, Dawkins' replaced the Australian Research Grants Committee with the Australian Research Council (ARC), supplying it with a professional, full-time leadership and a bigger budget. Its role was to broaden research activity, encourage partnerships outside the university sector and provide an avenue for research funding open to both the established universities and the newly created 'post 1987' institutions born of the institutes and colleges. Additionally, the formation of the ARC gave the government an opportunity to direct research to meet national priorities, provide funding to postdoctoral and early career researchers, support links between researchers and industry, and drive Australian universities into a position comparable to other OECD countries (Department of Employment, Education and Training 1988, pp. 90–91).

In *Excellence and Efficiency: The Vice-Chancellors' Response to the Green Paper*, the Australian Vice-Chancellors' Committee noted that 'Industry must accept more responsibility for funding research projects and must recognise the value of funding R&D in Australia rather than buying technology from overseas' (1988, p. 4). This was particularly relevant as Australia tried to move beyond an economy reliant on natural resources and agriculture. Both the Vice-Chancellors' Committee and Dawkins recognised that a significant volume of funding would be required to make Australian research comparable in depth and quality with other OECD nations. The plan was for the ARC to allocate $5 million in 1988, increasing progressively to $65 million in 1991 (Department of Employment, Education and Training 1988, p. 94). Dawkins was aware that the growth of the university sector would outstrip the available volume of government funding and to solve the problem, much to the chagrin of the universities, he doubled the ARC budget by clawing back 1 per cent of their operating grants. At the same time, he reinforced the vice-chancellors' argument by stating that 'research in higher education institutions cannot serve as a substitute for industrial research and development; nor should they be forced to assume this role' (Department of Employment, Education and Training 1988, p. 90). However, he wrote, the government 'seeks to promote greater responsiveness' within the university sector to both social and industry needs (1988, p. 90).

To help achieve this, the ARC established the Collaborative Research Grants Scheme to encourage universities and industry partners to work together on research projects. More significantly, in 1990 in its fourth term the Hawke government established the Cooperative Research Centres Program (CRCs) to bolster collaborative research between universities, government research laboratories like the CSIRO, and industry partners. The CRCs focused on big science programs to be funded at a level of at least $2 million per annum from the Commonwealth to be matched by an equivalent amount from the research and industry partners for an initial seven years with a possibility of renewal. Since their establishment, there have been ten selection rounds resulting in 168 CRCs involving an investment of $3 billion by the government and almost $9 billion in cash and in-kind contributions from participants. In the most recent review of the CRC program, Professor Mary O'Kane pointed out that they have become 'an iconic program in the Australian innovation system that has been copied in other countries' (O'Kane 2008, p. i). The CRCs have been an elegant solution to the issue of developing closer relationships between government research laboratories and industry, as well as leveraging considerable extra research funds from industry partners to address the chronic under-investment in research and development by the private sector.

At the same time as the Dawkins' review, the Committee on Higher Education Funding, led by former NSW Premier Neville Wran, attempted to negotiate a position between universities as accessible public institutions and organisations powerful enough to thrive in an increasingly competitive international environment. For both Dawkins and Wran, the goal was to make universities more competitive, provide a level playing field for the newer universities and detach higher education from a reliance on the public purse as they grew from relatively small organisations with thousands of students into major corporations with tens of thousands of students.

When the Committee on Higher Education Funding released its report, it specified that its goal was to provide 'a way of financing the further growth of the system that was fair to the students who benefited from education through future earnings' (1988, p. 19). The outcome was the Higher Education Contribution Scheme, or HECS, which involved undergraduate students paying a 'contribution', either upfront at a discounted rate or deferred and recouped through the taxation system when graduates' salaries reached average weekly earnings. Not surprisingly, the scheme was very unpopular with students but, like the CRC research program, provided an innovative solution to the need for increased funding in higher education and has been widely copied overseas. Although politicians from both parties have regularly tinkered with the two programs, both CRCs and HECS have survived to the present day and remain enduring parts of the Hawke legacy.

Higher education under Howard

By the early 1990s, it was clear to all involved in higher education that the world they had known was gone and the emergent, amalgamated universities were fashioned on corporate, rather than collegial, lines. Increasingly, they were led by a vice-chancellor and president, who was supported by a full-time senior management group which oversaw the development of the institution according to the strategies and targets articulated in its research management, equity and corporate plans. In 1997, after the accession of the Howard government, Minister for Education Amanda Vanstone commissioned a review led by Roderick West, the former Headmaster of Kings College in Sydney. He wrote:

> We think that it is desirable and necessary for the Government to take an industry perspective on the higher education sector ... Higher education institutions consume resources, provide services, manage assets and have customers. If these resources are not used effectively governments, students and the community will receive poor returns for the investments that they make in universities. (Higher Education Financing and Policy Review Committee 1998, p. 19)

By then, even though many academics were still uncomfortable with the corporate approach, universities were operating in a market environment involving enterprise bargaining, quality audits of teaching and research, and an increasing emphasis on the need for good governance, overseen by more streamlined councils populated by members who came from the corporate sector. While the West review had limited impact, Appendix 13 of the final report gained considerable notoriety in the sector. It argued that increased competition from international and online universities would have a devastating effect on Australian higher education and predicted that, by 2015, only a handful of local universities would survive (1998).

Looking back from the perspective of the end of the first decade of the twenty-first century, it is clear that Australian higher education has not only survived but prospered, despite the fact that it is 'the only OECD country where the public contribution to higher education remained at the same level in 2005 as in 1995' (Bradley et al. 2008, p. xv). While the unified national system has splintered into at least four power blocs[1] the sector has become much more internationally focused and competitive. It has assiduously pursued research and teaching links with institutions, both public and private, throughout the Asian region to complement its traditional focus on North America and Europe. To offset the lack of growth in public funding, the sector has increasingly relied on the significant growth in the private contribution to funding flowing from international student income as well as the continual tweaking of HECS, which has massively increased the debt load of Australian graduates. At the same time, Australian universities have developed suites of fee-paying undergraduate and postgraduate courses, including professional doctorates, delivered both online as well as face to face. As a result, the Commonwealth grant as a proportion of the total income of universities has declined substantially since the Dawkins reforms, representing only a relatively small fraction of total income in most institutions.

Throughout the Howard years, each new minister of education introduced reforms that aimed to reinforce the idea of universities as commercially sustainable institutions and continued the push towards a less regulated, more market-driven system with a lower reliance on public funding. Vanstone's successor David Kemp revamped the formulae for both research infrastructure and research training to tie funding to research performance more effectively in the Institutional Grants and Research Training schemes. In 2003 his successor, Brendan Nelson, initiated another review, *Our Universities: Backing Australia's Future*, in which he canvassed the idea of reintroducing a division between research-intensive and teaching-only institutions. During his tenure of the portfolio, Nelson established a number of measures to evaluate the quality of teaching and research, based on competition between institutions and tied directly to funding, noting that,

> In a partially deregulated higher education system, there will be strong demand among prospective students and their parents for information about institutional and course performance. (Department of Education, Science and Training 2003, p. 40)

The impact of these performance measures on universities was considerable, although there was much consternation in the sector around Nelson's penchant for publishing league tables on teaching quality, which often masked miniscule differences in the scores between institutions. More radically, he initiated a review of research infrastructure funding for universities that proposed measures of quality, based on publications and impact on the broader society.

The impact factor in the proposed formula split the universities, with the Group of Eight older institutions strongly opposed to its introduction, and the rest of the sector supporting it. While his successor as Minister for Education, Julie Bishop, continued with this proposal it was not implemented before the Howard government lost power in 2007.

The Rudd agenda

When the Rudd Labor government came to power in late 2007, it rejected Nelson's Research Quality Framework Working Party's recommendation of including a measure of community impact. Instead, it established a new review, Excellence in Research for Australia (ERA). This review aims to develop a formula for the distribution of research funding measured primarily by the quality and volume of publications with community impact reduced to a focus on knowledge transfer through commercialisation. The watering down of the focus on community impact in the formula appears to be a victory for the old established Group of Eight universities and a retreat from the Hawke legacy of a broader engagement with industry and the wider community. The ERA seems more reminiscent of the 1960s than the Hawke years.

However, the new government also established a review of higher education in Australia, chaired by Emeritus Professor Denise Bradley. Her *Review of Higher Education: Final Report*, delivered in December 2008, builds on the Hawke reforms as it starts from the premise that 'the reach, quality and performance of a nation's higher education system will be key determinants of its economic and social progress' in a more interconnected global environment (p. xi). It recommends setting a target of 40 per cent of 25 to 34 year olds to have university degrees, and 20 per cent of undergraduate enrolments from low socioeconomic backgrounds by 2020 (p. xiv). It also recommends

> a demand driven entitlement system for domestic higher education students in which recognised providers are free to enrol as many eligible students as they wish in eligible higher education courses and receive corresponding government subsidies for those students. (Rec. 29)

This is to be supported by an increase of 10 per cent in the base funding for teaching and learning from 2010 (Rec. 26). Equally, to address a longstanding deficit in funding, Bradley also recommends a significant increase in the Research Infrastructure Block Grant – from 22 cents to 50 cents in the dollar – to support the indirect costs of university research (Rec. 8). Further recommendations provide for a major increase in government-funded tuition scholarships for international research students in areas of skill shortage coupled with living allowance scholarships provided by each institution, as well as providing for an increase in the number of Research Training Scheme places and the value of the Postgraduate Award stipend for Australian students (Rec. 9, 10, 13, 14).

In contrast to Nelson's position, the Bradley review reaffirms the importance of the link between teaching and research 'as a defining characteristic of university accreditation and reaccreditation' (Rec. 22). While it canvasses the possibility of the need for some amalgamations in regional areas, it rejects any suggestion of a return to a two-tiered system. It also recommends strengthening the role of the national government in the oversight of the regulatory and quality assurance frameworks for both universities and the vocational education and training sector. In its recognition of the critical role of universities in the global marketplace, in its equity and access provisions and its commitment to a national system, the Bradley Review can be viewed as a direct descendant of the Hawke governments' higher education policies. The Rudd government's positive response to the review and its decision in its second budget to spend $5.7 billion on higher education, research and innovation should ensure that Bob Hawke's legacy lives on.

Notes

1   These include the Group of Eight older institutions, the Innovative Research Universities representing most of the rest of the pre-1987 universities, the Australian Technology Network comprised of the five former central institutes of technology in the mainland states, and the New Generation universities which represent the remainder of the post-1987 institutions.

References

Australian Vice-Chancellors' Committee 1988, *Excellence and Efficiency: The Vice-Chancellors' Response to the Green Paper*, Australian Vice-Chancellors' Committee, Canberra

Bradley, D., Noonan, P., Nugent, H. and Scales, B. 2008, *Review of Higher Education: Final Report*, Department of Education, Employment and Workplace Relations, Canberra

Committee on Higher Education Funding 1988, *Report of the Committee on Higher Education Funding*, Australian Government Publishing Service, Canberra

Committee to Review the Australian Overseas Aid Program 1984, *Report of the Committee to Review the Australian Overseas Aid Program*, Australian Government Publishing Service, Canberra

Davies, S. 1989, *The Martin Committee and the Binary Policy of Higher Education in Australia*, Ashwood House, Melbourne

Dawkins, J. 1987, *Higher Education: A Policy Discussion Paper*, Department of Employment, Education and Training, Canberra

Department of Education, Science and Training 2003, *Our Universities: Backing Australia's Future*, Department of Education, Science and Training, Canberra

Department of Employment, Education and Training 1988, *Higher Education: A Policy Statement*, Australian Government Publishing Service, Canberra

Higher Education Financing and Policy Review Committee 1998, *Learning for Life: Review of Higher Education Financing and Policy*, Department of Employment, Education, Training and Youth Affairs, Canberra

Nelson, B. 2002, *Higher Education at the Crossroads: An Overview Paper*, Department of Education, Science and Training, Canberra

O'Kane, M. 2008, *Collaborating to a Purpose: Review of the Cooperative Research Centre Program*, Department of Innovation, Industry, Science and Research, Canberra

Ryan, S. 1986, *Guidelines to the Commonwealth Tertiary Education Commission for 1987*, Australian Government Publishing Service, Canberra

Ryan, S. 1999, *Catching the Waves: Life in and Out of Politics*, HarperCollins, Sydney

Ryan, S. 2003, 'Women's Policy' in eds S. Ryan and T. Bramston, *The Hawke Government: A Critical Retrospective*, Pluto Press, Melbourne

Chapter 7

Hawke and Ryan: an acceleration of Indigenous education policy

Peter Buckskin

Introduction

In 2003 Bob Hawke wrote: 'Concern with equity during a time of economic reform was a reflection of our broader fundamental commitment to creating a society of equality of opportunity and non-discrimination' (Hawke 2003, p. vi).

Between the years 1983 and 1991, Prime Minister Robert Hawke, his ministers and the Labor government built on the Whitlam legacy in Aboriginal affairs, progressing the notions of self-management and self-determination by Aboriginal peoples through practical, representative bodies that were able to influence government policy more significantly than Aboriginal voices had ever done before.[1]

Unfortunately, Hawke did not fulfil all his promises to Aboriginal Australians – for example, his goal of statistical equity in employment and income status between Aboriginals and other Australians by the year 2000 (Hawke 1994, pp. 590–593), and a treaty and land rights by 2000 (Hand 1987, p. 3152) – and his limited actions on some such issues disappointed many in his own ranks (Ryan 1999, p. 197) as well as in the wider community. However, his government opened a new era in Aboriginal affairs by listening to and acting on the advice of representative Aboriginal groups like the National Aboriginal Education Committee (NAEC), the National Aboriginal Conference (NAC) and, later, the Aboriginal and Torres Strait Islander Commission (ATSIC).

By supporting the work of Susan Ryan and John Dawkins to improve Aboriginal education, and particularly by launching the National Aboriginal and Torres Strait Islander Education Policy in 1989, Hawke displayed leadership and humanity that gave Aboriginal leaders and educators confidence and encouraged them to continue speaking out for their peoples. By supporting the operations of the NAEC, Hawke set in train a process through which Aboriginal leaders developed networks and community support structures that created hope in communities and ensured that the minority Aboriginal voice calling for appropriate education services would be heard more clearly right across the nation.

Pre-Hawke background

Since 1788, when non-Indigenous people formally settled in Australia and claimed the land as their own, Aboriginal and Torres Strait Islander Australians have had little decision-making power over their lives or the mainstream education denied to or provided for their children. For more than a hundred years, individuals and small groups tried to change this, but it was not until after World War 2 that the calls for justice and equity for Aboriginal peoples became louder and more organised. In the 1967 referendum, the Australian electorate voted overwhelmingly in favour of the Commonwealth government having the power to make laws overriding the states for Aboriginal people.[2]

The Whitlam government of 1972, as the first Labor government since 1949, was swept into power on a promise of 'It's Time' – time for things to be different. Prime Minister Whitlam pronounced: 'Australia's treatment of her Aboriginal people will be the thing upon which the rest of the world will judge Australia and Australians not just now, but in the greater perspective of history' (Whitlam 1972). He established the Interim Committee for the Australian Schools Commission (the Karmel Committee), which allowed educators to make formal statements to government about the enormous problems facing Aboriginal education and to call for a separate investigation. To undertake such an investigation, the Commonwealth government established the National Aboriginal Consultative Group (NACG) in 1974, and then in 1977, acting on advice from the NACG, established the National Aboriginal Education Committee (NAEC). The NAEC was to provide informed Aboriginal and Torres Strait Islander advice to the Commonwealth Minister for Education, including monitoring existing policy and programs, developing new policy and programs, promoting investigations, reviews and studies, and advising on the education needs of Aboriginal people and the most appropriate ways of meeting these needs (see VAEAI no date).

The NAEC first focused on the importance of including Indigenous-Australian studies as a compulsory course unit in Australian schools and universities, saying it must be taught with a high degree of respect and understanding to develop an accurate knowledge of Australian history. It also called for increased tertiary funds to train more Aboriginal teachers, with the goal of one thousand Aboriginal teachers by 1990. (This was achieved, but, regrettably, many of the graduates were employed in jobs other than classroom teaching.)

Following the Schools Commission report of 1975 the Commonwealth government began funding special programs in the state and territory education systems to alleviate the disadvantages of Aboriginal students. The commission wrote to state departments to suggest programs that could increase the involvement of Aboriginal people in the education process. They offered financial support to establish Aboriginal Consultative Groups at the state level, and Victoria, Queensland and NSW were the first three states to establish consultative groups (see VAEAI no date).

By 1983, when the Hawke government was elected, there were Aboriginal Education Consultative Groups operating in most states, with charters to develop, plan, implement, coordinate and evaluate Aboriginal education programs, services, projects and activities at the state, regional and local level. Their impact on state education authorities was limited, due largely to their limited resources to support meetings and research, but their consultations and discussions ensured that when the opportunity came to work with members of the NAEC to draft a national Aboriginal education policy for consideration by the Commonwealth government, that policy reflected the needs and aspirations of the majority of Aboriginal and Torres Strait Islander Australians.

The members of the NAEC came from all states, the Torres Strait Islands, the Northern Territory and the Australian Capital Territory and shared a range of educational experiences including traditional Aboriginal and formal western-style education. The committee offered advice to the Commonwealth education portfolio agencies and the Department of Aboriginal Affairs on existing programs and on the development of educational programs and policies throughout Australia for Aboriginal and Torres Strait Islander peoples. They also offered advice to other institutions concerned with the education of Indigenous people.

Engagement with Aboriginal representatives

In the early years, apart from a full-time chair, the NAEC was comprised of part-time members – individuals travelling to Canberra from all parts of Australia and fitting their advisory work in between jobs and demanding family and community lives – but the Hawke government, keen to see the committee play a bigger role, provided extra support in the form of a full-time salaried position for the Deputy Chair, taken up by Errol West, and an enhanced secretariat to support the committee's work.

As a young Aboriginal teacher, Chairman of the South Australian AECG and a member of the NAEC, I was thrilled to be part of what seemed to be a positive future for Aboriginal education. I remember meetings with Susan Ryan when she was the Shadow Minister for Aboriginal Affairs before the 1983 election of the Hawke government. First and foremost a committed feminist, Susan Ryan had a strong sense of social justice and an appreciation of the importance of education to equal opportunity. I remember her keenness as a shadow minister to learn about Aboriginal communities and to listen to our views on improving educational opportunities for our children. I remember looking forward to a day when she might be Minister for Aboriginal Affairs and have the authority to act on our advice.

So it was with an initial sense of disappointment that I learned that in the new Hawke government Clive Holding would be Minister for Aboriginal Affairs. But this changed when it was announced that Susan Ryan would be Minister for Education, and she, in keeping with the NAEC's advice, secured Prime Minister Hawke's support to move Aboriginal education policy into the education portfolio (out of Aboriginal affairs).

I recall the excitement felt by NAEC members when Prime Minister Hawke authorised new administrative orders that brought

Aboriginal education into the mainstream education portfolio
(Commonwealth of Australia Gazette, No. S 46, 11 March 1983)
and made the NAEC a ministerial committee advising the Minister
of Education, rather than the bureaucracy. For us, this structure
symbolised that the education of our children was seen as a mainstream issue rather than a sideline issue, and that state education
systems could no longer leave it in the 'too hard' basket, along with
all other Aboriginal affairs, for the Commonwealth government to
'fix'.

Unfortunately, when Labor came to power in 1983, it inherited a
large deficit, and the perceived economic crisis informed much of the
Hawke government's policy making. Systematic economic reforms
saw the opening of Australian finance and industry to global competition and the restructuring of the role of trade unions. Hawke,
and his Treasurer Paul Keating, regarded good management of the
ailing economy as vital ('Robert Hawke in Office' no date). Though
some were critical at the time, many people have since expressed
admiration for the way these reforms positioned Australia internationally thereafter.

As Education Minister, Susan Ryan set up the Aboriginal and
Torres Strait Islander Capital Grants Program to build and renovate
school buildings in remote communities, and made efforts, with
the cooperation of the states, to provide suitably trained teachers
for Aboriginal children. However, the resultant budgetary pressure
took its toll as she sought additional funds for education, which, by
its very nature, was already a huge budget item (Ryan 1999, p. 240).
This culminated in her being over-ridden by the prime minister and
treasurer to introduce tertiary fees, and not long afterwards John
Dawkins was made Minister for Education.

What was important to the Aboriginal community at this time
was that they and their representatives on both the NAEC and
ATSIC were being encouraged to discuss issues like autonomy and
self-determination and that their advice on improving Aboriginal
well-being was being sought as the basis of government policy. We
thought that the Hawke commitment to consensus, seeking out
leaders in various sectors and securing consensus around major
issues, was being applied to Aboriginal education, and that ministers had confidence in us, and we responded to this with energy and
hard work.

We were always aware of the dependency on government that was inherent in bureaucratic structures like the NAEC and ATSIC, and the requirement they brought for Aboriginal people to learn about and work within non-Aboriginal structures and processes (as discussed by Hughes 1995), but we were buoyed by the fact that we were dealing with a government which for the first time, and without any legal obligation, seemed pre-disposed to supporting Aboriginal people and willing to articulate in the Parliament its awareness of Aboriginal prior ownership, invasion, dispossession and our entitlement to self-management and self-determination.

There was excitement in December 1987 when Aboriginal Affairs Minister Gerry Hand announced to the Parliament an intensive round of consultation with Aboriginal organisations Australia-wide to discuss reorganisation of Aboriginal and Islander affairs under a national Aboriginal and Torres Strait Islander Commission (ATSIC) based on elected regional councils. In 1989, after long parliamentary debate, the *ATSIC Act* became law, with objects that read:

> 3. The objects of this Act are, in recognition of the past dispossession and dispersal of the Aboriginal and Torres Strait Islander peoples and their present disadvantaged position in Australian society:
>
> > (a) to ensure maximum participation of Aboriginal persons and Torres Strait Islanders in the formulation and implementation of government policies that affect them;
> >
> > (b) to promote the development of self-management and self-sufficiency among Aboriginal persons and Torres Strait Islanders;
> >
> > (c) to further the economic, social and cultural development of Aboriginal persons and Torres Strait Islanders; and
> >
> > (d) to ensure co-ordination in the formulation and implementation of policies affecting Aboriginal persons and Torres Strait Islanders by the Commonwealth, State, Territory and local governments, without detracting from the responsibilities of State, Territory and local governments to provide services to their Aboriginal and Torres Strait Islander residents. (*Aboriginal and Torres Strait Islander Commission Act 1989* (Cwlth))

At the time, some Aboriginal groups did not support ATSIC in its final form. Certainly, it was not what was originally intended, as the final legislation was the result of long Senate debate and more than one hundred amendments proposed by the Coalition and the Democrats. There were also those who saw it as merely a forum through which the government would secure the views of the Aboriginal community, not as a body that would administer government services and be an agent of self-determination (Brennan 1990).

With the benefit of hindsight, we can be critical, but the creation of ATSIC, like the government's engagement with the NAEC, was an important step towards increased Aboriginal participation in decision making, and its operation, though later discredited, became an important vehicle for building the confidence of its Aboriginal members and the communities they represented.

Adoption of the National Aboriginal and Torres Strait Islander Education Policy

In 1987, portfolio changes saw Susan Ryan removed as Minister for Education and John Dawkins appointed as Minister for Employment, Education and Training. This began not only what was to be the most significant reform of tertiary education to date, but also the most significant opportunity for Aboriginal educators seeking a new approach to schooling for Aboriginal children.

Although it seemed to some that the new portfolio arrangements signalled a shift from the cultural and consultative emphasis under Ryan to the interventionist approach of Dawkins, driven more directly by economic considerations (McMorrow 2003), those who had been active within the AECGs and the NAEC were pleased that the change culminated in an admirable national policy initiative in Aboriginal education.

Dawkins established an Aboriginal Education Policy Task Force which was to report to him as Minister for Employment, Education and Training. Many Aboriginal people were reluctant to cooperate with this change, but thanks to the consultation and hard work undertaken by the NAEC in the preceding decade, the new task force was able to prepare the comprehensive Hughes Report of 1988 (named for Aboriginal educator Paul Hughes, who had earlier been a Chair of the NAEC and who now reported to Minister Dawkins as Chair of the new Aboriginal Education Policy Task Force) which then enabled Prime Minister Hawke to launch the first National Aboriginal and Torres Strait Islander Education Policy in 1989 (originally referred to as the ATSIEP and later more commonly as the AEP).

I remember the day Hawke launched the AEP in the Great Hall at Parliament House in Canberra. Aboriginal and Torres Strait Islander leaders from every education sector applauded the inclusive nature of the policy and the enacting legislation which coordinated all the specific targeted programs under the auspice of the one policy framework (*Aboriginal Education (Supplementary Assistance) Act 1989* (Cwlth)).

The AEP identified twenty-one long-term goals. Its main themes were increased access to and participation in education by Aboriginal people, involvement of Aboriginal and Torres Strait Islander people in educational decision making and the delivery of education services, and equitable and appropriate educational outcomes (Department of Employment, Education and Training 1989).

Endorsed in 1989 by all state and territory governments, the AEP came into effect nationally in 1990 as the Hawke government dedicated specific funds to Aboriginal education through programs such as the Indigenous Education Strategic Initiative Program (IESIP) and Aboriginal Student Support and Parent Awareness (ASSPA).

This policy stands out as a milestone in Australian history, uniting all states and territories with the Commonwealth in a commitment to pursuing national goals for Indigenous education, goals which, for the first time in postcolonial Australia, had been formulated by Aboriginal people themselves and professionally set down in writing by Aboriginal educators. It set benchmarks for achieving these goals and optimistically anticipated that there would be a noticeable increase in Aboriginal participation by the year 2000.

For the first time, and at last, through the AEP the Australian nation was formally expressing through government policy an awareness of the need to improve educational opportunities and outcomes for Aboriginal people and a strategy for achieving that which was based on increased Aboriginal input into education decision making.

Since then, although the policy has been reviewed several times and augmented by the 1992 Literacy Strategy, it remains the formal policy of Commonwealth and state governments to this day, still educationally and culturally relevant. The shameful fact is that the policy has still not been effectively implemented to benefit Indigenous children. In the 1990s, the reports of the Royal Commission into Aboriginal Deaths in Custody (1991) and the National Inquiry into the Separation of Aboriginal and Torres Strait Islander Children from their Families (1997) highlighted the failure of education and training systems to engage and achieve appropriate educational outcomes for Aboriginal and Torres Strait Islander Australians. The 1999 Human Rights and Equal Opportunity Commission Inquiry into Rural Education was similarly scathing in its assessment of the lack of provision of basic education, finding it an abuse of human rights. The fact that Indigenous Australians remain educationally and otherwise disadvantaged in relation to the rest of the Australian population is an offence against humanity.

The problem has been not with the policy but with the failure of governments to implement it, reminding us of the weaker aspects of our Australian federation. There are limits to the ability of the Commonwealth government to influence the quality of teaching and the delivery of education by individual state education authorities. Regrettably, it seems that no amount of money given to the states is yet able to ensure their sustained support for the principal changes required for improvement, namely systemic changes that will result in:

- engagement of Indigenous peoples in the governance of schools, to secure our active participation in school-based decision making;
- inclusion of cultural competency studies in pre-service and in-service training for teachers and education workers, to ensure the knowledge and skills required for building positive relationships with Indigenous children and their communities;
- training of more Indigenous Australians to be employed in teaching and support roles at all levels of care and education, and establishment of career paths and award structures that recognise their value to the learning process for Indigenous students, and indeed for all students; and
- establishment of a national council of Indigenous educators to provide professional, pedagogical advice to governments and education systems on the learning needs of Indigenous children, and to be involved in regular evaluation of the efforts

being made by politicians, administrators and schools to apply that advice.

A sustainable society is one within which all groups feel that their voices are heard and no groups are left behind while the majority enjoy educational and life success. While the current gaps between Indigenous and non-Indigenous Australians remain, the whole Australian society is weakened.

From my personal experience as an Aboriginal educator I know that it is difficult for disadvantaged individuals to maintain energy and motivation when they see no reflection of themselves in the governmental, judicial, health, education and other institutions of the nation. Any confidence to participate and accept ownership for change comes from seeing our own leaders and professionals confidently relating to governments and other influential mainstream community members, and at present Indigenous Australians are not seeing much of that.

In all areas, and especially in education, governments have failed to maintain the legacy of the Hawke era, to maintain the rigorous professional relationships between Commonwealth and state governments and Indigenous educators that were strengthened during the Hawke years, and to complement those high-level interactions by fostering local interactions between confident local Indigenous representatives and school leaders, between members of local AECGs, Indigenous teachers, Indigenous education workers and non-Indigenous teachers and principals.

The NAEC ceased functioning as a formal education advisor to the Commonwealth government in 1988. In 1989, the National Federation of Aboriginal Education Consultative Groups (NFAECG) was established by the various consultative groups around Australia, but it ceased its operations in 1996. Since then there has been no national Indigenous education consultative body or process established, and now AECGs exist in only some states.

Despite the heartfelt apology in early 2008, the Rudd government has not yet seen the need for a national Indigenous education body to advise the Commonwealth government, nor for any Indigenous educators to be employed at a senior level within the Commonwealth education bureaucracy. A number of Indigenous workers are employed within Indigenous education units in state education departments, but they are not always encouraged to provide 'frank and fearless advice' and their perceived inability to influence mainstream processes and attitudes has wearied the few Indigenous workers still in the schools.

Closing the gap in education and a range of other areas between Indigenous and non-Indigenous Australians will require the most constructive consensus between the Commonwealth and state governments and Indigenous educators and communities that Australia has ever seen. In education, the AEP launched in 1989 by Prime Minister Hawke provided a solid foundation for this consensus, and improved education outcomes will result if only governments once again engage with and support the involvement of Indigenous community leaders, professional educators, parents and teachers. Energetic and informed Indigenous individuals are keen to participate, and governments must genuinely seek out and support their participation. Whether Indigenous workers choose to be active within independent Indigenous policy groups, within government bureaucracies or in service delivery roles in schools, governments must champion them as advocates for change, not require their compliance with a system that fails to provide cultural safety and motivation for Indigenous children.

Insulted and demoralised by the behaviour of the Howard government, many Indigenous people remember the hope that was engendered by the Hawke government's attempts to make up for the colonial past by recognising and respecting Indigenous aspirations and trusting our capability to formulate effective advice. Current Australian governments need to reclaim the initiative that began with Whitlam and was progressed by Hawke. They need to once again extend trust, and to rekindle the confidence and ownership felt by Indigenous advisers and their communities during the Hawke era.

The post-Hawke 'discrediting' and abolition of ATSIC reminds us that there are challenging complexities for all Australians in moving from colonial domination to Indigenous self-determination, but this must not deter us from once again extending trust and finding an effective way forward for all our children. I hope that we will soon see some constructive initiatives from the Rudd government including the establishment of new Indigenous representative structures and processes.

Notes

1 Throughout the late twentieth century, the Indigenous peoples of Australia were referred to as 'Aboriginal and Torres Strait Islander peoples', and the word 'Aboriginals' alone was often used to describe all groups. In recent years, the words 'Indigenous Australians' are more commonly used to refer inclusively to all groups across Australia and the Torres Strait Islands, while 'Aboriginals' is preferred by those who traditionally lived in what the settlers called South Australia, 'Koori' by those in Victoria, and 'Murrie' by those in Queensland. This chapter uses the words 'Aboriginals' and 'Aboriginal and Torres Strait Island peoples' when describing events of the twentieth century, as those words were used at that time, and it uses the words 'Indigenous Australians' when looking to the future.

2 Until the 1967 referendum the Commonwealth Constitution, section 51(xxvi), expressly prohibited the federal government from making laws for Indigenous people. The referendum was hailed at the time as an opportunity for the government to make laws to improve Aboriginal people's lives, although in reality the federal government did not make much use of its new power for several years (Attwood and Markus 1998).

References

Attwood, B. and Markus, A. 1998, 'Representation matters: the 1967 referendum and citizenship' in eds N. Peterson and W. Saunders, *Citizenship and Indigenous Australians: Changing Conceptions and Possibilities*, Cambridge University Press, Cambridge

Brennan, F. 1990, 'ATSIC: seeking a national mouthpiece for local voices', *Aboriginal Law Bulletin*, Vol. 2, No. 43, pp. 4–5

Department of Employment, Education and Training 1989, *National Aboriginal and Torres Strait Islander Education Policy: Joint Policy Statement*, Commonwealth of Australia, Canberra

Hand, G. 1987, House of Representatives, *Debates*, 10 December, p. 3152

Hawke, B. 1994, *The Hawke Memoirs*, William Heinemann Australia, Melbourne

Hawke, B. 2003, 'Foreword' in eds S. Ryan and T. Bramston, *The Hawke Government: A Critical Retrospective*, Pluto Press Australia, Melbourne

Hughes, I. 1995, 'Dependent autonomy: a new phase of internal colonialism', *Australian Journal of Social Issues*, Vol. 30, No. 4, pp. 369–388.

McMorrow, J. 2003, 'Education policy' in eds S. Ryan and T. Bramston, *The Hawke Government: A Critical Retrospective*, Pluto Press Australia, Melbourne

National Inquiry into the Separation of Aboriginal and Torres Strait Islander Children from their Families 1997, *Bringing them Home: Report of the National Inquiry into the Separation of Aboriginal and Torres Strait Islander*

Children from their Families, Human Rights and Equal Opportunity Commission, Sydney

'Robert Hawke in Office' no date, Australia's prime ministers website, http://primeministers.naa.gov.au/meetpm.asp?pageName=inoffice&pmId=23, accessed 31 March 2009

Royal Commission into Aboriginal Deaths in Custody (Johnston, E.) 1991, *National Report*, Australian Government Publishing Service, Canberra

Ryan, S. 1999, *Catching the Waves: Life in and out of Politics*, HarperCollins, Sydney

Victorian Aboriginal Education Association Inc no date, website, http://www.vaeai.org.au, accessed 31 March 2009

Whitlam, G. 1972, Policy Speech for Australian Labor Party, Blacktown Civic Centre, Sydney, 13 November

Chapter 8

Delineating multicultural Australia

Alan Mayne

The year 2009 is not only the eightieth anniversary of Bob Hawke's birth; it is the twentieth anniversary of his government's launch of the National Agenda for a Multicultural Australia (Department of Prime Minister and Cabinet 1989). Hawke's prime ministership is sometimes criticised for focusing upon economic policy at the expense of social well-being, and for emphasising strategy rather than sustaining principles (see for example Walter 2001; Aplin, Foster and McKernan 1987). This chapter will test these assessments in relation to federal government policy on multiculturalism. It was during Hawke's prime ministership that multiculturalism received its greatest challenge, culminating in 1988 when the federal opposition abandoned the bipartisan consensus on immigration policy and explicitly rejected multiculturalism. Hawke energetically defended multiculturalism, and set in train a review process that in 1989 delivered its most eloquent articulation, the National Agenda for a Multicultural Australia.

Multiculturalism is not a contentious word in twenty-first century Australia. Indeed, its principles are so well established as the drivers of cross-cultural tolerance and a 'fair go' for all that the word itself is sparingly used today. However in 1988, when I wrote two feature articles in *The Age* newspaper defending it, multicultural policy was under siege (Mayne 1988a, 1988b; see also Mayne 1989). At that time, amid anxieties created by recession and the restructuring of the Australian economy, many Australians viewed with unease the nation's changing demographic face since the Second World War. They wanted immigration policy altered to put a brake on further rapid social change. Others felt that multicultural policy was giving unnecessary privileges to newcomers from regions of the world that until recently had not been significant sources of immigration to Australia. Still others, some speaking for the newcomers, others on behalf of the left, argued that multicultural policy was not doing enough. Influential voices declared that 'Multiculturalism is presently a source of confusion and division', and urged that 'it would be beneficial to the nation if the idea of multiculturalism was quietly abandoned' (Coleman and Manne 1989, p. 10).

Then, as now, multiculturalism had two overlapping meanings. One is descriptive: Australia is a multicultural nation. The other is active: government policy supports the cultural diversity of Australia's population as a healthy tonic of cross-cultural tolerance and national vigour. Some quibble that the two meanings represent 'a conceptual muddle of prescription and description' (Galligan and Roberts 2003, p. 16), but the significance of the National Agenda is that it made plain the two meanings, explained their positive and interlocking qualities, and established in practical and uncontentious ways what multiculturalism meant both in terms of government action and the rights and responsibilities of all Australians. As Hawke explained in 1988, the nation's bicentenary year,

> In a descriptive sense Australia is already multicultural. Some four out of 10 Australians are immigrants or their children. Half of them are from non-English-speaking backgrounds. Less than half the population is of purely Anglo-Celtic descent and almost a quarter has no such ancestry. One in eight Australians speaks a language other than English at home.
>
> In a policy sense multiculturalism is about managing that diversity in the interests of harmony, social justice and economic efficiency.
>
> Multiculturalism is concerned with three things: respect for individual difference, promotion of a fair go, and making the best use of all Australia's human resources. (Hawke 1988, p. 11)

Multiculturalism had gradually emerged as the basis for immigrant settlement programs during the 1960s as the White Australia Policy ended and evidence of the limitations of assimilationism accumulated (see Foster and Stockley 1984; Lopez 2000). Its influence upon federal government policy began cautiously during Gough Whitlam's prime ministership. Its clearest exponent in government was Al Grassby, Minister for Immigration and later Australia's first Commissioner for Community Relations. However the spark came from ANU sociologist Jerzy Zubrzycki, who had since the late 1960s proposed cultural pluralism as the proper framework for improving immigration settlement programs. Zubrzycki argued that 'it was important [to] keep in balance three objectives of multiculturalism: social cohesion, equality of opportunity and cultural maintenance' (*The Age*, 3 August 1988, p. 10). The term multiculturalism was borrowed from Canada, but developed different emphases in Australia as it addressed the outcomes of recent immigrant settlement that were being revealed by sociologists and demographers such as Jean Martin and W.D. Borrie, and which were highlighted by Ronald Henderson's Commission of Inquiry into Poverty which began in 1975.

The momentum for translating multicultural concepts into policy came from Malcolm Fraser, prime minister from 1975 to 1983. Fraser encouraged recognition of Australia's cultural diversity, establishing the Special Broadcasting Service (SBS), and introduced social welfare entitlements for migrants. He also sought to clarify the multicultural principles upon which these programs rested, setting up the Australian Population and Immigration Council (chaired by Borrie), the Australian Ethnic Affairs Council (chaired by Zubrzycki), and appointing Melbourne lawyer Frank Galbally to chair a review of migrant services. Galbally's 1978 report became the reference point for subsequent multicultural policy formulation. The report enunciated four guiding principles: equality of opportunity for all, recognition of cultural diversity, delivery of services through general programs augmented by special bridging programs to meet migrant needs, and the development of migrant services in partnership with their users. On Galbally's recommendation, Fraser also established the Australian Institute of Multicultural Affairs (AIMA) to provide a research base for policy development and to explain these policies to Australians.

On becoming prime minister in 1983 Hawke therefore inherited a set of multicultural programs. Until the late 1980s he seemed intent upon dismantling rather than augmenting them. On taking office the Hawke government substantially reduced the immigration intake, and the 1986 federal budget slashed funding for English language training and other multicultural programs. AIMA was abolished, and for a time a question mark hung over the SBS. Hawke's actions were grounded in pragmatism. AIMA was axed because it 'was seen as a creation of the Fraser government' (interview with Sir James Gobbo, 22 December 2008), and immigration intake was wound back in response to the recession and high unemployment of the early 1980s. The Hawke ministry were also well aware of the mixed signals from the electorate – expressed again during the 1987 federal elections – about multiculturalism, and consequently there emerged 'real concerns in Government … that multiculturalism was a recipe for ethnic division' (Shergold 1995).

By the late 1980s Hawke had to respond not only to anger among ethnic communities at the winding back of multicultural programs, but antipathy towards multiculturalism in the broader community and within his own government. He was also coming under increasing pressure over the size and composition of the annual immigration intake. Some critics complained that family reunion was taking precedence over skilled and business migration, and others worried that migrant selection procedures were causing 'the "Asianisation" of Australian society' (Collins 1984, p. 11). Popular historian Geoffrey Blainey brought the criticisms of immigration and multicultural policy together. Blainey had first voiced his concerns during 1984 (Blainey 1984). In 1988 he again posed 'the question that so worries many Australians: whether Australia should continue unthinkingly to select a majority of migrants from Asia and other Third World regions' (Blainey 1988b). Multiculturalism was in Blainey's opinion an unsatisfactory attempt to mediate the domestic frictions that were being created by this flawed immigration policy. Even commentators sympathetic to the government conceded that the principles behind multiculturalism had become unclear, and that explanation was urgently needed.

The Hawke government responded by attempting to distinguish between immigration and multicultural policy, and thus to provide clarity, a solid basis for consensus building, and a practical way forward for both. The government first established a Committee to Advise on Australia's Immigration Policies in 1987, chaired by China expert Dr Stephen FitzGerald. The government's hope was partly to provide a justification for its immigration program in terms of economic benefits, and also to debunk conservative assertions that immigrant selection was determined by a hidden multicultural government agenda 'to use immigration as some form of social engineering to achieve racial diversification in Australia' (Committee to Advise on Australia's Immigration Policies 1988, p. 59). The FitzGerald report (ibid.), published in June 1988, exposed this fallacy and also recommended enlarging the migrant intake and giving the selection process a keener economic edge.

The government turned next to multiculturalism and, by detaching consideration of it from the subject of migrant selection, Hawke sought to reassert the original multicultural ideal of Australia as a diverse but not divided society. A twenty-one-member Advisory Council on Multicultural Affairs was established in March 1987. Its chairman was Sir James Gobbo and the deputy chairman was George Wojak, head of the Federation of Ethnic Communities' Councils of Australia. Gobbo, a judge of the Supreme Court and chairman of the Australian Multicultural Foundation (he had been a member of the Australian Population and Immigration Council in the 1970s), had migrated with his parents from Italy, aged seven, in 1938. He would become Governor of Victoria in 1997. The Hawke government also created a full-time Office of Multicultural Affairs (OMA), located within the Department of the Prime Minister and Cabinet. Dr Peter Shergold, an economic historian, was recruited from the University of New South Wales to head it. Shergold directed the OMA until 1990 (he was replaced by Peter Vaughan), later becoming head of ATSIC and subsequently 'head mandarin of Australia' as Secretary of the Department of the Prime Minister and Cabinet from 2003 to 2008 (interview with James Gobbo, 22 December 2008). The joint task of the advisory council and the OMA was to define multiculturalism and provide a blueprint for policy development. Gobbo remembers that at his first meeting with Hawke the prime minister

> didn't speak at length about what he wanted, but I could sense what the problem was, namely that what should have been a subject where government should have been having a lot of friends, well he was getting a lot of aggro from different directions. He was getting aggro from what I might call the old Australian view … and he was getting aggro

from the communities, the ethnic communities, because … they were
left rudderless, without their own research body and without a direct
line … to a ministry. (ibid.)

Hawke's strategy worked. Many of the recommendations in
the FitzGerald report (the subtitle of which is *A Commitment to
Australia*) were incorporated into a revised immigration program
in December 1988. These included an enlarged annual immigration target, a revised points system which balanced family, skilled,
and business migration, and the establishment of a new bureau of
immigration research. Releasing the new policy, the government
reaffirmed its commitment to multiculturalism and to non-racial
criteria for immigrant selection. Welcoming the announcement,
The Age commented that 'Multiculturalism is important because it
recognises reality', and was being expressed in a policy framework
that acknowledged that the 'diversity of Australian society has been
one of the great achievements of post-war immigration' (*The Age*, 9
December 1988, p. 13).

The advisory council's initial report, *Towards a National Agenda
for a Multicultural Australia*, drew together eighteen months of consultations and research by the OMA, and was released by Hawke in
September 1988. The research findings established beyond question
the advisory council's first proposition, that 'Australia's ethnic and
cultural diversity cannot be ignored. It is a fact of life. In a descriptive sense there can be no question that Australia is now, and will
remain, a multicultural nation. We cannot turn back the clock. Nor
should we seek to do so' (Advisory Council on Multicultural Affairs
1988, p. 1). The council contended, secondly, that the 'variety of
our origins has not threatened our social cohesion. We remain a
united nation. We are, perhaps more than at any time in our history,
distinctively Australian' (p. 3). And the council proposed, thirdly,
to 'build … upon the traditional commitment of Australians to
a fair go for all' by setting an eight-goal social justice and social
inclusion agenda (p. 5; see chapters 1–8). Endorsing the report, the
prime minister clearly articulated what multicultural policy was not:
it was 'not about creating division – it is about promoting acceptance of difference'; it was 'not about providing special benefits for
immigrants or Aboriginal Australians – it is about providing equal
opportunity for all'. He also emphasised the conditions under which

multicultural programs were provided, insisting that multiculturalism 'is premised on an overriding and unifying commitment to
Australia.' And as he offered these qualifications he also praised the
'tremendous economic asset' – in the form of diverse talents fully
harnessed by Australian society – that multiculturalism represented
(Hawke 1988, p. 12).

After further community consultations, social surveying and
research the National Agenda, subtitled *Sharing Our Future*, was
jointly launched in Sydney by Hawke and – bridging the political
divide – New South Wales Liberal Premier Nick Greiner in July
1989. The agenda elaborated upon the eight goals that the advisory
council had identified in 1988, and based them upon three principles: 'cultural identity: the right of all Australians, within carefully
defined limits, to express and share their individual cultural heritage' (Department of the Prime Minister and Cabinet 1989, p. vii);
social justice; and economic efficiency. The agenda carried with it
$70 million to boost multicultural services and programs. These
would, the prime minister insisted, be available to all Australians:
'We are all equally entitled to a fair go, equally entitled to dignity
and self-respect, entitled to equal access to the services of the government'. All Australians should, he said, 'recognise diversity for what
it is – a great source of new talents and ideas, a catalyst for social
dynamism, a true source of wealth in both its cultural and economic
senses' (*The Age*, 27 July 1989, p. 3). Shergold later recalled that the
National Agenda 'was a winner in terms of balancing rights and
responsibilities and it cut off a lot of the opposition, particularly the
opposition that had come from academics, the right wing attack. It
essentially took the teeth out of that' (Shergold 1995).

Hawke's strategy had worked, then, but only just. The FitzGerald
report discomforted the government because, in attempting to distinguish between immigration and multicultural policy, FitzGerald
fuelled the simmering anxieties about multicultural policy in general
and Asian immigration in particular. The report suggested that the
word multiculturalism might be replaced by something more innoc-
uous, such as cosmopolitanism. Critics seized upon the suggestion,
warning that 'the advocates of multiculturalism should beware that
the culturally enriching virtues of diversity do not degenerate into
the socially damaging vices of divisiveness, breeding ghetto mentali-
ties and communal intolerance' (*The Age*, 8 June 1988, p. 13). Blainey

in particular used the FitzGerald report to bolster his long-running argument that 'immigration was a divisive and unpopular issue', and that 'the policy of multiculturalism is widely viewed as divisive and hostile to Australian traditions and values'. In Blainey's opinion, multicultural policy was turning Australia into 'a "phantom nation", a cluster of tribes in which the wishes of people who retained an allegiance to other countries were respected at the expense of most Australians' (Blainey 1988a).

A still more serious challenge came from federal opposition leader, John Howard, who was quick to realise that he had been 'given a springboard by the FitzGerald report' (*The Age*, 6 August 1988, p. 10). Howard boldly dumped the bipartisan agreement on immigration and migrant settlement policies that had endured since the end of the Second World War. Announcing this decision at a joint press conference with the leader of the National Party, Ian Sinclair, in early August 1988, the two men declared that multi-culturalism 'had run off the rails' and was causing confusion and mistrust (*The Age*, 1 August 1988, p. 1).

Howard was seemingly on safe ground, given the opinion polls and Blainey's sniping, when he declared: 'To me, multiculturalism suggests that we can't make up our minds who we are or what we believe in' (*The Age*, 2 August 1988, p. 1). Howard offered an enticing alternative to multiculturalism: he would go to the next elections with the slogan 'One Australia'. However Howard went a step too far when he followed up his attack on multiculturalism by saying that the rate of Asian migration in particular 'is so great that it is imposing social tensions and imposing a lack of social cohesion' (ibid.). These twin provocations – on multiculturalism and Asian migration – were too much for moderates within the Liberal Party, and Howard's tactics backfired. Premier Greiner bluntly declared that there was no acceptable policy alternative to multiculturalism, and his opinion was publicly supported by Victorian opposition leader Jeff Kennett and South Australian Liberal leader John Olsen. Retired prime minister Fraser added to Howard's embarrassment by demanding a return to bipartisanship and re-endorsement of multiculturalism.

Matters worsened when anti-Asian comments by Sinclair forced Howard to reprimand his Nationals colleague, an exercise in damage control that was dubbed 'hypocrisy' (*The Age*, 13 August 1988, p. 10).

Although Howard forced through his One Australia policy in the party room after a heated debate, and announced forcefully that 'the Opposition had "moved on" from the concept of multiculturalism', commentators agreed that it was 'a victory achieved at the cost of continuing bitter division within his own party' (*The Age*, 23 August 1988, p. 1; 24 August 1988, p. 13). That assessment was confirmed in mid September when Howard and Sinclair dumped the National Party's Senate leader, John Stone, from the shadow Cabinet because of his extreme comments about Asian immigration. An angry Stone hit back personally at Howard, declaring that 'My only fault has been to support too faithfully the position originally taken up, and never recanted, by the leader of the team' (*The Age*, 15 September 1988, p. 1).

Hawke was quick to capitalise upon these divisions. When Liberal deputy leader Andrew Peacock attacked the National Party leadership for their bellicose comments about Asian migration, and former immigration spokesperson Philip Ruddock criticised the joint-party leadership for 'hijacking' the Opposition's policy-making process, the prime minister theatrically appealed to 'decent Liberals' to reassert control over their immigration policy (*The Age*, 13 August 1988, p. 3). In a further bid to embarrass Howard, Hawke moved a motion in parliament reaffirming that racial and ethnic origin were not criteria for migrant selection (*The Age*, 25 August 1988, p. 3). Three of Howard's colleagues – former immigration minister Ian Macphee, Ruddock and South Australian Liberal Steele Hall – crossed the floor and two others walked out of the House 'in a humiliating rebuff' to their leader (*The Age*, 26 August 1988, p. 1). In October and again in November, as Hawke attacked the Opposition's immigration and anti-multiculturalism planks for costing Australia up to $350 million in lost Asian business migration and cancelled trade, Howard complained that the prime minister was 'trying to stir the pot on immigration' (*The Age*, 3 October 1988, p. 3; also 21 November 1988, p. 6).

And stir Hawke continued to do, with good effect. With political commentators agreeing that Howard's One Australia policy 'has, ironically, caused more division than the policy of multiculturalism he finds so unpalatable' (*The Age*, 9 December 1988, p. 13), the Opposition leader was becoming a liability. Howard was replaced early in the New Year by Peacock, who quickly announced a return to bipartisanship on immigration policy. Ruddock, the new coalition spokesman for immigration, reaffirmed the stance that he had taken when he crossed the floor in August 1988, that Australia 'is a multi-racial society', and he emphasised that the opposition's policy contained all 'the essential elements of multiculturalism' (*The Age*, 18 May 1989, p. 16). That assurance, jibed Hawke, smacked of prevarication, and at the launch of the national agenda in July 1989 he pilloried the opposition for its 'unwilling[ness] to commit itself openly, honestly and unashamedly to a multicultural Australia, with multicultural policies'. Peacock snapped back that the Prime Minister was engaging in 'partisan pre-electioneering' by 'playing politics on a sensitive policy area' (*The Age*, 27 July 1989, p. 3). As indeed Hawke was. He went on to win the 1990 federal election, and the Labor Party was returned to office in the election of 1993.

It is therefore clear that Hawke's support for multiculturalism during the late 1980s was conditioned in large part by political considerations. He was quick to take advantage of mistakes by his parliamentary opponents, and he was also intent to win back ethnic voters who had been antagonised by Labor's earlier curtailing of multicultural programs. Speaking at a citizenship ceremony in his electorate of Wills, Hawke conceded that the FitzGerald report had led to 'ill-informed criticism and crude stereotyping' of multiculturalism, but declared that while he remained prime minister there 'will be no return to the past. The White Australia Policy is dead and buried' (*The Age*, 20 July 1988, p. 3). Some painted him as an unprincipled opportunist for behaving so. Blainey accused him of claiming the moral high ground while scrabbling in the mud, and claimed that the multiculturalism being defended by the prime minister 'is unpopular because it is increasingly seen as a confidence trick, a clever and expensive and unpatriotic venture in propaganda and vote-catching' (1988c, p. 30). The accusation is unconvincing. Where was the propaganda advantage, if the opinion polls were right and the Australian public preferred Howard's One Australia to Hawke's multiculturalism? And where were the blocks of 'ethnic votes', since – as those who incited fear about ethnic 'ghettoes' emphasised – many immigrants had not become Australian citizens?

As a canny political strategist Hawke would privately have conceded the mileage that Howard initially seemed likely to win by appealing to anxiety and prejudice, but instead of accommodating himself to these feelings he confronted them. Taking advice from the OMA, he labelled as 'nonesense' suggestions that multicultur-alism was divisive (*The Age*, 21 July 1988, p. 15; Hawke 1988) but, in explaining what multiculturalism actually meant, Hawke drew as well upon two core principles of his own. One was his belief in consensus out of diversity. Hawke applied the term 'one nation' to the immigration debate before Howard did, asserting in July 1988 that 'the essence of multiculturalism and the Government's policy was that Australia was one nation, undivided and united in a com-mitment to a free and open society which welcomed people regard-less of the color of their skin, their language or religion' (*The Age*, 21 July 1988, p. 15). Hawke's other intuitive grasp of multiculturalism was that it should represent a 'fair go' for all. This was, said Gobbo, 'a personal thing' for Hawke, as neither the political nor the indus-trial wing of the Australian labour movement had a strong record historically of cross-cultural egalitarianism. The two men had previ-ously stood together on the issue of a fair go for migrants. In 1979, when an influx of Vietnamese 'boat people' caused alarm, Gobbo led an investigation by the Australian Population and Immigration Council. Hawke, then President of the ACTU, was also a member of the committee. When it recommended an orderly and humane processing of applications at source in the refugee camps, the federal government hesitated. Hawke strongly supported Gobbo, declaring that 'if you tell the Australian people the truth ... they'll wear it' (interview with James Gobbo, 22 December 2008). As they did.

It was to flesh out these personal concepts that Hawke asked Gobbo to chair the advisory council, and established the OMA to assist him (Gobbo made plain that as a Supreme Court judge he 'wasn't going to be at the beck and call of the media every time there was an issue': interview, 22 December 2008). The day-to-day devel-opment of the national agenda was left to Shergold and his staff at the OMA. It was fortuitous that in developing the agenda these three men held four important things in common.

Firstly, they shared a healthy dose of scepticism about the word multiculturalism. Gobbo had initially rejected Hawke's invitation to chair the advisory council because he thought that 'multiculturalism had lost its way'. Gobbo had little respect for the posturing about multiculturalism by some ethnic community organisations, which he blamed for antagonising Blainey in the first place. Nor did he like the 'verbose' characterisations of multiculturalism in government reports. He was sceptical of those who sought to create multiculturalism 'as … a philosophy in itself', and told Hawke when he accepted the chairmanship that 'if we do our job right, we should be able to reach a result where we don't need to use the word "multiculturalism", where you just become part of the landscape. He was very taken with that idea' (interview, 22 December 2008). Shergold, too, conceded at his valedictory lecture upon leaving the public service in 2008 that multiculturalism was 'a noun I always eschewed' (2008).

Secondly, the three men's impatience with multiculturalism as a creed translated into shared determination to bring it into the mainstream, to build a platform for it that was based upon a broad consensus of views. Gobbo was determined to shift multicultural policy formation 'away from the periphery of Australian life and bring it into the centre', and he insisted as a precondition for his chairmanship that the council include Simon Crean as president of the ACTU and a senior representative from the Business Council of Australia. For Shergold, mainstreaming meant emphasising the economic benefits of a culturally diverse society. As he later recalled, 'It was apparent to me pretty quickly that, as long as multiculturalism was either seen as ethnic dancing or social welfare, it really wasn't going to get the support that it required at senior levels [of government and the public service]. And so there was a conscious campaign to give it that economic dimension' (1995).

Thirdly, Gobbo, Shergold and Hawke agreed that the agenda must spell out the responsibilities of citizens in a multicultural society. Gobbo believed that multiculturalism had been 'all about rights and nothing about obligations' (interview, 22 December 2008). Hawke and Shergold sought to boost naturalisation rates, arguing that Australian citizenship not only had symbolic significance but was a prerequisite for full participation in society.

Fourthly, they were determined to set limits. Multiculturalism had to be subordinate to respect for the Constitution and the rule of law, for parliamentary democracy, freedom of speech and religion, English as the national language, and equality of the sexes. The national agenda emphasised that the 'Government's multicultural policies presume an overriding and unifying commitment to Australia, [its] values, customs and beliefs' (Department of the Prime

Minister and Cabinet 1989, p. 52). For Gobbo, however, the 'kernel' of the agenda lay elsewhere, in the parameters it drew for social inclusion and affirmative action. Although the advisory council had readily agreed to the need for legal, health and educational services for migrants, it was divided about the desirability of a US-style affirmative action strategy. Gobbo opposed the idea, arguing that 'the migration ethos is built around the fair go, about ... equality of opportunity not equality of outcomes'. With opinions deadlocked, Gobbo burst out: 'I can tell you, when I came out here with my father, my father was not looking for a favoured go, he was looking for a fair go, he wanted an opportunity' (interview, 22 December 2008). That carried the day.

The national agenda in its final form succinctly defined multiculturalism, established a clear roadmap for its future development, and offered a kick-start by providing 'a framework of concrete initiatives to build on the foundations laid by successive governments' (Vaughan 1989, p. v). The roadmap had begun to take shape at a two-day retreat that the council held shortly after its appointment, during which some members began to talk about multiculturalism in terms of 'a mini Bill of Rights, a Bill of Rights for Migrants'. Gobbo countered that such an approach would produce 'just a lot of words' and invite opposition (interview, 22 December 2008). Crean suggested that rather than words 'we need a stocktake', and so began the OMA's review of multicultural strengths and weaknesses which steered multicultural policy away from engrossment with a narrow range of social welfare entitlements and cultural activities, to a wide-ranging strategy 'for managing the consequences of cultural diversity in the interests of the individual and society as a whole' (Department of the Prime Minister and Cabinet 1989, p. vii). Two important consequences of this were the partial inclusion of Aboriginal people on the multicultural social justice agenda (at the start of the review process they had been ruled out of consideration because 'multiculturalism has not been seen as directly concerned with Aborigines': Jupp 1989, p. 2), and the reformulation of multicultural social inclusion thinking from a concern with residual social disadvantage to proactive programs designed, said Hawke, to 'fully harness the enormous wealth of human talent available to us' (Hawke 1989, p. v). The national agenda included concrete initiatives to streamline recognition of overseas workforce skills, assist the empowerment of women, support English language and LOTE teaching, reinforce access and equity practice by the Commonwealth bureaucracy, and strengthen the SBS. It initiated follow-up social justice reviews by the Law Reform Commission, Administrative Review Council, Attorney General's Department and the Race Discrimination Commissioner.

The national agenda was reviewed and updated – recognising the High Court's *Mabo* judgement – by a new advisory council in 1995 during Paul Keating's prime ministership (National Multicultural Advisory Council 1995; OMA 1995; and see Calma 2008). Another National Multicultural Advisory Council was appointed by the Howard government in 1997 and overseen by Ruddock, now Minister for Immigration and Multicultural Affairs. Its task was to devise a new agenda. How completely had the multicultural landscape changed since Hawke's Advisory Council was appointed a decade earlier. The Howard government now accepted that the 'term "multicultural" is an appropriate description for the cultural and linguistic diversity of Australian society and the term "multiculturalism" is an appropriate term to describe the public policies that address the issues raised by that diversity' (National Multicultural Advisory Council 1999, p. 10). Howard's personal discomfort with the 'M' word did not stop him from supporting multicultural practice, because as Gobbo had predicted to Hawke in 1987 good practice had become part of the landscape.

It is a credit to Gobbo, Shergold and their colleagues that in framing the National Agenda for a Multicultural Australia in 1987–89 they produced 'a document that would work, that could be a handbook' for all governments and all Australians (interview with James Gobbo, 22 December 2008). The agenda endures as the cornerstone for social inclusiveness and tolerance in a culturally diverse nation. It is a credit to Bob Hawke that he initiated, championed and implemented the National Agenda for a Multicultural Australia.

References

Advisory Council on Multicultural Affairs (ACMA) 1988, *Towards a National Agenda for a Multicultural Australia: A Discussion Paper*, Australian Government Publishing Service, Canberra

Aplin, G., Foster, S.G. and McKernan, M. (eds) 1987, 'Robert James Lee Hawke' in *Australians: A Historical Dictionary*, Fairfax, Syme & Weldon Associates, Broadway

Blainey, G. 1984, *All for Australia*, Methuen Haynes, North Ryde

Blainey, G. 1988a, 'Immigration debate will not go away', *Weekend Australian*, 11–12 June

Blainey, G. 1988b, 'Not good enough, Mr Holding', *The Australian*, 26 March

Blainey, G. 1988c, 'Racist: a word hijacking the immigration debate', *The Australian*, 20 August, p. 30

Calma, T. 2008, 'Human rights, multiculturalism and Indigenous rights', speech delivered to the Multicultural Development Association Reconciliation Strategy Launch, South Brisbane, 30 July, www.hreoc.gov.au/about/media/speeches/race/2008/20080730_MDA.html, accessed 26 March 2009

Coleman, P. and Manne, R. (eds) 1989, 'The perils of multiculturalism', *Quadrant*, vol. 34, no. 6, pp. 9–10

Collins, J. 1984, 'Why Blainey is wrong', *Australian Society*, vol. 3, no. 9, p. 11

Committee to Advise on Australia's Immigration Policies 1988, *Immigration: A Commitment to Australia*, Australian Government Publishing Service, Canberra

Department of the Prime Minister and Cabinet, Office of Multicultural Affairs 1989, *National Agenda for a Multicultural Australia: Sharing Our Future*, Australian Government Publishing Service, Canberra

Foster, L. and Stockley, D. 1984, *Multiculturalism: The Changing Australian Paradigm*, Multilingual Matters, Clevedon

Galligan, B. and Roberts, W. 2003, 'Australian multiculturalism: its rise and demise', paper presented to the Australasian Political Studies Association Conference, University of Tasmania, 29 September – 1 October, www.utas.edu.au/government/APSA/GalliganRoberts.pdf, accessed 26 March 2009

Hawke, B. 1988, 'Resisting the rallying call of fear', *The Age*, 9 September, pp. 11–12

Hawke, B. 1989, 'Foreword' in Department of the Prime Minister and Cabinet, *National Agenda for a Multicultural Australia: Sharing Our Future*, Australian Government Publishing Service, Canberra

Jupp, J. 1989, *The Challenge of Diversity: Policy Options for a Multicultural Australia*, Australian Government Publishing Service, Canberra

Lopez, M. 2000, *The Origins of Multiculturalism in Australian Politics, 1945–1975*, Melbourne University Press, Carlton

Mayne, A. 1988a, 'Diversity and conflict are signs of vitality', *The Age*, 27 July, p. 13

Mayne, A. 1988b, 'The ghetto myth', *The Age*, 14 June, p. 13

Mayne, A. 1989, 'What immigration policy for Australia?', *Overland*, no. 115, pp. 78–85

National Multicultural Advisory Council 1995, *Multicultural Australia. The Next Steps: Towards and Beyond 2000*, Australian Government Publishing Service, Canberra

National Multicultural Advisory Council 1999, *A New Agenda for Multicultural Australia*, Commonwealth of Australia, Canberra

OMA 1995, *Our Nation: Multicultural Australia and the 21st Century*, Commonwealth of Australia, Canberra

Shergold, P. 1995, 'A national multicultural agenda for all Australians', interview for *Making Multicultural Australia*, http://www.multiculturalaustralia.edu.au/library/media/Audio/id/424, accessed 26 March 2009

Shergold, P. 2008, 'Valedictory lecture', Canberra, 8 February 2008, Australian Public Service Commission, www.apsc.gov.au/media/shergold080208.htm, accessed 26 March 2009

Vaughan, P. 1989, 'Foreword' in J. Jupp, *The Challenge of Diversity: Policy Options for a Multicultural Australia*, Australian Government Publishing Service, Canberra

Walter, J. 2001, 'Robert James Lee "Bob" Hawke' in eds G. Davison, J. Hirst, S. Macintyre, *The Oxford Companion to Australian History*, revised edition, Oxford University Press, South Melbourne

Chapter 9

The Hawke legacy: social justice as a right not charity

Rosemary Crowley

In 1983 the Hawke Labor government came to power and I was elected to the Senate at the same time. I was the first woman the South Australian ALP had ever sent to Canberra, a mere 89 years after the right to vote and stand for parliament had been won by women in South Australia. I can still remember the energy, excitement and optimism of that time and the great feeling of the 'rightness' of the election. For a start, it redressed the awful injustice of the Whitlam dismissal. Further, it was the time and the opportunity to introduce the policy changes that we had all been campaigning for during the seven years of the Fraser government.

The Hawke government was responsible for wide-ranging reforms, from economics and industrial relations to education, health and social policy. Bob Hawke himself was uniquely placed to push the changes. From his time as ACTU president, he was well aware of the needs of working men and women, he was used to talking to business and he was used to pushing for change.

I want to highlight two areas to tell the story from within, rather than give a detailed analysis of how policy was turned into practice and became an enduring legacy of the Hawke government. The two areas are sex discrimination legislation and women and sport. The first is a great success story and a monument to the Hawke government; the second a story not finished.

As a new chum to government, I had much to learn about the

processes and procedures of government, of parliament and of the public service. I found the processes almost as interesting as the outcomes, and successful outcomes depended in very large part on managing the processes. Alongside the parliamentary ones, there were also the party procedures. All ALP members and senators were members of the full caucus and also a number of caucus sub-committees. I was a member of the health, education and social policy committees and the newly formed women's caucus committee. I also served on a number of Senate committees.

While I was learning about all these steps and stages so were the community and they often found their way into the system as part of their lobbying. The caucus committees, in particular, were a very useful tool for government members and senators to bring information into the debate about legislation. They were regularly host to persons or groups who had a message for government about any number of issues. I found this to be an important part of our democracy.

Sex discrimination

As the twentieth century drew to a close, it was popular to ask the question: what was the greatest thing, event or invention, in the century? There was no right answer, just an interest in what people thought. In India, to give a paper about the status of women for the fiftieth anniversary of Indian independence, I met a man whose answer was the changed status of women. Thinking about it, he could be right. The changes for women were remarkable, though they are uneven across the world. In Australia, at the start of the century, women had little access to education, few jobs, poor pay, poor health services and little protection under the law. By the end of the century things had changed.

It was the Whitlam government in 1972 that spoke to women, appointed a women's advisor, and introduced free tertiary education, equal pay and Medibank. However, those changes were not firmly established and many were watered down or deleted by the Fraser government. It took the Hawke government to re-establish and to build further rights, benefits and services for women.

One of the great contributors to the change in equity and justice in Australia was the introduction of the Sex Discrimination Bill in the federal parliament in 1984. It had been introduced as a private members bill by Senator Susan Ryan in opposition in 1981. She then introduced it in the Hawke Labor government. In government the bill was divided into two, with affirmative action split off into a separate bill. With the support of the Democrats and a number of Liberal senators who 'crossed the floor', the Sex Discrimination Bill was passed in 1984 through the Senate and the House of Representatives, and, after being signed in executive council, so became law.

In the lead-up to the bill being introduced, the debate in the community was characterised by truly outrageous and stupid claims. The world would change so as to be unrecognisable, no longer would men hold doors open for women, women would not want to have children, would not want to stay at home and much more. The public debate ranged all the way from ill-informed, ignorant and sexist, to vicious. The major misunderstanding was that the bill was all about women and that, of course, set the misogynist hares running. The arguments in parliament were no less silly, ignorant and sexist. Women would be required to ride alongside truckies across the Nullarbor and what would that lead to?

What the bill actually proposed was that the law would promote equality – remove discrimination – between men and women by prohibiting the differential treatment of men and women in housing, financial matters, employment, clubs and so on based on sex, marital status, pregnancy or family responsibilities.

In the Labor government, the process for the passage of bills took time; they went through Cabinet, the relevant caucus committee, the full caucus committee and sometimes a Senate and/or House of Representatives committee. The Sex Discrimination Bill got a thorough going over. When finally all channels were exhausted, the bill was ready to go to the parliament. What happened next was that the legislation was listed on the notice paper in the Senate or the House, and in the fullness of time came up for debate in the relevant chamber. Usually the bill was introduced into the House of Representatives first and then came to the Senate. However, if the relevant minister was in the Senate, then the bill was likely to be introduced into the Senate first. That was certainly the case with this bill. The opposition was waiting to throw everything at Senator Ryan, having seen what the papers and other media were writing and saying about this bill. But before they could get at her and the bill, it had to be listed on the Senate notice paper and time for it to be debated had to be set aside. That was another challenge.

Each sitting week of parliament, as well as all the other caucus meetings, the Labor senators would attend a Senate caucus committee to hear and discuss the coming week's agenda for debate, the speakers required, assessment of time for the bill to pass and so on. Usually it was a short meeting and all items were quickly agreed upon.

In the case of the Sex Discrimination Bill, something extra was needed. There was a challenge within the Labor ranks after it was on the notice paper to set aside further time for it to be debated and passed. I remember there was considerable discussion in that Senate caucus meeting. Not everyone in the Labor government was passionately in support of the bill particularly because the debate in the Senate was long and tedious, especially because the opposition was using filibustering to draw it out over many hours and days with nonsense arguments like the ones listed above. This meant that other legislation was delayed and it caused some frustration for Labor senators. There was considerable pressure for it to be left on the notice paper over the Christmas break and other things debated, but Susan Ryan knew that this would mean that the bill would probably never get passed. In the end, we agreed to sit on a Friday, when we usually left Canberra on a Thursday night, all day if necessary, to get the bill debated. This was just another challenge on the road to successful passage of the bill.

The design of this law had three significant innovations. First, it proposed that people who had a claim of unequal treatment or discrimination could go into an office of the Human Rights Commission and make their complaint – at no cost to them. Second, the process of settlement was by way of mediation, where possible, with the staff of the commission listening, to judge whether the complaint was mischievous or serious. If it were serious, the commission brought the people involved to the table to sit down and discuss it, with the aim of settlement. The commission also helped claimants to decide whether to bring their complaint under state or federal legislation. It was, and is, easy and affordable for people to make a complaint and to get a resolution, and it means that the considerable cost of litigation is avoided. This is of great significance!

Not too long after the law came into practice and the appropriate offices and staff were in place, I had a function organised through my office. Three young Aboriginal women attended and during the function they told us about a time when they went to a nearby hotel after their workday – they were public servants – and they were refused drinks there. They said to the barman, 'You can't do that. It is against the law and we know where to go to make a complaint against you.' Those of us listening to that account were much cheered. Not only did the young women know the law and their rights, they knew where to go to use the law for their protection. Bravo!

The third innovation was the requirement that the Human Rights Commission publish a report each year about the number and type of complaints brought under the legislation. At the end of the first year, the report showed that most complaints were from working-class girls and women against discrimination in employment and from men about discrimination in their housing in the army!

This report was of vital importance. First, because it showed that the law did what it was supposed to do – to protect people from discrimination – and second, because it refuted the understanding that the law was 'for women only'. This was an argument used often throughout the debate, in parliament and in the newspapers and on television. But a government report about these cases was another thing altogether. Not only did this help men to know they could make complaints under the law; it also made it imperative that the army provide better housing for its single men, who lived in dormitory huts and ate in mess halls, whereas married men got four-bedroom houses to live in. Over the years since the introduction of this legislation, the housing in the defence forces for single men – and women – has significantly improved.

The sex discrimination legislation was a challenge, as Susan Ryan so eloquently describes in her book, *Catching the Waves* (1999, pp. 240–245). She makes it clear how important was the support of Bob Hawke. He knew the policy promises to women in the lead up to his election victory.

Hawke's support was equally important for the affirmative action legislation, which addressed ways to improve the participation and promotion of women within industry and business and universities. Here his contacts and his experience with the ACTU

were invaluable. It was part of the Hawke government's commitment to justice, equality and good governance. It also corresponded
to other windows of opportunity. There was a growing need for
better trained and qualified staff and workers and, when opportunity presents, good government seizes the day.

The *Sex Discrimination Act* had a very wide impact. In all the
areas covered in the legislation, new rules applied and now people
were required to behave differently. They also began to think differently. Women, like in the example above, were supported by the law
and so they felt more confident and valued themselves more. Men
likewise learned when the law protected them and when it required
them to behave differently. They soon learnt that respecting women
and their skills did not demean them; rather it enhanced them.
Even the media began to change and now blatant sexism draws
wide criticism. There are more women in the media now; they read
the news and no-one complains about their voices anymore!

Women and sport

When the Labor government came into office, it had amongst its
proposals for reform a document called 'Towards equality'. In it
were 42 proposals regarding women. High up the list were items
like income security, freedom from violence, and access to health
and education. A little lower down the list was sport.

The Sport Minister, John Brown, had early on introduced modified rules of sports like cricket and hockey to ensure that all children
had an opportunity to get out there and play. Research had shown
that lots of children missed out, and that in the teenage years more
girls than boys dropped out of physical activity.

In 1984 Senator Susan Ryan and Minister John Brown set up
a committee to enquire into ways to assist women in sport and to
encourage more women to get involved. Susan Ryan appointed
me to head that enquiry. Our committee consisted of eight people.
We toured round Australia, both city and country, and produced
a report called *Women, Sport and the Media*, which was tabled in
parliament. It recognised that the problems that women faced were
well known and documented for a long time but little or no change
had happened; and that there were structural barriers as well as barriers of prejudice and discrimination for women to overcome.

The report made recommendations, in particular the establishment of a Women's Sport Promotion Unit (WSPU) in the Sports Commission in Canberra. I kept wondering why the letters 'WSPU' rang a bell until I recalled they stood for the Women's Social and Political Union in the UK – to my mind a delightful apposition!

Our report was tabled in parliament in 1985 and it was launched by Prime Minister Bob Hawke in the parliamentary committee rooms on the same day. I remember walking along the corridor with Bob and him saying that he never knew that Australian swimmer Linda McGill held the record for the fastest time for an Australian, man or woman, across the English Channel for many years.

Bob Hawke was interested in most sports, in particular cricket, so it was no wonder that he re-established the Prime Minister's Eleven to play various teams, usually visiting touring teams from other countries. The teams played at Manuka Oval in Canberra and the PM used to go and watch if he possibly could – as did we. After our report *Women, Sport and the Media* came out, a visiting New Zealand women's cricket team was playing an Australian women's team at Manuka. It so happened that the next day was to be the Prime Minister's men's team playing the touring West Indies team. When I asked the prime minister if he was going to the women's game he replied yes, he would be there – as would I.

Not only did he attend, but he presented the Australian team with $8000, acknowledged my presence and contribution, and quite stunned the visitors. 'Your prime minister came! … And gave the team money!' More than that, he stayed for quite some time and watched the Australian team batting. He was mightily impressed with one player in particular: 'great little batter!'

Sadly the next day it rained and so his team never got to play, though we all attended the reception for the two teams in parliament that evening. I spoke to Hazel Hawke that day and asked how Bob was. She replied that 'he was not good to talk to at the moment'.

In the evening I talked with Clive Lloyd, manager with the West Indian team at that time, about the team playing near the Oval in London, with the local kids, many of whom were black. He said it was one of the most rewarding things they did: seeing the joy of the children at being able to bowl at Viv Richards, or to try to hit their bowlers for six, or even hit them at all. Essentially, the children were just delighted to be out there playing with the great cricketers.

This had a special pungency for me because Bob Hawke had chosen an Aboriginal lad as wicketkeeper for Australia and the rain meant he never got his chance to play against the West Indian team. It also meant that Bob Hawke's commitment to equity and opportunity for all, especially Aboriginal people, did not get an airing.

Bob Hawke's love of sport was very well highlighted when Australia won the America's Cup for yachting in Perth. He was thrilled and voiced the delight of most Australians. And when he said, 'Any boss who sacks a person for coming late to work today is a bum', he spoke to and for most Australians, in a language they all understood.

So it seemed to me that Bob Hawke would be interested in my suggestion that, along with his men's cricket team, he could also put his name to a women's team. That team was the Australian women's netball team. Being a good sport and seeing its value, Bob agreed to the establishment of the Prime Minister's Cup for netball. Bob attended some of the matches and became a great supporter of netball. First and foremost, he recognised the skills, the beauty, the energy, the fitness and the athleticism of the players and the game. Then he also loved a winner. At the Entertainment Centre in Sydney, he watched Australia come from behind to beat New Zealand in a splendid game of netball. When, with one minute to go, Australian captain Michelle Fielke made an interception that turned the game, Hawkie nearly hit the roof with his excitement. Once again, he was in perfect sync with all the Aussies there.

On a visit to Port Adelaide, Bob and his team found themselves with a couple of spare hours on a Saturday afternoon. When he was asked what he might like to do in that time, he surprised everyone by asking whether there was a netball game he could go to. There was and he did, and it sent quite a message to some in the 'team' who were slow to catch on about women's sport and Bob's attitudes to it.

Netball was, and still is, one of the highest participatory sports in Australia, yet it got almost no TV coverage, and little sponsorship. This was a classic example of unfair practice and discrimination, and Bob's help to change that was very welcome.

The sport enquiry was also a great opportunity to learn more about the political process and how to achieve change. It also provided possibilities to pass on some of that learning to others. On my visits to learn about sporting matters in rural communities, I had the opportunity to meet with women who were battling for better surfaces on their netball courts. Compared to the local footie field, the netball courts were a disgrace and nothing they did seemed to change that. It was good to talk with the women there about when their local government had its meetings, when community members could put up resolutions, and their finding out how much their local government spent on sporting facilities. I might add here that throughout the enquiry, and for years after, I have never been able to get a gender breakdown of local government expenditure on sport – footie fields versus netball courts for example.

But I could and did ask the minister for sport, Senator Graham Richardson a question about funding for hockey. Did he know that there were twice as many women as men playing hockey and yet the women got half the funding that the men got? He did. In fact, these figures were recorded in the annual Sports Commission report and showed the value of gender-disaggregated figures. The minister agreed that those allocations should change.

This brings me to another highlight of the Hawke government: the women's budget paper. It came out with the budget and reported the allocation of every department on gender lines. It was a world first, later deleted by John Howard, but used as a model for other countries. I was at the UN and asked to support a resolution moved by South Africa and Japan proposing it for other countries. I was proud that they were following our initiative but I had to tell them that we no longer had it in Australia. It has been introduced in South Africa but not yet in Japan.

People have often asked me why I thought sport was an important issue for the Hawke government. The Women, Sport and Media enquiry touched on two things that mattered to Bob Hawke: sport and fairness. It is not sporting to have more than half of the population – women and girls – competing against stacked odds.

Conclusion

As these stories illustrate, the core policies of the Hawke government set out to address discrimination, inequity and unfairness. It was a government that made government an instrument for change, for betterment, for equity, for assessment and measurement. What it achieved was to see the policies about equal opportunity and

Medicare entrenched in the political landscape. No matter how he tried, Howard was not able to delete them, though he tried hard.

But, without a doubt, the greatest and most permanent changes are the sex discrimination changes. For women and men, for girls and boys, there is no going back. Our values and our attitudes are very different from 25 years ago. For women those changes have benefited family and community, the wealth of our nation and our future.

References

Ryan, S. 1999, *Catching the Waves: Life in and out of Politics*, HarperCollins, Sydney

Part 3

Health, housing and the environment

Chapter 10

Medicare and Australian health policy

Ron Donato

Today it is inconceivable to imagine that Australia would abandon the basic principle of universality embodied in its Medicare system. Yet Australia has the distinction of being the only major developed country to introduce a universal publicly funded health insurance system and then to dismantle it following a change of government. The pattern of vacillation between providing support for a universal tax-funded health system and supporting a subsidised *voluntary* private insurance sector has characterised much of Australian healthcare policy since the 1940s (Gray 2006). In the main this has reflected the historically significantly different views on healthcare financing held by the two major political parties and the different constituencies they represent (Duckett 1992). The Labor Party has established links with the trade union movement and traditionally supported an expanded public sector and tax-funded national health insurance scheme with an emphasis on free health care. In contrast, the Liberal Party places a high value on individual freedom and the virtues of self-initiative and personal responsibility, and consequently has encouraged private provision and financing of health care by subsidising private hospitals and voluntary private health insurance organisations.

However, it was not until the introduction of Australia's second universal health insurance system of Medicare by the Hawke Labor government in 1984 and successive election victories that a universal health insurance system was entrenched into the institutional landscape. In 1996 the Liberal Party under the leadership of John Howard finally abandoned the party's more than fifty years of opposition to a publicly funded universal health system and embraced Medicare. Had it not been for the electoral success of the Hawke government, enabling it to remain in office for as long as it did, a Liberal government most certainly would have dismantled the universal health system, as it did in 1976 following the short tenure of the Whitlam Labor government. It is the acceptance of universalism in health care by both major parties that renders the establishment of the Medicare system a fundamental and profound legacy of the Hawke Labor government. Bob Hawke himself, and his consensus-building approach to policy, played a significant role in the establishment and eventual entrenchment of the universal healthcare system.

Whilst the Australian healthcare system performs well by international standards it also has particular structural problems that have impeded the performance of the system and represent an increasing source of tension. First, there is the division of responsibilities on health matters between the Commonwealth and state governments, which causes fragmentation and consequent inefficiencies. Second, the health system possesses certain anomalies stemming from the failure to redefine the role of voluntary private insurance within a universal system following the introduction of Medicare. Future health policy developments are governed by these structural features. Here also the historical and socio-institutional context becomes important for understanding the nature of policy reform options aimed at improving health system performance in the Australian situation. I will conclude this chapter by considering the legacy of these socio-historical and structural issues and their policy implications for the newly elected Rudd Labor government.

Health financing policy: historical and institutional context

During the 1940s, following the extension of wartime powers and associated tax-raising capabilities of the Commonwealth, the then Labor government attempted to introduce a comprehensive national health service based on the British NHS, which had been introduced in that country in 1948. In 1946 a constitutional amendment (section 51(23A)) introduced by the Chifley Labor government was passed by referendum to enable the federal government to legislate on 'pharmaceutical, sickness, hospital benefits, medical and dental services (but so as not to authorise any form of civil conscription)'. The constitutional amendment was significant as it paved the way for the development of a federally funded welfare state (Duckett 2004; DeVoe 2001).

Earle Page scheme (1953–1972)

The defeat of the Labor government in 1949 meant that it was unable to implement its proposed national health system. The incoming Liberal coalition government, recognising the public popularity of the Labor party's proposal for a national health plan, introduced its own, and Australia's first, national health scheme in 1953 known as the Earle Page scheme. Developed in close collaboration with the medical profession, the scheme centred on subsidised *voluntary* private insurance for hospital and medical fees, the maintenance of the traditional doctor–patient relationship, and fee-for-service remuneration for medical services. The principles of the scheme ostensibly reflected the basic philosophies of both the Liberal Party and the medical profession of personal reliance, individual responsibility, and clinical and financial independence (Hunter 1980).

By the mid 1960s the Earle Page scheme was subject to mounting criticisms over the inequities and failures of the system. In particular, 17 per cent of the population (2 million people) was without insurance, significant population segments had inadequate coverage and there were increasing financial hardships associated with rising out-of-pocket costs (Scotton and MacDonald 1993; Sax 1984). Following a Commission of Inquiry in 1968 modifications were made to the scheme to address these problems although the basic principle of subsidised voluntary private insurance remained the central pillar of the national health scheme (Palmer and Short 2000).

Australia's first universal system: Medibank (1972–1975)

In 1972 a federal Labor government was elected for the first time in 23 years. Significantly, compulsory universal insurance featured prominently in its election campaign. The proposed system was based on the research work of two Australian economists, Richard Scotton and John Deeble (Scotton and Deeble 1968). Under Labor's universal plan, all citizens would be entitled to free public hospital treatment and medical benefits would be provided at 85 per cent of scheduled fees. The scheme would be financed out of general taxation. Private insurance would be relegated to a supplementary role providing coverage for private hospital charges and ancillary services not covered by Medibank. The scheme was vigorously opposed by the Australian Medical Association (AMA), which spearheaded opposition to the plan from health funds, private hospital groups and the opposition parties (which had control of the Senate), and so was able to obstruct the government's effort to pass the legislation (Scotton 2000). It took a two-year struggle and a joint sitting of both houses of parliament before the Medibank legislation was finally enacted in August 1974 and implemented in July 1975.

Dismantling of Medibank (1975–1983)

The severe economic recession stemming from the 1974 OPEC oil crisis coupled with controversial domestic political issues led to an election victory and return to power of a Liberal coalition government in December 1975. Despite the election promise to 'maintain Medibank', recognising its electoral support among voters, the Liberal government nevertheless systematically began to dismantle the scheme within six months of entering office. The period from 1975 to 1983 saw a number of major changes to Medibank driven by both partisan philosophical values and fiscal considerations (Duckett 1984; Najman and Western 1984). In all there were five versions of Medibank, the final one being a return to a subsidised voluntary insurance system virtually identical to the former Earle Page system of the 1950s. Not surprisingly many of the problems associated with the Earle Page scheme re-emerged, such as a growing uninsured and underinsured population, limited macro-level cost containment strategies, large out-of-pocket gaps and system complexity.

Medicare: Australia's second universal system (1984–)

When a Labor government returned to power in 1983 it reintroduced a compulsory national insurance system of Medicare. This had been a major plank of its policy platform. The Medicare arrangements were one outcome of the Prices and Incomes Accord the Labor party had negotiated with the trade union movement prior to the election. Under the Accord the trade union movement agreed to moderate money wage demands in exchange for enhancement in the 'social wage' of which a tax-funded universal health insurance system was the centrepiece (Duckett 2003; Carney 1988). Introduced in 1984, the basic structure of Medicare closely resembled the general features of the earlier Medibank system.

However despite strong electoral support for Medicare the newly elected government encountered considerable resistance in implementing its health policy agenda (Blewett 2000; Gray 1990). A bitter dispute erupted between the government and the medical profession, which centred around controls placed on private sector activities of surgeons in public hospitals principally in the speciality areas of radiology and pathology (Palmer 1989). The dispute was eventually concentrated in NSW where industrial action led to mass resignations of specialists from their positions as visiting medical officers in public hospitals, putting great strain on the public system (Larkin 1989). Although the federal health minister agreed to set up a committee of inquiry in an attempt to diffuse the rising industrial action, this did not appease the more militant procedural specialists in NSW.

It was intervention at the highest political level involving the prime minister himself, together with the NSW premier and the president of the federal AMA, that finally settled the dispute in April 1985 – more than twelve months after the introduction of Medicare. As part of the consensus approach adopted by the prime minister a compromise was found in which considerable concessions were made by the federal government to the AMA demands but the basic principles of Medicare remained intact. For the Hawke government the main strategy was to get Medicare established quickly and avoid the disastrous scenario of a stillbirth. Here, conflict resolution for Bob Hawke was not a matter of crash-through politics of winners and losers and standing off against the medical profession, but rather involved consensus politics and compromise with the aim of achieving a 'win-win' outcome for the parties concerned.

The Hawke Labor government legacy: the entrenchment of Medicare

Following the introduction of Medicare in 1984, successive Labor electoral victories in 1987, 1990 and 1993 saw a period of stability and the consequent entrenchment of Medicare within the socio-institutional landscape. By 1991 the universal system appeared to be firmly established with opinion polls showing public support steadily increasing from 52 per cent in 1984 to 71 per cent in 1991 (Gray 1996). Here it is interesting to note that the health minister, Dr Neal Blewett, in an interview in 1989 was of the opinion that if Labor was elected for another term, Medicare would have become a 'permanent part of the social fabric', which he believed would then be difficult to terminate (Gray 1990, p. 239). The Labor Party was able to achieve further electoral success under Bob Hawke in 1990 and again under Paul Keating in 1993. This was sufficient to entrench the Medicare system.

In 1996 after four successive election defeats the Liberal party abandoned its historical opposition to, and formally embraced, the Medicare universal health insurance system. At the launch of the Coalition's 1996 election health policy campaign, A Healthy Future, John Howard stated:

> I do not deny that in earlier years I was critical of Medicare ... The Australian public has grown to like Medicare. They find security in Medicare. They embrace Medicare. So does the Coalition and it is an absolute fundamental of our approach that Medicare stays come what may. (Howard 1996, p. 1)

Following its election victory in 1996, the Liberal government swiftly embarked on a series of subsidies, tax penalties and other regulatory measures to bolster private insurance membership, which had declined from 50 per cent in 1984 (when Medicare was first introduced) to a low of 30 per cent by 1998. The cumulative effect of these measures was an increase in private health insurance membership: from 2000 onwards around 44 per cent of the population have held some form of coverage.

A consequence of the private health insurance initiatives has been that for the first time in Australia's history considerable regulatory support has been given to underpinning *both* a universal health insurance system and a voluntary private health insurance system. Significantly, the newly elected Labor government is continuing the support for a pluralist healthcare system by maintaining private health insurance subsidies and also the tax penalties for high income earners who do not take out private health insurance. The then shadow (Labor) health minister, and now Deputy Prime

Minister, in an address to the private health insurance industry in July 2006 stated: 'Australians love their Medicare. But over 42 per cent of Australians have private hospital cover. The private health sector is embedded in our health system and is part of our mixed health landscape' (Gillard 2006, p. 1). A degree of policy convergence and bipartisan support for a pluralist universal health system has emerged over the past decade such that future health policy development in Australia is likely to be framed by these institutional features. Here there are prospects that the Rudd government may be taking a leaf out of Bob Hawke's consensus politics by recognising the socio-institutional significance of the private healthcare sector within the overall Australian healthcare setting.

Structural problems and tensions in the Australian healthcare system

Commonwealth–state responsibilities

A salient feature of the Australian healthcare landscape is the complex division of powers and patterns of joint involvement in the funding, provision and regulation of healthcare services between Commonwealth and state governments. This jurisdictional overlap continues to have major policy implications.

The limited revenue-raising capacity of the state governments relative to their services provision responsibilities and their consequent reliance on Commonwealth fund transfers to meet their obligations gives rise to what is known as 'vertical fiscal imbalance'. The fiscal imbalance and the division of responsibility between Commonwealth and state governments has resulted in a complex, fragmented and uncoordinated system and has created problems of cost shifting between the two levels of government. Specific problems of inadequate delineation and blurring in the roles and responsibilities between the two levels of government have been well documented and include: overlapping and costly duplication of resources and effort; cost and risk shifting; barriers to effective coordination across service programs and reduced accountability as governments give attention to political point scoring and blame shifting (Commonwealth of Australia 2006; Productivity Commission 2005a; 2005b). Both the Productivity Commission and a parliamentary inquiry on health funding identified waste, duplication and cost shifting occurring between jurisdictions and an inherent bias in funding arrangements towards treating illness rather than preventing illness which impeded continuity of care (Productivity Commission 2005a; 2005b; Commonwealth of Australia 2006). Current structural arrangements, with separate 'institutional silos' around funding and service provision, create significant barriers that prevent individuals from receiving a coordinated and seamless continuum of healthcare services.

Unfortunately, in the absence of system-wide structural reform, improvements in health system performance must rely on a level of cooperation and goodwill between the two levels of government that override the incentives within the system to do otherwise (OECD 2006). The recent establishment of the Hospital Reform Commission by the newly elected Labor government in February 2008 can be seen as a response to the structural problems associated with the Commonwealth–state divide in funding and provision of healthcare services. Whilst Prime Minister Kevin Rudd emphasised that the purpose of the commission was not just 'tinkering' with the health system but to address its problems 'root and branch', whether this translates in practice into a comprehensive national health reform agenda that deals with longer term performance and structural issues has yet to be determined. At the time of writing, the commission has released its interim report, in which it strongly emphasised the need to address the structural problems associated with the division of healthcare responsibilities between Commonwealth and state governments (Commonwealth of Australia 2009).

Voluntary private health insurance

A particular problem with healthcare policy in Australia is that the appropriate role of voluntary private insurance was not redefined when Medicare was introduced in 1984. Prior to 1984, the Commonwealth government coopted the private health insurance sector to effectuate its social welfare objectives. With the introduction of a universal system the need for community rating, cross-subsidisation and anti-competitive regulation is greatly reduced as the government's welfare objectives are pursued through the universal system (Scotton and MacDonald 1993). However the regulatory features governing private health insurance remain a legacy of when voluntary private insurance was the basis of Australia's national health insurance scheme and consequently, given its extensive overlap in coverage with Medicare, sits incongruently in the context of a universal system (Paolucci et al. 2008; Donato and Scotton 1999).

In order to underpin the community rating principle, mandatory reinsurance arrangements enable funds with a high proportion of designated high risk members to be compensated through a reinsurance pool shared by all funds on an actual cost reimbursement basis. Market signals are distorted, which weakens the incentive for health funds – when contracting with private hospitals – to control costs for the older and higher-cost population cohorts (Owens 1999). Another significant limitation of private insurance arrangements has been their lack of integration with the broader health system particularly with regards to primary and preventative care (Willcox 2005). The federal government (in April 2007) attempted to address these issues to some extent by allowing benefits to be paid to the prevention and substitution of hospitalisation. However it is uncertain whether insurers will have sufficient incentives and capabilities to be able to engage in appropriate primary care and disease management activities and direct resources away from institutional care. Moreover, the system-wide problems of duplication and lack of coordination of primary care services between the private sector (for those individuals covered by voluntary private health insurance) and the universal tax-funded universal sector (for those who are not) are not explicitly addressed.

A number of empirical studies have questioned the effectiveness of the insurance incentives and policy design in general aimed at reducing public hospital use (Fiebig et al. 2006; Lu and Savage 2006; Dawkins et al. 2004). Empirical studies have highlighted that particular services provided within the private sector may be less technically efficient, more costly or may not be strictly necessary (Savage and Wright 2003; Duckett and Jackson 2000). Attention has also been drawn to the supply side of hospital services, as surgeons often work in both the public and private sectors. A transfer of doctors to meet the increased demand in the private hospital sector attracted by greater workload and higher sector prices can decrease the supply of doctors for public patients. Moreover, uncontrolled demand in the private sector (known as moral hazard) may more than offset declines in public hospital demand, such that changes in physician supply induced to meet the demand differential could see a *worsening* of waiting lists in the public sector (Duckett 2005).

The interaction of anti-competitive regulatory arrangements, moral hazard and the uncapped dimension of a fee-for-service private sector that is underwritten by Commonwealth subsidies raises concerns over the longer-term (publicly funded) affordability of current arrangements and the ability to control macro-level costs of the system. Consequently, the large duplication between public (Medicare) and private financing of services remains an increasing source of structural instability and inefficiency for the health system as a whole.

Health policy challenges: structural reform – the next legacy

Growing concerns over structural problems associated with Commonwealth–state responsibilities have led to calls to consolidate all public funding into a single funding stream (Podger 2005; 2006; Fitzgerald 2005; Richardson 2003; 2005; Allen Consulting Group 2004). The key structural features of such an approach involve the allocation of funds to area-based purchasing authorities based on the healthcare needs of the defined population group. The government purchasing agency is mandated to make informed decisions on behalf of its population to purchase from capitated funds the most appropriate mix of health services that best meets their particular healthcare requirements. In theory, funding all healthcare services under a single pool removes the boundaries between healthcare programs and the consequent structural impediments to the cost-effective substitution and integration of healthcare services (Segal et al. 2002). Although there would be no fundamental changes to the core principles of Medicare the single fundholding framework does constitute major changes at the organisational level within the healthcare system through the establishment of government regional purchasing agencies responsible for the health of their population.

Whilst a single funding stream deals with Commonwealth–state structural issues, it does not explicitly address the role of private insurance and associated regulatory structure between public and private financing. It is in this context that *managed competition*, representing a more comprehensive reform approach involving competing third-party purchasers, has been advocated in Australia by Richard Scotton, the co-architect of Australia's Medibank/Medicare system (Scotton 1999; 2000; 2002). Here capitated payments through the form of publicly funded 'universal entitlements' are tied to the healthcare needs of the individual. Health plans, acting as third-party agents, must compete for enrolees to receive capitated funds and purchase the appropriate mix of services from competing providers (Paolucci et al. 2008; Segal et al. 2002). Supplementary insurance cover would not attract public funding and would be paid entirely by the individual. In theory, the competitive purchasing framework offers the potential of greater purchaser accountability and an integrative role for private insurance, and accords with the pluralistic nature of the Australian healthcare landscape. Notwithstanding its conceptual appeal, Scotton's managed competition model is generally considered to be the more 'radical' of the reform options as it requires greater structural and organisational changes to the health system as well as posing particular technical challenges (Segal et al. 2002).

In the absence of a systematic approach, incremental policy adjustment reduces to adhocracy (Podger 2005; 2006). A coherent longer-term strategic framework would allow more comprehensive policy reforms to be pursued through a series of systematic incremental changes guided by empirical evidence and evaluation.

Conclusion

A profound legacy of the Hawke Labor government affecting every Australian citizen was the implementation of a publicly funded universal health insurance system. Here the role of Bob Hawke as a former ACTU president and as newly elected Labor Party leader was crucial in ensuring that the proposed Medicare system was accepted as part of the 'social wage' by trade unions and represented the centrepiece of the Prices and Incomes Accord. Moreover adopting a consensus approach, a personal trademark of the Hawke era, was instrumental in ensuring that Medicare overcame considerable political resistance following its implementation as well as entrenching it into the Australian socio-political fabric through continued electoral success. Whilst Medicare is now firmly embedded within the Australian institutional landscape, history shows that a Liberal coalition government would not have introduced a universal healthcare system.

Interestingly, Richard Scotton, the co-architect of the Medibank/

Medicare system, has argued that the basic objective of Medicare was equity and it was designed to meet the needs of the 1960s– 80s when the policy focus was on expanding insurance coverage to the entire population (Scotton 2002). Apart from having a certain degree of macro-level cost control, which comes with significant public funding, the pursuit of allocative and dynamic efficiency, according to Scotton, was never explicitly incorporated into the design features of the Medicare system. It is in this context that the Rudd Labor government has the opportunity to address longer-term structural issues of the Australian healthcare system and focus on system performance and the ability to meet challenges of the twenty-first century. Whether the new Labor government will be able to embrace a strategic framework to guide longer-term health policy reform and provide a legacy for the next generation of Australians – as the Hawke government did in its time – remains to be seen.

References

Allen Consulting Group 2004, *Government Working Together: A Better Future for all Australians*, report prepared for the Victorian government, Allen Consulting Group, Melbourne, http://www.allenconsult.com.au/ publications/download.php?id=287&type=pdf&file=1, accessed 15 July 2006

Blewett, N. 2000, 'The politics of health', *Australian Health Review*, vol. 23, no. 2, pp. 10–19

Carney, S. 1988, *Australia in Accord: Politics and Industrial Relations under the Hawke Government*, Sun Books, Melbourne

Commonwealth of Australia 2006, *The Blame Game: Report on the Inquiry into Health Funding*, House of Representatives Standing Committee on Health and Ageing, Commonwealth of Australia, Canberra

Commonwealth of Australia 2009, *National Health and Hospital Reform Commission*, Commonwealth of Australia, Canberra, http://www.nhhrc. org.au/, accessed 15 February 2009

Dawkins, P., Webster, E., Hopkins, S. et al. 2004, *Recent Private Health Insurance Policies in Australia: Health Resource Utilization, Distributive Implications and Policy Options*, Melbourne Institute of Applied Economic and Social Research Report no. 3, University of Melbourne, Melbourne

DeVoe, J. 2001, *The Politics of Healthcare Reform: A Comparative Study of National Health Insurance in Britain and Australia*, Australian Studies in Health Service Administration no. 88, School of Health Services Management, University of New South Wales, Sydney

Donato, R. and Scotton, R. 1999, 'The Australian healthcare system' in eds
    G. Mooney and R. Scotton, *Economics and Australian Health Policy*, Allen
    and Unwin, Sydney

Duckett, S. 1984, 'Structural interests and Australian health policy', *Social
    Science and Medicine*, vol. 18, no. 11, pp. 959–966

Duckett, S. 1992, 'Financing health care' in ed. H. Gardner, *Health Policy:
    Development, Implementation and Evaluation*, Churchill Livingstone,
    Melbourne

Duckett, S. 2003, 'Making a difference in health care' in eds S. Ryan and
    T. Bramston, *The Hawke Government: A Critical Perspective*, Pluto Press,
    Melbourne

Duckett, S. 2004, *The Australian Healthcare System*, 2nd ed., Oxford University
    Press, South Melbourne

Duckett, S. 2005, 'Private care and public waiting', *Australian Health Review*,
    vol. 29, no. 1, pp. 87–93

Duckett, S. and Jackson, T. 2000, 'The new health insurance rebate: an
    inefficient way of assisting public hospitals', *Medical Journal of Australia*,
    no. 172, pp. 439–442

Fiebig, D., Savage, E. and Viney, R. 2006, *Does the Reason for Buying Health
    Insurance Influence Behaviour?*, CHERE working paper 2006/2, Centre for
    Health Economics and Research and Evaluation, University of Technology
    Sydney, Sydney

FitzGerald, V. 2005, 'Health reform in a federal context' in *Productive Reforms
    in a Federal System*, Roundtable Proceedings, 28 October 2005, Productivity
    Commission, Canberra

Gillard, J. 2006, Speech to 5th Private Health Insurance Summit, http://www.
    juliagillard.alp.org.au/news/0706/spad06-01.php, accessed 14 November
    2006

Gray, G. 1990, 'Health policy and the Hawke government: a watershed?' in eds
    C. Jennett and R. Stewart, *Consensus and Restructuring: Hawke and Public
    Policy*, Macmillan, Melbourne

Gray, G. 1996, 'Reform and reaction in Australian health policy', *Journal of
    Health Politics, Policy and Law*, vol. 21, no. 3, pp. 587–615

Gray, G. 2006, 'Health policy' in eds A. Parkin and S. Woodwards,
    Government, Politics and Policy in Australia, Pearson Education Australia,
    Frenchs Forest, NSW

Howard, J. 1996, *A Healthy Future: Launch of the Coalition's Health Policy*,
    transcript, 12 February 1996, Brisbane, http://http//parlinfoweb.aph.gov.au/
    piweb/repository1/media/pressrel/%20JNQ201.pdf,
    accessed 15 October 2006

Hunter, T. 1980, 'Pressure groups and the Australian political process: the case of the Australian Medical Association', *Journal of Commonwealth and Comparative Politics*, vol. 18, no. 2, pp. 190–206

Larkin, J. 1989, 'The New South Wales doctors' dispute 1984–85: an interpretation', *Politics*, vol. 24, no. 2, pp. 67–78

Lu, M. and Savage, E. 2006, *Do Financial Incentives for Supplementary Private Health Insurance Reduce Pressure on the Public System? Evidence from Australia*, CHERE working paper 2006/11, Centre for Health Economics and Research Evaluation, University of Technology Sydney, Sydney

Najman, J. and Western, J. 1984, 'A comparative analysis of Australian health policy in the 1970s', *Social Science and Medicine*, vol. 18, no. 11, pp. 949–958

OECD (2006) *OECD Economic Surveys: Australia*, OECD, Paris

Owens, H. 1999, 'Health insurance' in eds G. Mooney and R. Scotton, *Economics and Australian Health Policy*, Allen and Unwin, Sydney

Palmer, G. 1989, 'Health insurance and financing' in eds B. Head and A. Patience, *From Fraser to Hawke*, Longman Cheshire, Melbourne

Palmer, G. and Short, S. 2000, *Health Care and Public Policy: An Australian Analysis*, 3rd ed., Macmillan, Melbourne

Paolucci, F., Butler, J. and Van de Ben, W. 2008, *Subsidising Private Heath Insurance in Australia: Why, How, and How to Proceed?*, ACERH Working Paper no. 2, Australian Centre for Economic Research on Health, Canberra

Podger, A. 2005, 'Directions for health reform in Australia', in *Productive Reforms in a Federal System*, Roundtable Proceedings, 28 October 2005, Productivity Commission, Canberra

Podger, A. 2006, 'A model health system for Australia', paper presented at the inaugural Menzies Health Policy Lecture, 3 March 2006, http://www.ahpi.health.usyd.edu.au/pdfs/events2006/apodgerlecture.pdf, accessed 9 December 2006

Productivity Commission 2005a, *Productive Reforms in a Federal System*, Roundtable Proceedings, 28 October 2005, Productivity Commission, Canberra

Productivity Commission 2005b, *Review of National Competition Policy Reforms*, Inquiry Report, no. 33, Productivity Commission, Canberra

Richardson, J. 2003, *Financing Health Care: Short-Run Problems, Long-Run Options*, Working Paper no. 138, Centre for Health Program Evaluation, Monash University, Melbourne

Richardson, J. 2005, 'Priorities of health policy: cost shifting or population health', *Australian and New Zealand Health Policy*, vol. 2, no. 1, http://www.anzhealthpolicy.com/content/2/1/1, accessed 19 November 2006

Savage, E. and Wright, D. 2003, 'Moral hazard and adverse selection in Australian private hospitals: 1989–1990', *Journal of Health Economics*, no. 22, pp. 331–359

Sax, S. 1984, *A Strife of Interests: Politics and Policies in Australian Health Services*, Allen and Unwin, Sydney

Scotton, R. 1999, 'Managed competition' in eds G. Mooney and R. Scotton, *Economics and Australian Health Policy*, Allen and Unwin, Sydney

Scotton, R. 2000, 'Medicare: options for the next 25 years', *Medical Journal of Australia*, no. 13, pp. 41–43

Scotton, R. 2002, *Managed Competition in Health Care*, Workshop Proceedings, 23 August 2002, Productivity Commission, Canberra

Scotton, R. and MacDonald, C. 1993, *The Making of Medibank*, School of Health Services Management, University of New South Wales, Sydney

Scotton, R. and Deeble, J. 1968, 'Compulsory health insurance for Australia', *Australian Economic Review*, vol. 68, no. 4, pp. 9–16

Segal, L., Donato, R., Richardson, J. et al. 2002, 'Strengths and limitations of competitive versus non-competitive models of integrated capitated fundholding', *Journal of Health Services Research and Policy*, vol. 7, suppl. 1, pp. 1–9

Willcox, S. 2005, 'Buying best value health care: evolution of purchasing among Australian private health insurers', *Australian and New Zealand Health Policy*, vol. 2, no. 6, http://www.pubmedcentral.nih.gov/picrender.fcgi?artid =1079790&blobtype=pdf, accessed 20 August 2006

Chapter 11

Work in progress: developing new directions for affordable housing policy in the Hawke/Keating governments

Brian Howe

The catalysts for change

My time in the housing portfolio of the Hawke/Keating governments came at a crucial period when postwar housing policies were manifestly unable to meet the new economic and social realities of the last decades of the twentieth century. Australian social policy has always tended to demonstrate a preference for the poor, and this had been reflected in the first Commonwealth State Housing Agreement (CSHA) of 1945 with its focus on slum clearance and the rehousing of the poor especially in Australia's inner city areas. However, following the election of a conservative government in 1949, priority had been given to home ownership. This, combined with rapid population and industrial growth, would mean that public housing was directed to providing rental housing for a largely immigrant industrial workforce. Generally located in proximity to the new heavy engineering and manufacturing plants, new public housing estates offered thousands of working families secure housing, often in a well-planned and pleasant environment. However by the early seventies new investment in manufacturing was beginning to slow and housing authorities began again to turn their attention to urban renewal in the inner suburbs, influenced by overseas trends favouring high-rise housing. Ronald Henderson in his poverty enquiry (1969–1975) criticised the lack of attention being given by public housing authorities to the poor and argued that the subsidies implicit in public housing (controlled rents and a system of rebates) might be better directed towards the person rather than the building (Commission of Inquiry into Poverty 1975). However, the early demise of the Whitlam government and the onset of an economic crisis, unresolved during the years of the Fraser government, meant that no large-scale reform such as housing vouchers was introduced.

When the Hawke government was elected in 1983, the state of the economy dominated Cabinet discussions. Although increased funding for public housing was made available and a First Home Owners Scheme was introduced, lasting housing policy reform was not a high priority. Ministers were critical of Whitlam's failures in macroeconomic policy and there was little support for establishing anything like the controversial Department of Urban and Regional Development, which had been central to Whitlam's housing and urban agenda. It was not until the 1990s that the Hawke and then the Keating governments turned to housing policy and urban reform. This interest was not driven by housing reform per se but rather part of an agenda to reform federal–state relations built on the recognition that the states were crucial to national sustainable economic and social reform.

Building a new economic model: implications for housing

The Hawke government in the 1980s realised that it would not be able to address the underlying problems facing the Australian economy without effectively creating a very different economic and social paradigm than that which had been dominant through to the mid-seventies.

Few areas in Australia were untouched by structural change during the 1980s and this change had enormous impact on the postwar model of financing and building housing. Financial deregulation had enormous implications for housing: Lionel Orchard has observed that 'the decision to deregulate took away one of the central pillars of postwar housing achievement without much action to compensate its effects' (Orchard 2003). There was little emphasis on compensation due to a feeling that an over-emphasis on home ownership was one source of distortion in the Australian economy which lacked other incentives for domestic savings. While some efforts were made to protect home owners, protecting renters was a more complex problem. The focus of conservative governments on private ownership of housing had also limited the growth of public housing, which in the postwar period had never exceeded 5 per cent of the housing stock. The preferential treatment of home purchasers and the limits placed on public housing had left a large group of people in the private rental market, often occupying housing that was poorly maintained and located. Budget pressures at the same time were restricting the supply of new public housing thus increasing targeting of the limited stock to the very poor.

State housing authorities were under increased financial pressure, leading officials to suggest the need for radical changes in housing policy. Rob Carter, a senior Victorian housing official, broke ranks with many other housing administrators in the mid eighties, arguing for a means-tested housing benefit and for its extension to public housing. According to Carter, such a housing benefit scheme would also make the flow of income to renters in difficult circumstances more even, regardless of whether they were in public or private housing. Arguments for the introduction of a housing benefit were also put by Hal Kendig and Chris Paris in a study undertaken as part of the International Year of the Homeless (Kendig and Paris 1987). They proposed that introducing a housing benefit in combination with the Family Allowance Supplement would represent a major contribution to reducing child poverty. I found these arguments convincing and, as the then Minister for Social Security in the 1980s, sought at every opportunity to increase rent assistance as both a contribution to equity and to the reduction of poverty and especially child poverty.

During the late 1980s my colleague Peter Staples, then Minister for Housing, had carried out a National Housing Policy Review which looked at the cost effectiveness of housing allowances as well as the possibility of encouraging private investment in public housing. Staples encouraged the states to invest more of their own funds in public housing. However, the increased targeting which led to the high cost of rebates in public housing meant that there remained an acute shortage of funds to add to stock. The increasing pressure from the Department of Finance to place more social security beneficiaries in public housing added to the cost of rebates, effectively placing state housing authorities in financial crisis. There was a desperate need for policy reform.

Canberra academic Michael Jones set out the issue clearly in 1990:

> Public housing authorities cater for a lucky minority of the housing needy, providing subsidies of up to $200 a week in high cost areas such as Sydney. Unlucky needy tenants cannot gain similar subsidies; and even with increases in rental allowances announced in 1988, private low income renters will continue to be a major high risk poverty group. (Jones 1990, p. 198)

The National Housing Strategy

After being elected to the ministry in 1990 I discussed my portfolio responsibilities with the Prime Minister, Bob Hawke. I suggested that I was especially interested in housing both because of my long-term interest in this area and my concern at the lack of progress during the 1980s in moving towards comprehensive reform. In early discussions with Hawke and the Treasurer, Paul Keating, it was agreed that federal–state relations should be a major focus of reform in the 1990s. In appointing me as the Minister assisting the Prime Minister on Federal–State Relations the Prime Minister was signalling his view that there was scope for significant improvements in the way the Commonwealth worked with the states across a range of social policy areas including housing. The government's decision to create the Council of Australian Governments (COAG) recognised that if Australia, with its relatively small population, was to build a sustainable economy/society the committed participation of the states was a necessity. Of course in some areas of policy the states were quick to recognise their interest in national reform. However in the area of social policy the states wanted the Commonwealth to remove tied grants and essentially hand the money and responsibility over to them.

In these circumstances, I appointed Dr Meredith Edwards as a consultant to undertake a review of national housing policy (described as the National Housing Strategy), which was carried out in 1990–92. Dr Edwards, an academic economist and public servant, had already undertaken a leading role in several important reforms in our government in creating Austudy and creating a very innovative and sensitive child support scheme. She had a broad knowledge of social policy and brought this much needed perspective to her examination of national housing policy directions. As a result of research carried out by the Henderson Poverty Inquiry and from my own experience as a minister and activist in inner city Melbourne, I understood that many of those pushed into poverty as a result of housing costs were renting privately. I indicated to Dr Edwards that I was especially keen to understand the depth of problems experienced by those living in private rental accommodation. I believed that the strength of the Hawke government was that it was not ruled by past models and stereotypes. I wanted some fresh thinking.

Dr Edwards made her approach clear in an early paper:

> Past deliberations of housing policy in Australia have often focused on various mechanisms of housing provision such as evaluating the relative merits of various housing tenures. To adopt a tenure focus as a starting point for analysis brings with it a danger of ether defending or attacking what exists; attention is taken away from the need for a wide range of housing choices as possible, to reflect the diverse needs of Australian households. (National Housing Strategy 1991b, p. 11)

Given the primary focus on the housing user, the National Housing Strategy identified two major objectives for future housing policy:

- the need for housing that is affordable for all Australians; and
- the need for housing that is appropriate in terms of quality, design, privacy, security and location.

In addition, one focus of the strategy was to be 'the identification or development of principles for evaluating standards of affordability and appropriateness which are acceptable to the community' (National Housing Strategy 1991b, p. 12).

The strategy published seven main issues papers along with a large number of background papers. Dr Edwards worked on a broad canvas, spelling out the impacts on housing programs and policies of the economic, social and environmental changes of the 1990s. The strategy recognised the growing mismatch in Australia between the ever-expanding supply of detached houses increasing in size and the diminishing size of households. Issues of equity were most obviously demonstrated in the large numbers of people in private rental paying too high a share of their family income on rent. This trend was increasingly impacting on younger people, who were often forced to remain longer in the family home or in inadequate private rental accommodation.

The National Housing Strategy emphasised the importance of the life course in understanding the new challenges for housing, and of diverse employment patterns leading to the need for different types of housing at differing stages in the life course. Dr Edwards found that, while public housing was increasingly targeted at the very poor, the private sector was not providing affordable housing for people who at different stages of their lives may have very low incomes. The degree of polarisation between the public and the private sector left public housing authorities, with most tenants on rebates, unable to generate a surplus on their investments while the private building sector was reluctant to play a part in affordable housing. In an early issues paper for the strategy, Dr Judith Yates from Sydney University suggested the need for tax subsidies to encourage the private sector to play a role in affordable housing (National Housing Strategy 1991a). However, this was opposed by Treasury which favoured increased targeting for public housing but failed to recognise the realities of market failure in the private rental market, with hundreds of thousands of low-income tenants paying more than 30 per cent of their income on rent. Most of these people lived in private rental accommodation where landlords' reason for investment was realising a capital gain rather than rental income and providing decent sustainable accommodation for low-income renters.

Overall, the National Housing Strategy sought to overcome the public–private dichotomy that had bedevilled housing reform in the seventies and eighties. Clearly for very large numbers of people, especially renters, there were serious problems in the affordability and appropriateness of the housing they were able to access. The National Housing Strategy recognised that the failure to mobilise the finance sector to invest in affordable housing for low-income people was a major failing of Australian housing policy. Affordable and appropriate housing needed to be promoted within broader urban and regional strategies that were inclusive of low-income people.

Choices for a changing nation

Largely as a result of the research findings of the NHS our government was able to spell out the reasons why radical change was needed. This did not result in immediate reform. The leadership struggle in 1990 and 1991 took some of the gloss off Hawke's agenda. It was confusing to members of caucus as Keating supporters encouraged the impression that we were about to cave in to the states. Difficult economic conditions encouraged a focus on short-term as opposed to longer-term policy. Nevertheless I was able in the 1992/93 budget to announce the core policies that had been agreed to by the government and that might set the direction for future discussions with the states. This was the first opportunity following the work of the NHS to embody the principal thrust in government policy and programs, which was set out in *Housing: Choices for a Changing Nation*, a portfolio statement accompanying the budget:

> By the year 2000 Commonwealth assistance to low income households renting their own accommodation will be paid according to a benchmark of affordability. As a result low income households should not be faced with unaffordable rents. (DHHCS 1992, p. 4)

And, on increasing the supply of housing for low-income people, the statement declared:

> The Commonwealth will establish a new Social Housing Subsidy program which will contribute towards the cost of borrowing for the provision of the public equity component of shared home ownership and other rental accommodation for low and moderate income earners. (DHHCS 1992, p. 3)

Both of these principal new policy directions had a tentative quality about them. On the one hand Treasury had defeated my proposal for a housing bond or equity instrument as a new mechanism to attract private sector funding into social housing and on the other hand there was no solid endorsement of our proposals on housing affordability benchmarks ahead of CSHA discussions with the states. The issue of benchmarks or standards is contentious because it defines a standard against which a government may be subsequently judged. It carries a political risk. The NHS had suggested an overall benchmark of between 25 and 30 per cent of household income for all renting households, effectively suggesting that subsidies payable for renters should be similar whether in the public or the private sector. Linked to this suggestion was also the proposal of the NHS that rent assistance might be paid in respect of public housing tenants. As rent assistance during this period, the early nineties, was nowhere near the value of rental rebates there would need to be considerable increases in private rental assistance to make this attractive to the states.

Federal–state negotiations on housing

The principal discussions with the states on public housing reform took place during the last term of the Keating government (1993–1996). The context was still the issue of the respective roles of the Commonwealth and the states in housing. The Commonwealth was due to sign a new Commonwealth–States Housing Agreement (CSHA) in 1995 and wanted to achieve some reform in line with the positions it had announced in *Housing: Choices for a Changing Nation*. During the late eighties the government had asked the Industry Commission to report on public housing, which it did in 1993. Its report, while supportive of public housing, advocated greater targeting of public housing and recommended the separation of property and landlord functions in public housing administration. The Industry Commission Report recommended Commonwealth responsibility for all income support including recurrent support for all rental housing. It also recommended the gradual withdrawal of the Commonwealth from capital funding for public housing, which, it said, should be able to generate income for the government at a commercial rate (Industry Commission 1993). This report would *not* have been received well by state governments and housing officials fearful that this had been the Commonwealth's agenda from the beginning.

The discussions with the states were progressed through meetings of portfolio ministers (mostly housing and planning ministers) but there was an understanding because of COAG's overarching interest that it would sign off on an agreed understanding with the states, which it did in 1995.

COAG, in a report summing up the work during the first half of the nineties on the respective roles of the Commonwealth and the states in housing, stopped short of fully endorsing the Industry Commission's recommendations and instead proposed reforms of the CSHA along the following lines:

- clearer roles and responsibilities for the Commonwealth, state and territory governments, with increased flexibility for jurisdiction to invest in resources across a mix of housing assistance
- measures to improve transparency of financial arrangements
- an outcomes focus with clear measures of performance, including an 'agreed needs' methodology for planning and setting targets
- a clearer emphasis on commercial management of housing stock, and a diversification of supply and providers
- potential for contestability of supply
- consumer choice in types of assistance.

COAG's conclusions were reflected in a new CSHA signed in that year which was for the first time a clear performance-based agreement specifying the outcomes that it was agreed should be achieved over the ensuing five years. It was, as Caulfield (2000) has noted, decidedly managerial in tone but it also anticipated the proposals announced by the Commonwealth later that year in its *Community and Nation* statement (Keating 1995).

Community and nation

Towards the end of 1995 the Keating government announced a radical plan to transform the delivery of public housing in Australia. The main thrust of the plan included the Commonwealth taking full responsibility for all rent assistance (that is for both public and private tenants), while the states and the private sector would be responsible for the supply of housing in their various jurisdictions. The proposed reforms also included a provision to allow rent assistance to be converted to a lump sum to be used as a deposit for home purchases, greater private sector involvement, a reduction in housing industry regulations, an evening up of the subsidy provided to both public and private renters, and differential rates of rent assistance depending on geographical location and the state of the real estate market. The Keating government was announcing its intention to negotiate with the states to shift the focus nationally from the direct funding of bricks and mortar and for the Commonwealth to take responsibility for housing assistance payments for low-income renters in both public and private rental housing. This would involve substantial increases in rent assistance payments to approximately 500,000 people depending on the design of the payment. As rent assistance is both demand driven and indexed, this plan would mean over time substantial increases in the flow of funds from the Commonwealth to the states. Furthermore the extension of an affordability benchmark from the public sector to private sector rental housing represented a major step towards a more universal response to housing need.

This proposal was only made possible by the steady increases in the real value of private rent assistance over the life of the Hawke/ Keating governments. It was the combination of real increases in family payments together with rent assistance that social policy experts such as Ann Harding saw as the reason for the decreases in poverty that were achieved over the life of these governments. The increases in rent assistance together with the ongoing government support of the CSHA created a financial envelope that made possible the policy proposals I have outlined above. The core of these proposals were initially endorsed by the Howard government at COAG in 1996 but were later not pursued partly because of opposition from some premiers but principally because the relief of poverty was not a core commitment of the Howard government.

It was thus left to the Rudd government to address the issue of affordable housing. It has on the one hand sought to assist first home buyers through grants and a matched savings scheme while seeking to address the future of the CSHA and affordable housing on lines similar to those set out in the 1995 COAG decision. Initially developing a national rental incentive scheme to encourage private investment in social housing, the Rudd government, now facing a global financial crisis, has committed more than $6 billion dollars to affordable rental housing over two years. Most of the funds will be leveraged through community housing associations working in partnership with private developers. It has made a commitment to increase the rental housing stock, public and non-government, by an additional 20,000 units. This commitment however is conditional on reaching agreement with the states on a number of reforms designed to build a much more diverse rental housing sector subject to national regulation and registration as well as encouraging contestability in the allocation of funds to encourage a range of new providers to offer housing options to a broader range of housing types. This emphasis on greater transparency was anticipated in the 1995 COAG agreement, foreshadowing a more universal approach in providing housing assistance to all low-income renters. However, the Rudd government has not addressed the important issue of rent assistance, either in terms of reducing the cost of rebates for state housing authorities or in tackling the issues related to providing rent assistance in very different housing markets. There are considerable differences in rent costs between cities and also between urban and rural areas. These issues of detail are crucial if there is to be sustainable reform in affordable housing.

Conclusion

Bob Hawke as prime minister is rightly recognised for his economic reforms in the 1980s where his focus on consensus building made possible the acceptance by the Australian public of the most radical changes in macroeconomic policy since the Second World War. In creating COAG he also made possible an inclusive national agenda which gave the states and territories a much larger role in setting national policy directions in areas of social policy such as that of access to affordable and appropriate housing. This issue that Hawke placed firmly on the agenda has been left to another Labor government to resolve in consultation with the states. Bob Hawke will be remembered as a Prime Minister committed not only to reaching accord but also for realising very substantive and lasting reforms. In housing and urban reform this remains the challenge of the Rudd government.

References

Caulfield, J. 2000, 'Public housing and intergovernmental reform in the 1990s', *Australian Journal of Political Science*, vol. 35, no. 1, pp. 99–110

Commission of Inquiry into Poverty 1975, *Poverty in Australia*, First Main Report, Australian Government Publishing Service, Canberra

Department of Health, Housing and Community Services 1992, *Housing: Choices for a Changing Nation*, Commonwealth of Australia, Canberra

Industry Commission 1993, *Public Housing*, Report no. 34, Australian
Government Publishing Service, Canberra

Jones, M. 1990, *The Australian Welfare State: Origins, Control and Choices*, 3rd
ed., Allen and Unwin, St Leonards, NSW

Keating, P.J. 1995, *Community and Nation*, Commonwealth of Australia,
Canberra

Kendig, H. and Paris, C. with Anderton, N. 1987, *Towards Fair Shares
in Australian Housing*, National Committee of Non-government
Organisations, International Year of Shelter for the Homeless, Canberra

National Housing Strategy 1991a, *Financing Australian Housing*,
Commonwealth of Australia, Canberra

National Housing Strategy 1991b, *Framework for Reform*, Commonwealth of
Australia, Canberra

Orchard, L. 2003, 'From saviour to summit: theory and practice in Australian
housing policy in the 1980s', unpublished manuscript

Chapter 12

Environment: 'What was right was also popular'[1]

Joan Staples

In 1989, Environment Minister Graham Richardson took a submission to Cabinet for a 20 per cent reduction in greenhouse gas emissions by 2005. He was not successful in persuading the resource and finance ministers on this first occasion, although a similar proposal was adopted soon after by the same Cabinet. From today's perspective, it is remarkable that the Hawke government was addressing climate change twenty years ago. Its action on the issue emphasises that this was the most progressive period in Australia's environmental history. However, it was also a missed opportunity on climate change and on continuing an environmental agenda.

Some publications on the Hawke legacy choose to ignore the whole environment story of the Hawke years or make only cursory references to it (Johnson 1989; Maddox 1989; Mills 1993; Steketee 2001). In publications where the environment is mentioned, all the initiative for the relationship is given to the Labor Party (Hawke 1994; Kelly 1994), or the emphasis is strongly narrative (Richardson 1994; Toyne 1994; Toyne and Balderstone 2003) and there has been little analysis of why this remarkable period of progressive environmental action did not continue.

In re-evaluating the significance of environment to the Hawke legacy, I will explore the main reasons why the government's unique environmental stance was not sustained into the Keating and Howard administrations, particularly focusing on the relationship between the government and environment groups. These groups, particularly the Australian Conservation Foundation (ACF) and the

Wilderness Society (TWS), were proactive in the relationship. Both government and environment organisations benefited and vigorously tried to optimise the relationship for their own ends, so that I would describe it as symbiotically pragmatic. Ignoring the relationship hides the fact that it was the electoral work of the environment organisations that returned the ALP to government in 1990, contributed to their record win in 1983 and helped to improve their position in the 1987 election. At the same time, the environment organisations achieved some iconic environmental gains. However, the relationship's reliance on electoral endorsement was a key factor making it unsustainable in the long term. Other factors that caused it to end were its dependence on particular individuals and their working relationships, opposition from the Labor resource and environment ministers influenced by a neo-liberal perspective, the rise of the Green Party, the concerted backlash from industry groups after the Coronation Hill mine decision in 1990 and Keating's strategic removal of the environment from his government's agenda. I will also review the Hawke government's actions on climate change, which, in retrospect, now assume much greater significance.

There is no doubt that the Hawke government was a remarkable period in Australia's environmental history. Toyne and Balderstone (2003) claim that it achieved more to protect the environment than any national government before or since. They list eleven key achievements:

- stopped the damming of the Franklin River;
- expanded enormously the Kakadu National Park, adding Stages 2 and 3 (and getting the World Heritage Area extended), and blocked the proposed Coronation Hill mine;
- blocked international moves to allow mining in Antarctica;
- protected the wet tropic rainforests of North Queensland by nominating them to the World Heritage List;
- handed back ownership of Uluru-Kata Tjuta National Park to its traditional owners;
- introduced Landcare, the first real attempt to deal with Australia's massive land degradation problems in a comprehensive way, and the One Billion Trees program – both part of the country's first prime ministerial environment statement, *Our Country, Our Future*;

- secured the protection of the Lemonthyme Forests in Tasmania, and tens of thousands of hectares of other icon forests around Australia;
- added a vast area to the Great Barrier Reef Marine Park;
- stopped the proposed Wesley Vale Pulp Mill in Tasmania;
- added other important parts of Australia to the World Heritage List, such as Shark Bay in Western Australia, Uluru-Kata Tjuta National Park and the Central Eastern Rainforest Reserves (around the escarpment of north-eastern New South Wales); and
- established the ecologically sustainable development (ESD) process, with a discussion paper, and then nine working groups being set up to consider the implementation of ESD principles in sectors of Australia's economy with major impacts on the environment. This was particularly remarkable, pre-dating as it did the Earth Summit in Rio de Janeiro by several years. (Toyne and Balderstone 2003, p. 170)

However, an environmental emphasis was not a consistent theme of the government. Ten of these eleven very significant actions occurred between 1987 and 1992, and almost all of them were in the three-year term of Environment Minister Graham Richardson, from 1987 to 1990.

The strategic ability of ACF and TWS first became apparent during the Franklin Dam campaign in the decade leading up to the 1983 federal election. That long campaign was important for demonstrating the organisations' mobilising power and their strategic political ability, and it was the training ground for a generation of environmental campaigners who developed a sophisticated understanding of the intersection of grassroots activism and the inside workings of the Australian political process. They ensured that they had support across the community, including in marginal electorates, and at the same time learned how to lobby at the highest levels of government. For example, towards the end of the campaign, TWS and ACF brought enormous pressure to bear on the Fraser government to intervene and Fraser responded with an unsuccessful offer of $500 million to Tasmania. At the same time, they put in place a grassroots marginal electorate strategy for the election the following year, in case the Fraser government did not intervene. This was after having ensured that the appropriate Labor Party policy was in place via a resolution at the 1982 ALP conference. So, forward planning, sophisticated strategic political analysis and grassroots support were the background against which ACF and TWS began their relationship with the Hawke government.

The support ACF and TWS brought to Labor in 1983 in fifteen marginal electorates was not crucial in winning the election, but it is widely conceded that it contributed to the election delivering the ALP's best postwar result (Hogg 2003). However, the earlier years of the Hawke government between the 1983 and 1987 elections provided little joy for the environment movement. From the government point of view, they faced the immediate challenge of assuming power during a recession that challenged economic orthodoxies. The environment was still a relatively new issue that was viewed as discrete and the concern of a specific interest group. Barry Cohen was a cautious environment minister and the big issues of the day called for intervention in state affairs, something he was not prepared to countenance.

After the 1984 election when seats were lost there was a perception in the ALP that it had failed to consolidate its position (Hogg 2003), and there were many recriminations related to the massive structural changes being introduced into the economy (Maddox 1989, p. 47). It was in this period of soul searching that some members of the government began to re-examine the ALP's environmental credentials (interview with Craig Emerson, 2008). However, it was not until Graham Richardson was elected to the Senate in 1984 and assumed the position of co-leader of the parliamentary right faction that environment organisations found a champion to take up their issues seriously. That process began in 1985.

I was ACF National Liaison Officer in Canberra from 1983. Together with TWS activist Dave Heatley, in 1985 I began talking to Graham Richardson about Tasmanian woodchip licences, which were due for renewal at the end of the year. They seemed to be fruitful discussions and Richardson's door was always open to us. However, I was disappointed at a November 1985 meeting with him that he chose a date in the following April to go to Tasmania to look at the forests, rather than intervening in the immediate woodchip decision. My disappointment was greatly tempered by knowing he was still interested in environmental issues and was prepared to learn more. The outcome of his Tasmanian visit has been well recorded and by the time Richardson arrived back in Hobart after visiting the forests in April 1986 he 'was a convert' (Richardson 1994, p. 214). Behind the scenes in the early part of 1986 Richardson began to take an interest in the other big issues of Kakadu and logging in Queensland's rainforests. The first that the public knew of his environmental interest was a speech he made in the Senate on Kakadu in mid 1986. The press gallery was immediately agog. This first showing of his hand on environment issues seemed incongruous to the cynical gallery who knew Richardson as a heavy hitter on the big issues. The story of his visit to Tasmania soon became public, but behind the scenes Richardson had been engaging on environmental issues since the previous year.

The extent to which individuals are important in history is widely debated, but it is clear there was a conjunction of individuals in government and ACF/TWS who saw the political synergies in the environment organisations and the ALP developing a relationship. On the government's side, Hawke, Richardson, Emerson and Balderstone were the key people. Richardson's commitment was crucial, as was the support he enjoyed from the prime minister. Craig Emerson, Hawke's newly appointed economic advisor in June 1986, willingly also took on the new role of environment advisor (interview with Craig Emerson, 2008) – a position he held for the next three eventful years of environmental activity. Simon Balderstone, a former journalist, worked briefly for ACF during the 1987 election, then become environmental advisor to Richardson, Hawke and Keating. On the ACF/TWS side, in the early period leading up to the 1987 election, Jonathan West moved between positions as TWS and ACF lobbyist, advisor to Minister Barry Cohen and Director of TWS before leaving the scene for a position at Harvard. I was ACF Canberra representative until after the 1987 election and was proactive in the early development of the Richardson relationship. Phillip Toyne became ACF director in 1987 and it was his close partnership with Simon Balderstone that underpinned much of the government and ACF's relationship from 1987 to 1990 – the period of most activity. From 1990, all these key players gradually lost their positions or moved elsewhere, so that by 1993 only Simon Balderstone remained (as Keating's environment advisor). Most of these players evaluate the period in terms of the importance of the role of individuals (interview with Graham Richardson, 2008).

Significantly, the relationship between ACF/TWS and the Hawke government was underpinned by electoral endorsement. The 1983 Franklin Dam endorsement of Labor by ACF/TWS grew out of a bipartisan approach to both major parties, with ACF/TWS believing up until the last minute that Fraser would intervene. When the Liberals did not do so, it was only then that ACF/TWS activated their alternative strategy of endorsing Labor after extracting a promise from Hawke. At the 1987 election, there was consensus that they should endorse the ALP because of the opportunity to make very significant gains. Within the environment organisations, supporters of this position argued that the threatened destruction of virgin forests, and particularly rainforest in the case of the wet tropics, made the case exceptional because, once destroyed, virgin, old-growth forests were lost for eons. Four issues were negotiated: logging in the wet tropics; woodchipping in Tasmania; extensions to Kakadu National Park and its World Heritage nomination; and stopping sandmining at Shelbourne Bay on Cape York. It was ACF and TWS having a 'clear finite and manageable agenda' of four issues that made the government prepared to deliver (interview with Craig Emerson, 2008).

The least prominent issue was Shelbourne Bay, which I had been promoting for ACF. It involved a Japanese company wanting to mine for silica sand on a pastoral lease that was the traditional land of the Wuthathi. Ironically, it turned out to be the hardest issue for the government as it involved using its foreign investment powers against a Japanese company. Australia was going through a collapse in its terms of trade in 1986 and serious current account problems, resulting in Keating's 'banana republic' warning. The last thing they 'needed was a bad international reputation on foreign investment and Paul [Keating] was very anxious on that' (interview with Craig Emerson, 2008). However, the government delivered and so did ACF and TWS. Despite an Australia-wide swing against Labor of 1.31 per cent, in the TWS/ACF-targeted marginal seats there was a swing *towards* Labor of 0.89 per cent which led the environment organisations to claim they were able to provide a 2 per cent swing. A pragmatic and symbiotic relationship had begun.

However, despite the opportunity to secure very significant gains from Labor's election promises, not everybody in ACF and TWS was entirely happy. ACF President Hal Wootten, the distinguished jurist, was one of seven who opposed the 1987 endorsement, out of a total of 36 ACF councillors. Writing in the ACF journal, *Habitat*, he said:

> Regular support for a particular party brings special problems. It will lead environment groups to be seen as captured, with nowhere else to go and not as important as other competing groups which will now be wooed. Similarly regular opposition will cause the party opposed to write off the opposing group as unwinnable and best sacrificed to competing interests. (Wootten 1987, pp. 5–7)

He also reminded ACF that governments change and the party that has not been endorsed will come to power (Wootten 1987, pp. 5–7).

After the 1987 election, Graham Richardson received his first portfolio and became the Environment Minister with responsibility for fulfilling the election promises he helped negotiate. Not only did he do this, but he also produced the remarkable number of achievements listed earlier. This was done using his considerable deal-making skills, with the support of advisers such as Balderstone and importantly with the support of his prime minister. Many of the gains of the productive three years of his period as minister were achieved against state governments of a different political persuasion and against great odds. For example, nominating the wet tropics for World Heritage listing involved identifying boundaries for hundreds of different landholdings, negotiating each and every one of them and also suffering physical confrontation when Richardson and his staff were attacked by an angry mob at Ravenshoe in far north Queensland.

The electoral involvement of ACF/TWS at the 1990 election came at a time of very high environmental awareness by the public; in fact environment was rated the second most important issue after the economy. ACF/TWS played a critical role in delivering government to the ALP, but, ironically, the election also marks the beginning of the end of the relationship. Richardson proposed a strategy to Hawke of relying on Democrat preferences.[2] His approach was vindicated when the ALP received only 39 per cent of the primary vote, the Coalition 43 per cent but the Democrats almost doubled their vote to 11 per cent and their preferences gave victory to the ALP. In the nine marginal electorates where ACF and TWS campaigned for a vote for the Democrats with second preferences to Labor, the Democrat vote was a high 13.4 per cent, which was critical in returning Labor candidates. It was conceded by commentators that the environment vote had won the election for Labor (Kelly 1994).

After the 1990 election, Richardson moved from the environment portfolio and Hawke's influence began to wane under the debilitating leadership tension. However, three major factors also combined to produce strong opposition within the ALP to further environmental gains. They were the attitude of the resource and economic ministers, the strengthening of neo-liberal thinking both within sections of the ALP and more widely, and a coordinated backlash by industry and resource interests.

There were four Cabinet decisions that were opposed by some key economic and resource ministers even when public opinion was in favour. They related to Shelbourne Bay, the Commission of Inquiry into Tasmanian forests, Wesley Vale pulp mill and Coronation Hill. The Shelbourne Bay issue, as indicated earlier, went against the advice of Treasury and the Treasurer. The outcome of the Commission of Inquiry into Tasmania's forests was overthrown by Cabinet in favour of a dissenting report by Commissioner Hitchcock, but only after fourteen hours of Cabinet debate with the resource and economic ministers opposing. It was the longest Cabinet discussion of the Hawke government (interviews with Graham Richardson and Simon Balderstone, 2008). The Wesley Vale pulp mill did not proceed because the Commonwealth imposed such stringent approval criteria that the proponent abandoned the project – a strategy that gained Cabinet support only because it did not actually stop the proposal. However, it was the blocking of a gold mine at Coronation Hill in Kakadu National Park that was a watershed decision in the government's environmental legacy. It was prevented from going ahead only by the prime minister using the full prestige of his office and abandoning his usual consensus style. It is also credited with being the cause of his loss of both caucus and Cabinet support and the 'nail in his coffin' as leader (Toyne 1994). This was despite the decision being politically popular with the electorate and being credited as the issue that helped the ALP win the 1990 election (Kelly 1994).

Although these environment decisions were won in Cabinet,

the opposition of key resource and finance ministers began to take its toll. At the same time, the rise of neo-liberal thinking and public choice theory and the work of conservative think tanks were influencing both sections of the ALP and the wider political debate.[3] This coincided with industry and mining interests mounting a coordinated media and lobbying blitz after the Coronation Hill decision, promoting it as a 'test case' in their relationship with the government (Toyne 1994). Elements in the ALP echoed this call. From the 1990 election and the Coronation Hill decision, the importance of the environment began to wane.

The end did not come with a change of the political party in power, but with a change of leader. Judy Lambert, adviser in Environment Minister Ros Kelly's office, tells of an election strategy meeting for the 1993 election when Keating was leader. She was representing the Environment Minister when Prime Minister Keating walked into the meeting and made a comment along the lines, 'This, this and this are the priority issues ... and the environment will NOT be one of the priority issues in this election' (interview with Judy Lambert, 2008). Throughout his prime ministership, Keating actively tried to disengage the Commonwealth from environmental decisions, so that Richardson could say, 'By the 1996 election we were not very green at all. We had moved back a long, long, long way' (interview with Graham Richardson, 2008).

Another factor that previously has not been taken into account as contributing to the end of the relationship with ACF/TWS is that the 1993 election was the first at which the Greens appeared as a national party. Richardson and Emerson assure me they were not trying to head off the formation of a Green Party when they went into the relationship with ACF and TWS, and Judy Lambert confirms she never heard talk of this concern. This is despite the formation of a Green Party inevitably being at the expense of Labor electorally. Personally, I always felt it was the 'elephant in the room' that was not being mentioned as I negotiated with Labor. However, the ALP representatives claim they were looking for electoral endorsement for the ALP and it was a bonus that 'what was right was also popular' (Richardson 1994, p. 214). Chris Puplick, Opposition Environment Minister opposing Richardson, identifies the Green Party as providing a natural home for the environment vote and so reducing the influence of the environment organisations (interview with Chris Puplick, 2008). Judy Lambert raises the interesting conundrum of whether the environment movement's feeling of being shut out after 1990 might have accelerated the formation of the Greens as a national party or whether the formation of the Greens led to the environment movement being shut out because Labor could now negotiate directly with the Green Party for preferences (interview with Judy Lambert, 2008). It is possible both proposals are true. Chris Puplick certainly believes the development of the Green Party was 'an absolutely critical factor' in the environment movement losing its influence with the other parties (interview with Chris Puplick, 2008).

Climate change

It would be misleading to suggest that climate change policy was a significant issue for the Hawke government. For example, Toyne and Balderstone did not mention it in their retrospective assessment in 2003. But the dominance of the issue today gives the Hawke initiatives new significance, as well as identifying a missed opportunity.

Throughout the 1980s there were a number of Australian and international scientific conferences on climate change. However, it was in 1988 in Toronto that the international scientific community was sufficiently confident in the science to set targets, calling for a 20 per cent reduction of carbon dioxide emissions worldwide by the year 2005, with the brunt of this to be borne by developed countries. In Australia, the CSIRO and the Commission for the Future held two joint conferences in 1987 and 1988, which were widely publicised including on a number of current affairs television programs and in *The Age*, which did a four page lift-out (Lowe 1989). The ACF employed a climate change officer to direct their campaigning and the indefatigable Ian Lowe, currently President of ACF, and acting Director of the Commission for the Future at the time, did much in communicating the issue to the public.

In 1989, in this context of international calls for action by scientists and the UN, with Australian scientists playing a leading role, and the public showing increasing interest, Richardson took a submission to Cabinet to reduce greenhouse emissions by 20 per cent by 2005 – the so-called Toronto targets (interview with Graham Richardson, 2008). His submission was rejected. However, the prime minister did release a greenhouse statement in 1989, which provided funding for research. Later in the year, in the lead up to a federal election, a major environment statement, *Our Country, Our Future*, covered many traditional 'green' issues, but gave prominence to climate change, supporting international action, promising to look for ways to reduce carbon dioxide emissions, including cooperating with the states on transport use, and providing $350,000 for public awareness and education (Hawke 1989).

The following year in 1990, the Hawke Cabinet did agree to a climate change submission similar to that sponsored by Richardson, but resource and finance ministers ensured it carried a significant proviso that no action would be taken if it affected the economy in any way. The decision was made in the context of an inducement to the environment movement to remain in the Ecologically Sustainable Development (ESD) process, which had been changed by the resource and finance ministers to the dismay of the environment groups. The proviso about the economy and the lack of commitment to the Cabinet decision meant it was quietly ignored in following years by the Keating government as the environment slipped from the public policy agenda. Keating declined to attend the Rio Earth Summit in 1992 which saw the ratification of the UN Framework Convention on Climate Change. One hundred and seventy two governments participated in the summit, and one hundred and eight heads of state or government attended, including US President George Bush senior. Australia's Prime Minister Keating was notable in his absence.[4]

Conclusion

The Hawke government can take credit for implementing an incredible environmental agenda. At the same time, ACF and TWS were proactive in promoting and shaping that agenda, such that the relationship between ACF/TWS and the government was symbiotically pragmatic. However it was not sustainable because of its dependence on electoral endorsement, and on the role of like-minded individuals. It also fell foul of deep-seated opposition from within the ALP and to coordinated opposition from industry and mining interests which coincided with the rise of neo-liberal thinking and a public choice agenda, as well as a changing political environment with the formation of the national Green Party.

Throughout the Hawke years, the environment was treated as

the concern of an interest group, not as integral to other portfolios or to the long-term health of the economy. It is debatable whether that analysis has changed significantly in the intervening years. With the election of the Rudd government, the environment lobby has not returned to the influence it had under Hawke, despite climate change being the dominate issue for vote changers at the 2007 election (Browne 2008). A decade of neo-liberal thinking, including public choice theory impacting on the status of non-government organisations, has influenced politicians (Staples 2006). However, of even more significance is the impact of a concerted campaign by the energy and resource lobby to weaken any emissions trading scheme proposed by the Rudd government. Rudd's decision to leave Howard government appointments undisturbed also left intact the power and influence of the 'greenhouse mafia', eloquently described by Pearse (2007). There are striking parallels between the concerted campaign by this lobby after the 1990 Coronation Hill decision and the unprecedented lobbying that took place throughout 2008 to block the development of an effective emissions trading scheme. Twenty years hence, the Rudd government's legacy may rest significantly on its response to climate change. We can only hope that their response will not be seen as another missed opportunity.

Notes

1   Richardson (1994, p. 214).

2   The ALP also looked to Tasmania, where in 1989 the five 'Green independents' led by Bob Brown had secured the balance of power and put the ALP into government with only 34.7 per cent of the primary vote. As coordinator of this Tasmanian campaign, I observed that this electoral success also enhanced national environmental awareness.

3   Refer to Shanahan (this volume) for their effects on economic policy. Public choice theory uses neo-classical economics to describe the behaviour and motivation of interest groups as rational self-interested actors. It does so independently of any consideration of historical experience, political tradition or institutional structure. For a discussion of public choice theory as it came to affect the Australian non-government sector see Staples (2006).

4   For a more complete discussion of climate change initiatives in the 1980s see Staples (2009).

References

Browne, P. (2008) 'Environment the key poll issue?', *Australian Policy Online*, 18 September, http://www.apo.org.au/webboard/results.chtml?filename_num=230903, accessed 1 April 2009

Hawke, B. 1989, *Our Country, Our Future: Statement on the Environment*, Australian Government Publishing Service, Canberra

Hawke, B. 1994, *The Hawke Memoir*, William Heinemann, Melbourne

Hogg, B. 2003, 'Hawke the campaigner' in eds S. Ryan and T. Bramston, *The Hawke Years: A Critical Retrospective*, Pluto Press, North Melbourne

Johnson, C. 1989, *The Labor Legacy: Curtin, Chifley, Whitlam, Hawke*, Allen and Unwin, Sydney

Kelly, P. 1994, *The End of Certainty: Power, Politics and Business in Australia*, rev. ed., Allen and Unwin, St Leonards, NSW

Lowe, I. 1989, *Living in the Greenhouse*, Scribe, Newham, Vic

Maddox, G. 1989, *The Hawke Government and Labor Tradition*, Penguin Books, Ringwood

Mills, S. 1993, *The Hawke Years: The Story from the Inside*, Viking, Ringwood

Pearse, G. 2007, *High and Dry: John Howard, Climate Change and the Selling of Australia's Future*, Viking, Camberwell, Vic

Richardson, G. 1994, *Whatever it Takes*, Bantam, Sydney

Staples, J. 2006, 'NGOs out in the cold: the Howard government policy towards NGOs', Discussion Paper 19/06, *Democratic Audit of Australia*, http://democratic.audit.anu.edu.au/papers/20060615_staples_ngos.pdf, accessed 1 April 2009

Staples, J. 2009, 'Australian government action in the 1980s' in ed. H. Sykes, *Climate Change on for Young and Old*, Future Leaders, Albert Park, Vic

Steketee, M. 2001, 'Labor in power: 1983–1996' in eds J. Faulkner and S. Macintyre, *The Story of the Federal Parliamentary Labor Party: True Believers*, Allen and Unwin, Crows Nest, NSW

Toyne, P. 1994, *The Reluctant Nation: Environment, Law and Politics in Australia*, ABC Books, Sydney

Toyne, P. and Balderstone, S. 2003, 'The environment' in eds S. Ryan and T. Bramston, *The Hawke Government: A Critical Retrospective*, Pluto Press, North Melbourne

Wootten, H. 1987, 'Elections and environmental politics: the search for consensus', *Habitat*, vol. 15, no. 5, pp. 5–7

Part 4

The economy, work and industrial relations

Chapter 13

Economic policy of the Hawke years

Martin Shanahan

Introduction

> The difficulty lies, not in the new ideas, but in escaping from the old ones. (Keynes 1949, p. vi)

The restructuring of the economy promoted by the Hawke government signalled a significant shift in Australia's economic development. The changes not only altered institutional structures and protection; they ultimately altered Australian attitudes to competition and markets, and the nature and direction of its economic growth.

Many of the changes were supported by both sides of parliament and were later described as overdue. Others have suggested they were an inevitable response to globalisation. These interpretations, however, come with the benefit of hindsight, and undervalue the power of the conservative forces and ideas that were current at the time.

This chapter provides a brief overview of the major economic policy changes initiated under the Hawke government, and emphasises the change in economic thinking that became accepted during this time.[1]

The context

> Where economics is involved, history is highly functional. The present is not to be understood in neglect of the past ... It will also ... be ...

clear that economics does not exist apart from context – apart from
the contemporary economic and political life that gives it form or the
interests, implicit or explicit, that shape it to their need. (Galbraith 1987,
p. 299)

When the Hawke Labor government was elected it faced the challenge of high unemployment and high inflation, a depreciating
current account, high interest rates, and increasing social division
and confrontation. It was elected in a period when overseas conservative governments, especially in the United States and United
Kingdom, had adopted aggressive monetarist policies aimed at
breaking opposition and shocking their economies out of lethargy.
The Fraser government (1975–1983) had adopted similar policies,
but with less ruthlessness than its overseas counterparts. The Hawke
government also carried a legacy of the grand social experiment
that had been the Whitlam government (1972–1975) but which had
stigmatised Labor as poor financial managers.

In addition to the immediate circumstances of the early 1980s,
however, the Hawke government was also faced with important long-term considerations. International financial certainties
were breaking down. New technologies, new sources of financial
capital and new economies had transformed the global landscape.
Australia's internal economic structure, heavily reliant on primary
production, had not responded strongly. While the nation's standard
of living was still First World, it was becoming evident that not only
was the standard slipping but that the previously reliable commodities that underpinned much of its prosperity were, in relative terms,
becoming less valuable. Whether Australia would become a 'client
state' of others was a question many were pondering.

The Hawke Labor government, therefore, needed to construct
economic policies that addressed both unemployment and inflation
and the longer-term structural issues facing the economy. Ideas and
attitudes, as well as policies, had to be changed.

The changes

In the early 1980s institutions such as protection, restricted migration, and conciliation and arbitration remained strong totems for the
belief that Australia could operate independently from international
markets. In reality many of these institutions had been progressively

modified over decades, but the collective economic view was still remarkably close to one expressed in the 1930s:

> The mechanism of international prices, which signals the world's need from one country to another and invites the nations to produce more of this commodity and less of that, belongs to an entirely different order. It knows no rights, but only necessities. The Australians have never felt disposed to submit to these necessities. They have insisted that their Governments must struggle to soften them or elude them or master them. In this way they have created an interesting system of political economy. (Hancock 1961 [1930], p. 67)

In floating the exchange rate, in December 1983, the Hawke government chose to allow international prices to set the price of the currency.[2] There are several consequences of floating the exchange rate. First, as the international market sets the price, its judgment on the currency's value becomes critical. Economies where the inflation rate is higher than others or where productivity is lower will find their currency being lowered in value. Second, as the balance of trade underpins the overall supply and demand for currency, producing goods that are relatively less valuable (agricultural commodities) will result in long-run devaluation. Conversely, high value goods (i.e. elaborately manufactured goods) will be price competitive. The net result is to encourage a more diversified economy with high-value industries exporting goods and services. Third, as the currency's value varies in response to international forces, the domestic economy is more insulated from external shocks.[3] While market forces may quickly change the price of the currency, the quantity impact on exports and imports operates more slowly, giving businesses time to respond to price signals.

Most importantly, however, floating the exchange rate had a significant symbolic impact. It signalled a decisive break from the previous 'interesting system of political economy' and sent a clear signal to all Australian citizens that the necessities of the international market could not be denied.

A range of changes were made to capital controls, interest rate setting and the rules for foreign banks. These changes not only helped create a faster and more responsive financial system, they allowed Australia (particularly Sydney) to become a larger player in international finance markets.

While the government exposed the finance sector to quite rapid change, through the Prices and Incomes Accord, it signalled a slower and more consultative process in the labour market. After a period of high unemployment and inflation in the late 1970s, and attempts to suspend wages growth under Fraser, the Hawke government embraced a strategy of negotiated accords between the union movement, corporate Australia and the government.[4] The first Accord initially focused on preventing automatic wage rises via arbitration. The aim was to break the wage–price spiral that had developed in the 1970s, and prevent a reoccurrence of wage explosions. Not only did the Accord achieve this, it evolved to encompass a range of economic reforms. Critically, it broadened the wage debate from prices and take-home pay to include the social wage, superannuation policy, productivity and microeconomic reform. This was to prove important over several years in advancing economic reform. It also signalled the Hawke government's commitment to negotiating and operating policy with a broad range of groups, rather than relying entirely on individual self-interest and specialist groups.[5]

Over a decade of government, economic challenges change. By the end of the government's first term, the combined effect of the Accord, a break in the drought, an end to the international recession, targeted programs of assistance and cuts in government spending had created over 500,000 new jobs and almost halved inflation. These early gains, however, were later offset as prices rose with the devaluing currency, the stock market crashed in 1987 and another international recession occurred. Domestic challenges such as industry restructuring, microeconomic reform and unemployment provided the government with a new set of problems. As Galbraith reflects, 'Economics is not, as often believed, concerned with perfecting a final and unchanging system. It is in a constant and often reluctant accommodation to change' (1987, p. 299).

Along with other economic policy changes, the push to restructure institutions and have Australians view markets as setting inescapable constraints continued. The government bound itself to operate with the constraint of not increasing government expenditure, income tax revenues or the budget deficit (Willis 2003, p. 145). This self-imposed trilogy, while advantageous politically, also demonstrated its commitment not 'to struggle to soften … or elude' international constraints, but to work within them.

Increased international exposure of domestic industry brought more challenges. Could Australian firms compete? Could they improve their efficiency? Long-term prosperity would depend on the economy's capacity to produce what the rest of the world wanted. The government began examining policies that impacted on market efficiency. These included taxation reform, national competition policy and reform of national infrastructure.

Taxation reform was only partially successful during the Hawke government. Capital gains taxes and fringe benefits taxes were imposed, and some tax loopholes removed. Income taxes were cut and the double taxation of dividends removed. A consumption and wealth tax were not introduced. Although incomplete, these changes did raise public debate, especially about the influence of government on the efficiency of the economy. Despite linking some tax cuts to Accord agreements, and using this to redistribute income, the tax system was not fundamentally altered to improve both competitiveness and equity.

The Hawke government faced two major challenges in office. The first was the need to convince the electorate that major structural reform was necessary. In this it was mostly successful. The second challenge was to have the electorate fully realise the consequences of this decision. In this the government was less successful, partly because the end of the process was unclear and because the changes were so large that reform fatigue was inevitable. Having made breathtaking reforms to the financial sector, significant changes to the labour market, and basic structural reforms to industry, ongoing reforms began to pall with the community.

Opening the economy brought with it the danger that international judgement about Australia's relative competitiveness would outstrip the capacity of the economy to adapt. This appeared to be what happened in the mid 1980s as the currency devalued rapidly. Despite continued labour market reform that linked wages to productivity, first at the industry and then the enterprise level, attention turned to the more difficult task of microeconomic reform. Having removed one layer of protection, the government aimed to reduce the overall cost of production by lowering domestic barriers. Transportation, communication, business regulation, trade union demarcation and work practices were all targeted, though not with the same success. Political considerations meant that some areas changed slowly (such as the car industry) while other changes (such as the privatisation of government authorities) were either incomplete or did not occur until later. Waterfront reform, rail freight and coastal shipping reform caused significant pain as the Labor Party sought to change the working conditions of union members. Other sectors, such as textiles, manufacturing and steel, were changed far more quickly. The message – that competition brought both winners and losers – was clear, as was the government's approach: to assist, but not completely shield, sectors subject to reform.

Privatisation became an increasing preoccupation as the government sought to ensure international comparability; it was also an ideological lightning rod. The Hawke government moved to privatise, often in stages, via commercialisation or partial privatisation. The result was similar: a reorientation of the authorities to respond to market signals and a diminution of their broader social considerations.

The evolution toward a more internationalised economy occurred in the face of major swings in economic conditions. Initially, wage cuts, reduced government expenditures and reduced inflation increased employment opportunities. But economic conditions changed as depreciation increased inflationary pressures and the government struggled to control the current account deficit. A boom in asset prices, especially house prices, much of it funded by overseas debt, was not initially met with increases in interest rates, in part because of the fear of recession resulting from the share market crash. Thus a period of rapid expansion was belatedly followed by the Reserve Bank's increasing interest rates. The result was 'the recession we had to have' and increases to both unemployment and inflation.[6]

The changing economic environment not only forced the government to make changes to economic institutions; it partially facilitated the process by removing alternatives. Just as the government's efforts to convince the population of the need for change was partly assisted by the more extreme policies of the opposition (who argued for faster labour market deregulation and more privatisation), harsh judgments by international markets allowed the government to argue for more extensive microeconomic reform.

Adjustment difficulties

The shift to a more market-oriented economy required many adjustments. Many participants made mistakes. More reliance on markets and less on government regulation allowed the inexperienced and the opportunistic to react badly. The finance sector, for example, made more than its share of errors, with banks seeking market share and quick profits ahead of long-run stability. Individual companies and directors, driven by dreams of fast profits in new markets, expanded; sometimes too aggressively, sometimes illegally. Naivety, opportunism and inexperience were a potent mix, as seen in the case of wheat farmers who borrowed funds offshore to expand their farms. Some lost everything as currency fluctuations wiped out the advantage given by lower interest rates. Others successfully sued financial advisors for not fully explaining the risk.

After a few years of glittering success (and, for some, excess) a number of headlines in the late 1980s and early 1990s relayed stories of corporate collapse. While some argued these resulted from the new challenges of unfettered market capitalism, others suggested the real cause was the old story of greed (Sykes 1996).

Nor did rapid depreciation of the dollar in the mid 1980s quickly produce an export-led recovery as first hoped. There were too many management, production, distribution and marketing lessons that had to be learned incrementally by individual firms inexperienced in international competition. The costs of depreciation came quickly while the benefits arrived more slowly.

Increased reliance on markets and restructuring of economic institutions affected areas many had previously considered insulated from market forces. In particular, housing markets were affected by variations in interest rates in a manner previously little experienced by the average Australian. House prices rose and affordable accommodation fell more quickly than had occurred in recent experience. Tariff cuts rapidly translated into cuts in employment as firms restructured or shifted offshore. Cost-cutting competition saw the rapid shedding of labour and its replacement with new technology. Youth unemployment increased as low-skill jobs contracted and demand for better trained workers increased. Productivity rather than experience became the basis for hiring labour. Outsourcing changed the rules of the game in a way that left many floundering.

While market signals impacted quickly across the economy, the ability for individuals, firms and sectors to respond varied greatly.

The government, mindful of the social impact of change, instigated a range of welfare policies to assist those at most risk. For example, it increased safety net provisions for the unemployed, initiated home assistance packages, and expanded health care for the least well-off so as to balance economic reform with social support. But with market downturns such policies also led to a rapid increase in government commitments, reducing its ability to respond.

The legacy: a change in economic thinking

If pressed for the single most important contribution made by the Hawke government, many commentators would proffer deregulation of the exchange rate. This, however, confuses a change in economic institutions with the more important legacy of a change in thinking. In the case of Australia the Hawke government promoted the view that a failure to respond to international market signals would result in a long-term decline in living standards. The government built its policies on the view that collectively Australians could meet the challenge of responding to international markets and, in the process of restructuring the community, compensate the losers while advancing the opportunity of winners to succeed.

While critics highlighted the naivety of promoting a level playing field in a world of realpolitik and special interest groups, one mark of the change in attitude is the difficulty in now imagining Australians would ever accept a return to a policy world of exchange rate controls, regulated interest rates, restricted borrowings, centrally determined wages, less competitive industry and more expensive consumer goods.

Deregulating the economy also reduced the government's role in setting macroeconomic policy. Rather than fiscal and monetary settings being the centrepiece of economic policy, the focus shifted to microeconomic reform. Unemployment and inflation, which had been the direct targets of government policy 25 years earlier, now became measures of how successful the government had been in microeconomic reform, or how independently the Reserve Bank had set interest rates.

Deregulation did not proceed smoothly. The roller-coaster adjustments of a newly deregulated exchange rate, less predictable responses to new national and international opportunities, and the personal impacts on families as their housing, work and education adjusted to less regulated environments brought with it a sense of unease and fatigue. After the years of Hawke and then Keating governance, many Australians sought refuge from continual change. The electorate began to view government as aiding elite winners over less successful battlers. Although John Howard won the 1996 election with the promise of calmer, less radical and more conservative government, the electors received continued market reforms. The result was a decade of still more profound shift to market-based solutions, and a greater emphasis on the individual. The marginalisation of unions, increased self-regulation in financial and service sectors, increased privatisation, more free trade agreements and more microeconomic and taxation reform would have been less significant had the ground not already been turned under Hawke.

The conservative period also consolidated the acceptance of another set of changes to economic thinking that had been initiated under Hawke. The early 1980s under Labor were characterised by a consensus approach to policy making, and the use of corporate structures to deliver outcomes. While market signals and incentives directed resources, government too played a role in ensuring just and equitable outcomes. Over time, however, the focus on market-based solutions also saw a shift in perceptions about the role of government. In 1986 Wilenski could argue without fear of derision:

> The expansion of government under electoral pressure has greatly widened the opportunities and choices for most people by providing them with education, basic health support and so on – all services which the market had failed to supply … the growth of government, both by its provision of services and by laws which changed the power relationships between large businesses on the one hand, and workers and consumers on the other, has been the greatest force in the past century for the expansion of individual freedom of ordinary people. (1986, p. 19)

By 1995, John Howard, as leader of the Opposition, would argue:

> The prevailing mood towards governments around the world today is one of mistrust … There is a widespread belief that governments

have few answers for contemporary problems. They are variously seen as the puppets of special interests or composed of people bent on self-promotion rather than the enhancement of the national interest.

This harsh judgment has a strong resonance in Australia …

Australians may not want government out of their lives, but they do want it off their backs. (Howard 1995)

With this shift in attitude to government came a deeper public acceptance of the role of individual success. Rather than focus on a social wage or community support programs, take-home pay (assisted by regular cuts to personal taxation) and public account-ability came to the fore. Government's role in redistributing income, or requiring equity as well as efficiency goals for statutory authori-ties, was downplayed in favour of ensuring maximum productivity and individual entrepreneurial opportunity.

Such a change in thinking also meant a change in the com-munity's acceptance of inequality. While protection all round had, in effect, pushed inequality offshore, commentators suggested the Australian national character lay great store in a fair go and mate-ship. 'This then is the prevailing ideology of Australian democ-racy – the sentiment of justice, the claim of right, the conception of equality, and the appeal to Government as the instrument of self-realisation' (Hancock 1961, p. 57). In the 1970s the Whitlam gov-ernment expressed this view by delivering 'equality of opportunity', especially in education, health and job creation, while maintaining much external protection. After the economic storms of the 1970s, the rise of market solutions under Hawke and minimal government under Howard, much of the Australian concern for mates and the fair go appeared to shift from being a government responsibility to one held by charities, churches and volunteers.[7] Certainly by the late 1990s market forces saw more citizens' votes determined by their hip-pocket nerve rather than a concern for equity. Australians' preference for governments that lowered taxes and provided imme-diate short-term benefits, despite the potential longer-term social, economic or environmental costs, suggested that Australians' com-mitment to the fair go was not as deeply entrenched as previously thought.

Conclusion

> The ideas of economists and political philosophers, both when they
> are right and when they are wrong, are more powerful than is com-
> monly understood. Indeed the world is ruled by little else. (Keynes
> 1949, p. 383)

Twenty-five years after the election of the Hawke government, the
world has changed and so has Australians' view of their place in that
world. Domestically, their views on the role of markets, government,
inequality, and economic and social policy have changed. Many of
these can be traced to shifts initiated during the Hawke Labor government. Some were perhaps inevitable and would have occurred
anyway; some were the result of courage, pragmatism and ideology.
Change when it occurs rarely follows a straight line.

The long-term legacies of these changes are still being worked
through. Some have assisted in diversifying the economy, increasing
productivity and making firms and sectors more efficient. There
have been winners and losers. Increased market exposure has
increased pressure on individuals and families to invest in education
and work harder and longer. There have been intended and unin-
tended consequences. Most significant, however, has been the shift
in how Australians think about markets, the role of government, the
importance of the individual and the extent to which they expect
governments to help others.

One key to this shift in thinking has been the realisation that,
while Australia remains a lucky country for most, the reality of scar-
city in all things and the need to make choices is a binding constraint
that no amount of protection can shield against. Australians now
appreciate they cannot live as if the rest of the world did not matter.
They also understand more personally the interrelated nature of
markets and their impact on all sectors of society.

There is evidence to suggest that the material benefits of the
changes initiated under Hawke will ultimately outweigh their costs.
How these benefits are to be distributed, and how Australians will
craft their own, national solution to balancing market outcomes
with social equity remain problems we have yet to solve.

Notes

1   Other studies of these changes include Ryan and Bramston (2003); Kelly (1992); and Jennett and Stewart (1990).

2   With the end of the Bretton Woods system in the 1970s, the Australian dollar was pegged to the US dollar, and later to a basket of currencies. Pegging permits some movement in value; it also obliges a government to buy the currency when its price falls.

3   Examples include the Asia 'meltdown' of 1997–1998 and the SARS outbreak of 2003. As external economies slowed the dollar devalued. Under a pegged system the government buys dollars thus increasing domestic interest rates and slowing the economy. Under a floating regime, the currency devalues, making exports more attractive and raising import prices. While the external shock is still felt domestically, the impact is dampened.

4   Between 1983 and 1996 there were eight Accords. For five years the Accord operated through the Arbitration Commission. From 1987 to 1991 it was decentralised to industry agreements. After 1991 enterprise agreements dominated.

5   This approach changed especially after the Hawke era, when conservative government policy became more reliant on markets altering individuals' behaviour and special interest groups sought to influence government policy.

6   The recession's label was given by Treasurer Paul Keating, who had already argued that restructuring was needed to prevent Australian becoming a 'banana republic'. The Treasurer's phrases often communicated the central issues more powerfully than any technical economic explanation.

7   While the recent economic crisis may signal the end of unfettered faith in the free market, it is still unlikely that increased government intervention will be accompanied by a return to the levels of protection removed under Hawke (see Rudd 2009).

References

Galbraith, J.K. 1987, *A History of Economics: The Past as the Present*, Penguin Books, London

Hancock W.K. 1961 [1930], *Australia*, Jacaranda Press, Melbourne

Howard, J. 1995, 'The role of government: a modern Liberal approach', The Menzies Research Centre 1995 National Lecture Series, Canberra, 6 June, http://www.ozpolitics.info/guide/elections/fed2004/the-policies/role-of-govt/, accessed 14 October 2008

Jennett, C. and Stewart, R.G. (eds) 1990, *Hawke and Australian Public Policy: Consensus and Restructuring*, Macmillan, Melbourne

Kelly P. 1992, *The End of Certainty: The Story of the 1980s*, Allen & Unwin, Sydney

Keynes, J.M. 1949 [1936], *The General Theory of Employment, Interest and Money*, Macmillan and Co., London

Ryan, S. and Bramston, T. (eds) 2003, *The Hawke Government: A Critical Retrospective*, Pluto Press, Melbourne

Rudd, K. 2009, 'The global financial crisis', *The Monthly*, February, pp. 20–29

Sykes T. 1996, *The Bold Riders: Behind Australia's Corporate Collapses*, 2nd ed., Allen & Unwin, Sydney, 1996

Willis R. 2003, 'The economy: a perspective from the inside' in eds S. Ryan and T. Bramston, *The Hawke Government: A Critical Retrospective*, Pluto Press, Melbourne

Wilenski, P. 1986, *Public Power and Public Administration*, Hale and Ironmonger, Sydney

Chapter 14

The best of times, the worst of times: the Hawke and Rudd governments, employment and industrial relations

Barbara Pocock

Introduction

Prime ministerial legacies are made in part by the times in which they find themselves. John Curtin, one of Bob Hawke's heroes (and he was not given much to heroes), had to rise to the challenge of war in the Pacific and a dramatic realignment of Australia's foreign alliances. Bob Hawke's legacy was partly of his own making, reflecting amongst others his particular interest in consensus and the terms of working life and employment. But his legacy was also a child of the times – times that saw high unemployment and significant changes in the composition of industry and employment and growth in global trade. Bob Hawke had to rise to these times and Kevin Rudd's prime ministership is likely to be similarly shaped by the way he meets the crises of his times: the world's most significant economic recession in seventy years, as well as the new elephant in the room: climate change.

How does Hawke's situation and his approach to employment and industrial relations compare with that of Rudd's, twenty-five years later? In this brief contribution, I consider two areas: industrial relations and employment, reflecting on the Hawke years and subsequent events. These developments throw the institutional frameworks, values and alignments of the Hawke years in comparative perspective. Circumstances and arrangements have changed dra-

matically since 1983, in ways and degrees that many of us would not
have predicted or expected.

Employment and industrial relations issues were amongst Bob
Hawke's signature arenas of government. This reflects Hawke's own
long history as an active member of the industrial wing of the labour
movement and his influence on industrial relations machinery in
Australia, as well as his commitment to addressing inequality, especially the inequality that marks the relationship between worker
and boss. One cannot imagine a prime minister today, flushed with
excitement, exclaiming on Australia winning the America's Cup,
'Any boss that sacks an employee for taking today off is a bum!' It
is impossible to imagine John Howard or Kevin Rudd encouraging
the whole workforce to take a 'sickie'. However, it is the kind of
comment that made Bob Hawke one of Australia's most popular
prime ministers. He did not lack colour before, during or after his
term as prime minister. Before ascending to leadership he was often
a larrikin. However, like his hero Curtin, Hawke took the office of
prime minister seriously, giving up the drink, if not his active socia-
bility with many in the union movement and beyond. This socia-
bility and public rapport made him an exceptional prime minister
in many ways (Hogg 2003).

The times: employment change in the Hawke years and since

Since the Hawke prime ministership ended in 1991, Australians
have experienced a second postwar boom, with positive growth in
gross domestic product in every quarter up until the end of 2008
with the exception of one (December 2000) (Figure 1). While the
onset of the global financial crisis in 2008 will break that long boom,
the post-Hawke/Keating years proved to be a sustained period of
economic growth.

The Hawke term itself was not so lucky. Two low points
occurred: five quarters of negative economic growth in the lead-up
to Hawke's election in March 1983 and another downturn beginning
in September 1990 lasting until June 1991 which saw four quarters
of negative economic growth. Together these periods of recession
contributed to sustained levels of unemployment in the Hawke term
and beyond and created serious policy challenges.

Figure 2 shows the unemployment levels in the period from
1980 to January 2009. The recessions of the early eighties and nine-

Figure 1: Per capita GDP, Australia, 1980–2008 ($ per capita)

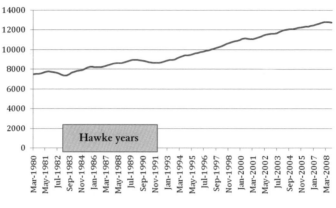

Source: ABS (2009a)

ties were associated with high and sustained rates of unemployment with official rates hovering around 8 per cent for most of Hawke's prime ministership. Official unemployment reached over 10 per cent in 1983, affecting more than 700,000 people, and it returned to close to this level as Hawke left office, and surpassed it in the ensuing months.

Figure 2: Official unemployment, Australia, 1980–2009 (per cent)

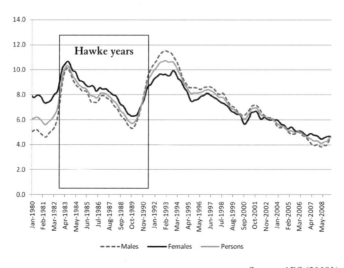

Source: ABS (2009b)

Figure 3: Employment by industry, Australia, 1984, 1991, 2008 ('000)

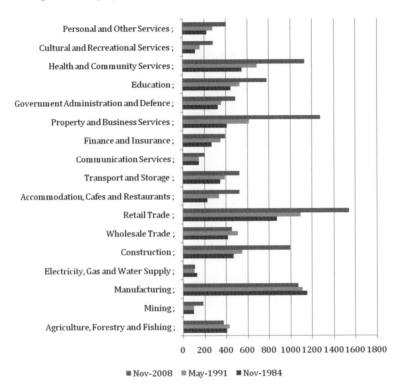

Source: ABS (2009c)

These years were also associated with significant industry restructuring, as manufacturing shrank (especially manufacturing for domestic consumption) and the services sector grew. This had important implications for the structure and nature of employment, with permanent, full-time manufacturing-based employment in decline. Figure 3 illustrates the decline in manufacturing and agricultural employment over the past quarter century, with rapid growth in employment in retail, property and business services, and health and community services. This transformation is sometimes called a shift to 'the knowledge-based' economy. However, it is not always clear how much of the services sector is truly 'knowledge-based' with much of it amounting to hard labour in the traditional sense (in care services, for example), as well as work requiring high levels of emotional intelligence (in health, education and management, for example) and 'performativity' (the calculated adoption of

Figure 4: Men's and women's employment, 1978–2009, trend ('000)

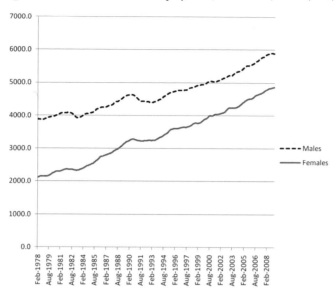

Source: ABS (2009b)

a style or approach in the process of offering a service or labour) for example in the retail and financial sectors.

The relatively high rates of unemployment in the Hawke years affected employment growth. However, these pauses were small dips in the long-run upward trend in total employment, as Figure 4 shows.

Both women's and men's employment expanded significantly in the Hawke years – and since. However, the period saw rapid increases in employment rates for women in particular. The employment to population ratio for women increased from 39.9 per cent in March 1983 to 47.1 per cent in December 1991. It has climbed much further again in the years since to reach 55.5 per cent in January 2009 (Table 1). While we lack good historical data about the effects of holding down a job as well as carrying out domestic and caring work, we know that in the Rudd years at least the majority of women are feeling pressed for time. In 2007, 56.3 per cent of working women felt often or always rushed or pressed for time (42.7 per cent of men also felt this) (ABS 2007b). The main reason for this is the pressure of combining work and family.

Table 1: Employment to population ratio, per cent, by sex, 1981, 1991, 2009

	Males	Females	Persons
Mar 83	69.4	39.9	54.4
Dec 91	66.6	47.1	56.7
Jan 09	68.8	55.5	62

Source: ABS (2009c)

The shift in industry structures illustrated in Figure 3 is clearly associated with the feminisation of the Australian labour force, as well as a steady shift away from full-time to part-time work. Figure 5 illustrates the shift to part-time work in the Hawke period and since, most of it concentrated amongst women.

Rapid growth in casual jobs has accompanied the growth in part-time work and the shift in industry employment to the services sector, especially during the Hawke and Keating years. Table 2 shows that casual employment grew by 4.7 percentage points in the Hawke years, and by 5.3 percentage points in the Keating years. The upward trend continued in the Howard period, but much more slowly, to peak at close to a quarter of all employees in late 2007. This level of precarious employment is unusual in the OECD area, with only Spain close to Australia's share.

Figure 5: Part-time and full-time employment, 1983, 1991, 2009 by sex, Australia ('000)

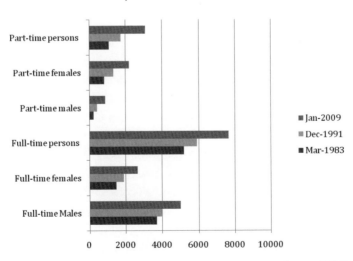

Source: ABS (2009b)

There was also growth (of 2.7 hours a week) in the average length of the weekly hours of full-time employees in the Hawke and Keating years. A much smaller increase characterised the Howard government. By the time of the 2006 census almost one in five Australians – most of them men – were working more than 49 hours a week: a quarter of men worked these long hours (ABS 2007a). Many of these extended hours were unpaid.

Table 2: Proportion of workforce that is casual and average actual hours of work of full-timers at commencement of prime-ministerial terms 1981–2007

	Date	% casual*	Average actual weekly hours of work for full-timers
Beginning of Hawke government	Mar 83	13.1	38.4
Beginning of Keating government	Dec 91	16.8	39.7
Beginning of Howard government	Mar 96	22.1	41.1
Beginning of Rudd government	Oct 07**	23.2	41.2

* Definition of '% casual' = casual employees in waged work
** Figures are for late 2006 rather than October 2007

Source: Campbell (2007, p. 49).

The transformation of employment extended to the institutional representation of workers: union density fell steadily in the 1980s. It halved again after Hawke's prime ministership when it fell from 40.5 per cent in 1990 to just 18.9 per cent in 2007 (ABS 2007c). The factors explaining this partly lie in the rapid change in the industries, occupations and forms of employment, but they also lie in the privatisation of some large organisations, and government hostility and legislative barriers to recruitment that were set in place in the Howard years (Peetz 1998; Peetz and Pocock 2009).

Accordingly, the Hawke government years witnessed great change in the workplace, and subsequent years have seen the continuation of these trends, although with slower rates of change under Howard on some factors like casualisation and long hours.

Recession in the Rudd years: what's different?

This background means that the Rudd government meets a potentially deep international recession in 2009 in the context of a very different labour market than that of the early Hawke years – one that is internationally distinctive in the incidence of part-time and casual work.

In 2009 Australia is entering a recession in a context of historically high rates of services sector employment, of women at work, and of part-time and casual employment. This means that this new recession is likely to affect women's employment more than those in the past. Also the new primacy of the services sector might mean that recession hits this form of employment more than in the past.

It is possible, also, that some effects of economic slowdown are below the radar of official labour force data, given the greater role of casual and part-time workers in the labour market. These types of workers are rarely formally retrenched because their jobs are not formally ongoing, unlike jobs in manufacturing where downturns result in headline-creating retrenchments such as occurred on the retrenchment of 1850 Pacific Brands workers across Australia in early 2009. Service sector workers – many of them long-term casual workers – lose their jobs by other means. They are simply not offered further shifts. Many others experience more under-employment as they are offered fewer shifts than before. Remembering that the average period of casual employment in Australia is over two and a half years, this represents the loss of long-established, regular employment. It will have a significant effect on household circumstances and expenditure given that the earnings of 'second earners' are far from 'pin money' for non-essentials in many households, but the bedrock on which large mortgage obligations are built.

We saw some signs of these effects early in the downturn in late 2008, with underemployment – which especially affects women and service sector workers – officially rising in advance of unemployment. The labour force underutilisation rate (which includes the unemployed and the underemployed, that is those who would like to work more) rose from 10.1 per cent in May 2008 (12.4 per cent for women) to 10.6 per cent in November 2008 for all persons (13.2 per cent women): in late 2008, one in five of Australia's part-time workers wanted and was available to work more hours (ABS 2008b).

It is also possible that a recession in the current context will dampen the level of long hours worked. However, the way in which this labour market indicator will go is uncertain. Economic security is a partial driver of long hours, as employees who fear for their job security attempt to 'stay sweet' with the boss by putting in extra unpaid efforts. Others may find that a cooling economy, and cooling demand for time, relieves job demands that drive long hours.

Overall, however, the Rudd government is likely to face a relatively high rate of underemployment and unemployment, coming after a long boom, not unlike the situation that confronted the Hawke/Keating governments in 1983–1996. However, the background and composition of un- and under-employment has changed because of structural shifts in employment and the labour market. The rapid decline in unionisation in Australia, in particular, distinguishes the role and voice of unions in the Labor governments in the two periods. It was partly this high level of voice that explained the Hawke government's close relationship with the leadership of the ACTU, notably Bill Kelty, in crafting economic policy.

Hawke, the Accord and summits

The Hawke period was especially marked by economic reforms, as the government enacted changes to the tax, trade and financial systems (Ryan and Bramston 2003). In industrial relations law, specifically, the Hawke government established the Hancock Committee to examine the operation of the industrial relations system and to recommend on its reforms. This led to the enactment of some changes in 1993. However, essentially the committee and the subsequent legislation did not materially disrupt the long-established architecture of arbitration and conciliation.

When the Hewson-led Liberal opposition proposed radical industrial relations changes as part of its 'Fightback!' program in 1991, Hawke characterised these as lunacy, and even business lacked confidence in or support for radical change in Australia's industrial institutions' arrangements. All this was to change in the following decades.

Rather than legislative change, the defining industrial relations initiative of the early Hawke years was the Accord (the *Statement of Accord by the ALP and the Australian Council of Trade Unions Regarding Economic Policy in 1983*'). It was a cornerstone of the new government. According to Ross Gittens 'the Hawke Government without the Accord would be like Samson with a crewcut' (*Sydney Morning Herald*, 31 July 1985). The Accord included responses to the coincidental evils of inflation and rising unemployment, essentially trading money wage increases for increases in the social wage.

The 1983 statement recognised 'the destructive nature of the current economic crisis' and had full employment as its prime objective (The Accord 1983, included in Stillwell 1986, p. 59). It promised 'that living standards of wage and salary earners and non-income earning sectors of the population' would be 'maintained and through time increased with movements in national productivity' (The Accord 1983, in Stillwell 1986, p. 59). The Accord's ambitions were modified in the subsequent National Economic Summit in April 1983 as business entered the conversation.

The overall cost–benefit calculation of the fruit of the Accord and its distribution has been much debated (Stillwell 1986; Ewer et al. 1991). While the Accord's merits for different classes of interests are contested, there can be no doubt of its political success in allowing the Hawke government to exercise considerable power in restraining wage growth and to reshape social policy significantly, not least the health system.

National conversations, changing times

It is striking in retrospect how central wages, industrial arrangements and employment were to the 1983 national conversation, led by Hawke, and key events like the National Economic Summit. This is in marked contrast to, for example, the much wider canvass of the Rudd government's 2020 Summit, a quarter of a century later. Rudd's 2008 summit included discussions about international affairs, Indigenous affairs, sustainable communities and the environment, education, productivity and other themes, without any specific reference to work or industrial relations (Commonwealth of Australia 2008). The 2020 Summit was a much less industrial, male, be-suited affair, with very significant representation from outside Canberra and peak lobby groups (Pocock 2008).

Nonetheless, industrial relations and the regulation of work figured very significantly in the election of the Rudd government in 2007. This followed vigorous contest around these issues in the Howard years (1996–2007). In this period, the Howard government significantly reshaped and weakened protection against unfair dismissal, encouraged individualised bargaining, reduced the award system to a safety net and then thinned out its protections, reduced unionisation and collective bargaining, and attempted to restrain wages growth. The government also led straightforward anti-union initiatives like the attacks on unionisation on the waterfront and in the building industry. Howard's personal commitment to the individualisation of industrial bargaining led to the folly of WorkChoices, a set of industrial reforms that went much further in transforming the industrial system, weakening the roles of tribunals, lowering minimum standards and workers' protections, and strengthening the hands of employers.

Thus, between 1996 and 2007 the Howard government moved inexorably towards a decentralised industrial system that shifted power towards employers. Some of the seeds of this shift had been planted in the late 1980s and early 1990s with Labor's move towards productivity-based enterprise bargaining that saw cuts in conditions in exchange for pay rises in some workplaces.

These seeds were evident in Paul Keating's speech to the Institute of Company Directors on 21 April 1993 when he suggested that industrial awards should become safety nets, and the primary industrial emphasis should be upon bargaining at the workplace, and that such bargaining would especially focus on productivity improvements (Keating 1993). Keating foreshadowed a much reduced role for industrial tribunals, which would make 'rare' use of compulsory arbitral powers, with parties expected to bargain in good faith with close harmony between the state and federal systems. Sixteen years later, in 2009, Keating's vision is very close to the Rudd government reality as set out in *Forward with Fairness* (Rudd and Gillard 2007).

This radical shift was made possible by the intervening Howard years, when John Howard was intent on a radical industrial revolution, culminating in WorkChoices. WorkChoices was the unexpected and radical child of Howard's surprise success in winning a majority in both houses of federal parliament in 2004. However, in the end WorkChoices and the vulnerability it created for women, casuals, young people and the disadvantaged – much exploited in the union movement's very successful 'Your Rights at Work' campaign of 2005–2007 – proved a step too far for the Australian public. The electorate turned on Howard, voting him out of his own seat, and electing the Rudd government. However, the Howard years had done their work: the Rudd government's vision on industrial relations law was a long way from the regime prevailing under Hawke a quarter of a century earlier (Rudd and Gillard 2007).

The industrial relations pendulum swings and swings

Howard's experiment with industrial radicalism was a step too far even for some of his own Cabinet. For example, former industrial relations minister Joe Hockey said in retrospect that the laws 'went too deep' despite being introduced with 'the best intentions' (ABC 2007). After the election, Hockey conceded that WorkChoices was dead and that the Rudd government had a mandate for a new system.

That said, the Rudd government has worked to de-emphasise industrial issues in its first term, diligently implementing its election mandate in minimalist ways. It has sought to take industrial relations off the agenda of public contention by adopting its election undertakings to the letter, in the form of Fair Work Australia. Essentially the direction of the Rudd reforms in industrial relations are very different from the regime in Hawke's time. It represents a turning back of the most extreme elements of the Howard government's radical WorkChoices legislation but is far from a return to the centralised, comprehensive, award-based, conciliation and arbitration system of the 1980s.

Employment creation in the Hawke years

One of the Accord's significant inclusions, undertaken in response to the rise in unemployment in the early 1980s, was job creation. As Australia sets out in 2009 to confront what may be a much more serious economic recession than that of the early 1980s, it is perhaps timely to consider this aspect of the Hawke legacy.

The Accord promised to create over 500,000 jobs. In the face of high unemployment a significant instrument established to assist the long-term unemployed in particular was the Community Employment Program (CEP), a demand-side labour market initiative designed to address cyclical unemployment directly. CEP operated between 1983 and 1987, and was at that time the largest public-sector-led employment creation effort ever undertaken in Australia (Howe 2008, p. 55). The Hawke government aimed to create the equivalent of 70,000 full-time jobs for an average length of six months in the program's first iteration (Australian Audit Office 1987); 65 per cent of funds were required to be for wage-related costs. The CEP used public funds to create full-time jobs of at least thirteen weeks duration, paid at award rates, mainly in local government and community organisations – termed 'project sponsors' – on projects offering community benefits that would not otherwise be undertaken (some were also directly created in the Commonwealth government). It particularly focused on disadvantaged job seekers. The labour market goals, administrative arrangements and evaluation of contracts were specified in considerable detail, to ensure the program's goals of targeted, net job creation through socially useful projects were met.

Based in the Hunter Valley in NSW, I was one of many state public servants working with Commonwealth officials, local governments and community organisations, developing and reviewing project ideas, and preparing recommendations on their funding. Commonwealth public servants worked to match long-term unemployed to the jobs created. CEP was structured partly in response to the bad press that had accumulated around the Whitlam government's Regional Employment Development Scheme of the mid-1970s. REDS was terminated in 1975, having created 32,000 short-term jobs designed to help meet high unemployment in regions especially associated with technological change and tariff reductions (Howe 2008, p. 57). REDS had developed a reputation for 'make work' jobs. However, like many labour market programs, REDS was short-lived and never robustly evaluated.

The CEP was characterised by the targeting of funds to create jobs in areas of high unemployment, with particular attention to ensure that the funds created jobs for the unemployed. Projects had to be labour intensive, offer employment for more than very short periods, incorporate training, and meet targets in relation to the long-term unemployed, women and other groups disadvantaged in the labour market like those with disabilities. Projects that were not labour intensive or might employ consultants or contractors were not favoured.

The CEP was discontinued in 1987 in favour of more supply-side 'active' labour market programs under the Keating government, which placed greater emphasis on formal training (Kirby 1986;

Cook 2008). Then, under the Howard government, much greater emphasis was given to subsidised private sector employment and 'mutual obligation', which required labour market participation in exchange for government support through, for example, the 'Work for the Dole' scheme. The latter has been described as 'punitive workfare' which stigmatised and disciplined the unemployed (Cook 2008, p. 8). This supply-side approach, with its focus on the behaviours and attributes of the unemployed or beneficiary, stands in strong contrast to the counter-cyclical public sector employment creation of the early Hawke years.

The Rudd government and counter-cyclical employment interventions

In the face of impending economic recession, the Rudd government has also turned its attention to counter-cyclical measures that take the national budget into deficit, responding on two fronts: funding very significant expansion in training-based 'productivity places' and spending programs designed to counter the economic slowdown. The Productivity Places initiative aims to create 645,000 training places (253,000 of them to be allocated to job seekers) over five years from 2008 'to ensure that Australians develop the skills that industry needs' (DEEWR 2008). The training places are to be delivered through industry to ensure that training is 'more responsive to the needs of enterprises and individuals' (DEEWR 2008).

Counter-cyclical employment generation measures have included a $10.4 billion 'Economic Security Strategy' in October 2008 funding infrastructure and making cash payments to households, aiming to create 'a stimulus of around 1 per cent of GDP and up to 75,000 additional jobs'. Three months later, the government announced a further $42 billion 'nation building and jobs plan' designed to create 90,000 jobs in 2008/09 and 2009/10 through funding building insulation in 2.7 million homes, upgrading 9540 schools, building 20,000 social and defence homes, making cash payments to households, giving temporary tax breaks to small business and increasing funding to local councils to build 'town halls, libraries, community centres and sport centres', with an emphasis on quick starts to projects (Swan 2009).

These initiatives attempt to address the short-term demand-side problems generating increasing un- and under-employment, while also 'delivering the long term investments needed to strengthen future economic growth' (Swan 2009). The focus of some of this spending also reflects the growing interest in reducing energy use in response to the threat of climate change. However, the building, road and infrastructure orientation of the Rudd stimulus packages (Rudd 2008) at the onset of the 2008/09 downturn will compli-cate – and perhaps retard – their capacity to generate jobs quickly. Construction-related projects require skilled workers and experi-enced supervisors, they are very oriented to male employment and they are often capital rather than labour intensive, with long delays in commencement. In this sense, the Rudd response to the downturn is in strong contrast to the demand-side response of the early Hawke period with its emphasis upon community and public-sector based employment as well as quick, targeted job creation, focusing upon specific groups especially the long-term unemployed and women. Counter-cyclical 'nation building' can mean long delays and uneven job creation, without careful attention to net new job creation. This approach continues the trend away from government involvement in direct provision of employment services and job creation that Howe (2008, p. 207) identifies as having characterised the policy trajec-tory since the Community Employment Program. Instead, govern-ments are increasingly involved in 'promoting or facilitating desired labour market behaviour amongst non-government actors' including employment creation through taxation regimes, wage subsidies and the training system, rather than direct job creation (Howe 2008, p. 207). Whether this works in a timely way, and responds to a more service-oriented labour force that is increasingly feminised, remains a test of the Rudd government's response to a downturn that may make the challenges faced by the Hawke government in the 1980s pale into insignificance.

Conclusion

In the quarter century between the Hawke and Rudd governments the labour market has changed a great deal. Much of this reflects the influence of changes in patterns of global trade and government pol-icies that have exposed Australian workplaces to international com-petition. Rapid expansion in services sector employment has seen the decline of life-time employment, of the full-time male breadwinner, of permanent jobs and of unionism. Labour market changes also

reflect changes in households and in gender politics as women have
turned to work as a means of boosting household income, their
financial independence and to make use of their increasing professional and vocational skills. However, while women have increased
their paid contributions diligently, they have not been rewarded with
relief on the home front, continuing to do double the hours spent
by men in unpaid domestic work (ABS 2008a). The consequences
of these inequities are very significant, especially in latter life as
women's share of superannuation earnings remains so much lower
than men's. The long revolution for women at work shows no sign
of ending soon.

The decline in unionisation in Australia – such a feature of the
way in which the Hawke government governed – has cast a long
shadow over the regulation of the labour market, as has the seismic
shock of WorkChoices. While WorkChoices was shortlived and
politically disastrous for its architects, its legacy might live longer
than some expect. The Howard years saw an inter-generational
rupture in the expectations of new generations of workers about
their entitlements, voice at work and the form of regulation of their
jobs. These younger workers have early experiences in casual work,
little knowledge of unionism and collectivity, and weaker parental
links to unions as lower rates of union density roll through the generations. They are encouraged to see themselves as independent
actors and authors of their own destiny. Whether they are able to
craft the work and life they seek, in a labour market that might be
characterised by higher unemployment, and where labour regulation
is crafted in terms of a minimalist safety net, remains to be seen.

Labor governments face particular challenges: can they craft
forms of labour market regulation that rise to the challenges of a
new century, and foster productive workplaces that are fair? This
means governing to create a decent working time regime, for pay
equity and fair rewards for work and for limits on pernicious long
hours and insecure work contracts. Can they renovate systems of
work regulation that respond to workers' changing circumstances
over the life cycle, recognise their care responsibilities, and at the
same time ensure that the growing population of low-paid services
sectors do not become an underclass of working poor?

References

Australian Audit Office 1987, *Department of Employment and Industrial Relations: Community Employment Program*, Auditor General Efficiency Audit Report, Australian Government Publishing Service, Canberra

Australian Broadcasting Commission (ABC) 2007, 'Bishop defends "dead" WorkChoices', ABC News, Sydney, 28 November 2007, http://www.abc.net.au/news/stories/2007/11/28/2104003.htm?site=elections/federal/2007, accessed 4 March 2009

Australian Bureau of Statistics (ABS) 2007a, *Census Tables*, Cat. no. 2068.0, ABS, Canberra

ABS 2007b, *Employment Arrangement, Retirement and Superannuation, Australia*, Cat. no. 6361.0, ABS, Canberra

ABS 2007c, *Employee Earnings, Benefits and Trade Union Membership, Australia*, Cat. no. 6310.0, ABS, Canberra

ABS 2008a, *How Australians Use Their Time, 2006*, Cat. no. 4153.0, ABS, Canberra

ABS 2008b, *Underemployed Workers, Australia*, Cat. no. 6265.0, ABS, Canberra

ABS 2009a, *Australian National Accounts: National Income, Expenditure and Product*, Cat. no. 5206.0, ABS, Canberra

ABS 2009b, *Labour Force, Australia*, Cat. no. 6202.0.55.001, spreadsheets, ABS, Canberra

ABS 2009c, *Labour Force, Australia, Detailed, Quarterly*, Cat. no. 6291.0.55.003, spreadsheets, ABS, Canberra

Campbell, I. 2007, *Globalisation and Changes in Employment Conditions in Australia*, Report Produced for the ILO Work and Employment (TRAVAIL) Program, Centre for Applied Social Research, RMIT University, Melbourne

Cook, B. 2008, *National, Regional and Local Employment Policies in Australia*, working paper no. 08-06, Centre of Full Employment and Equity, University of Newcastle, Newcastle, NSW

Commonwealth of Australia 2008, *Australia 2020 Summit, Final Report*, Commonwealth of Australia, Canberra, http://www.australia2020.gov.au/docs/final_report/2020_summit_report_full.pdf, accessed 27 March 2009

Department of Education, Employment and Workplace Relations 2008, *Productivity Places Program*, DEEWR, Canberra, http://www.dest.gov.au/sectors/training_skills/programmes_funding/Programme_categories/key_skills_priorities/productivity_places_program/, accessed 5 March 2009

Ewer, P., Hampson, I., Lloyd, C., Rainford, J., Rix, S. and Smith, M. 1991, *Politics and the Accord*, Pluto Press, Sydney

Hogg, B. 2003, 'Hawke the campaigner' in eds S. Ryan and T. Bramston, *The Hawke Government: A Critical Retrospective*, Pluto Press Australia, Melbourne

Howe, J. 2008, *Regulating for Job Creation*, Federation Press, Melbourne

Keating, P. 1993, Speech to the Institute of Company Directors, Melbourne, 21 April

Kirby, P. 1986, *Report of the Committee of Inquiry into Labour Market Programs* (the Kirby report), Australian Government Publishing Service, Canberra, http://www.voced.edu.au/docs/landmarks/TD_LMR_85_649.pdf, accessed 27 March 2009

Peetz, D. 1998, *Unions in a Contrary World: The Future of the Australian Trade Union Movement*, Cambridge University Press, Cambridge

Peetz, D. and Pocock, B. 2009, 'An analysis of workplace representatives, union power and democracy in Australia', *British Journal of Industrial Relations*, vol. 47, http://www3.interscience.wiley.com/journal/122384120/abstract, accessed 6 August 2009

Pocock, B. 2008, 'A view on the 20:20 Summit', Centre for Work + Life, Adelaide, http://www.unisa.edu.au/hawkeinstitute/cwl/documents/2020-commentary.pdf, accessed 27 March 2009

Rudd, K. 2008, *Nation Building: Rail, Road, Education and Research and Business*, a statement by K. Rudd, J. Gillard, W. Swan and A. Albanese, Department of Infrastructure, Transport, Regional Development and Local Government, Canberra

Rudd, K. and Gillard, J. 2007, *Forward with Fairness: Labor's Plan for Fairer and More Productive Australian Workplaces*, Australian Labor Party, Canberra, http://www.alp.org.au/download/now/forwardwithfairness.pdf, accessed 5 March 2009

Ryan S. and Bramston, T. 2003, 'Introduction' in eds S. Ryan and T. Bramston, *The Hawke Government: A Critical Retrospective*, Pluto Press Australia, Melbourne

Stillwell, F. 1986, *The Accord ... And Beyond*, Pluto Press, Sydney

Swan, W. 2009, *$42 Billion Nation Building and Jobs Plan*, joint media release with the Prime Minister, Canberra, 3 February, and associated fact sheets, http://www.treasurer.gov.au/DisplayDocs.aspx?doc=pressreleases/2009/009.htm&pageID=003&min=wms&Year=&DocType=0, accessed 14 May 2009

Chapter 15

The super revolution

Rhonda Sharp

Introduction

During the thirteen-year era of the Hawke and Keating Labor governments, Australia's retirement incomes system was transformed through the establishment of a private occupational superannuation funds industry. The assets of this industry exceeded $1 trillion by 2006, greater than the value of Australia's annual GDP, and comprised the largest capital market in the region. These changes not only spread superannuation coverage to over 90 per cent of the workforce but transformed the role of occupational superannuation in the Australian economy.

This chapter explores key factors that shaped the development of occupational superannuation policy in Australia during 1983–96. I argue that when the Hawke government came to office a range of policy options were available to it but as events unfolded the goals of superannuation policy shifted considerably. Prior to taking office in 1983, Labor had promoted the idea of a national superannuation scheme and, once elected, it initially discussed superannuation within the broadly Keynesian economic framework of the Prices and Incomes Accord. However, a turning point was the decline in the international economy which revealed the structural weaknesses that existed in the Australian economy. Following Keating's 1986 declaration that Australia was in danger of becoming a 'banana republic', and a marked shift towards a neo-liberal policy framework (Broomhill 2008), superannuation policy increasingly reflected this

economistic neo-liberal approach. The concept of a national superannuation scheme gave way to a less equitable occupational superannuation policy approach that served multiple economic policy
agendas. These included the reduction of budgetary pressure caused
by the demographic crisis of an ageing population, the maintenance
of the wages and incomes accord to contain the growth in real wages
and, finally, a higher level of national savings. The chapter will conclude with a critical assessment of the legacy of the Hawke/Keating
changes to the role of superannuation in Australia.

The policy environment inherited by the Hawke Labor government

The Australian Labor government's policy approach to superannuation was both influenced and constrained by a series of factors that
existed before it came to power. The policy environment inherited
by the incoming Hawke Labor government contained the seeds for
significant policy changes in the area of superannuation, some of
which developed into a wider policy program under Labor.

*Rising levels of superannuation coverage and the role
of the trade unions*

When the Hawke Labor government was elected in March 1983
superannuation coverage of the workforce, while still low and
uneven, had undergone a significant rise historically. Since the 1950s,
superannuation had increasingly become a supplement to the age
pension not only for the high-income groups but also for unionised
male employees (McCallum and Shaver 1986, p. 7).

Under the presidency of Hawke, the Australian Council of
Trade Unions (ACTU) adopted superannuation as an industrial
issue in 1979. This heightened union interest in non-wage working
conditions had also been facilitated by wage indexation introduced
in the early 1970s under the Whitlam Labor government, which
had restricted opportunities for wage increases. Clearly, by the end
of the 1970s superannuation was being targeted by the union movement as an important source of non-wage benefits.

Structural changes within the industry

At the time the Hawke Labor government took office in 1983,
major structural changes within the superannuation industry were

also emerging. The concentration of equity ownership within the industry had risen significantly, so that by 1977 life offices and superannuation funds were responsible for more than half of the net acquisitions of equity (Hancock 1983, p. 152). This created significant shifts in the ownership and distribution of equity capital in Australia.

Moreover, by 1983 superannuation had become the major part of the life insurance industry's new business. Superannuation constituted 65 per cent of the business of the life insurance industry by the end of the 1980s with two mutual life firms, AMP and National Mutual, accounting for nearly 70 per cent of the superannuation monies (Klumpes 1992, p. 124). In 1978 the first industry superannuation fund, LUCRF, was established by the Storeman and Packer's Union, followed by the building union industry fund, CBUSS, in 1984. These union funds with their low fee structures were fundamentally different entrants to the industry. Superannuation funds were growing in power and economic significance to the Australian economy.

Key new policy-making contexts

The Hawke Labor government took office at a time when the role of government in economic and social policy making was the subject of international debate and re-evaluation. In particular, lower levels of government intervention via income tax cuts and welfare expenditure cutbacks were firmly on the New Right policy agenda of the Thatcher and Reagan conservative governments. This resurgence of the more conservative strands of neo-classical economic thinking had been dominating Australian Treasury advice throughout the late 1970s and early 1980s, parallel to developments overseas (Whitwell 1986).

Nowhere was the policy pressure for less government intervention greater than in the financial sector. The idea of deregulating the financial sector had gathered momentum in the late 1970s. Instrumental in the debate was the Campbell Committee of Inquiry into the Financial System spearheaded by John Hewson when he was advisor to then Treasurer John Howard (Love 2008, pp. 21–28). The inquiry reported in 1981 and was unequivocal in its view that the dictates of economic efficiency required that economic activity be organised through a 'competitive market system which is subject to a minimum of regulation and government intervention' (Campbell 1981, p. 1). The committee advocated wholesale deregulation of the financial sector, implying that a central problem of the system was the level of government intervention. These views, slightly reworked by the Martin Committee established by Labor's Treasurer Paul Keating in 1983, provided the philosophical framework for two major policy changes in Labor's first year of office, namely, floating the dollar and moves to deregulate the financial sector. The deregulated exchange rate and financial sector affected all areas of government policy as well as creating a favorable context for the rapid expansion of private sector superannuation funds.

The Prices and Incomes Accord

A crucial and potentially opposing policy influence with which Labor began office was the *Statement of Accord Between the Australian Labor Party and the Australian Council of Trade Unions Regarding Economic Policy, February 1983*. The Accord gave the government an active role in the economy and committed Labor, if elected, to examine as a priority the possible role of a national superannuation scheme (Stilwell 1986).

The rise and fall of a national superannuation scheme

There have been several attempts this century to replace the age pension with a national superannuation scheme funded by earnings-related contributions from employees and/or employers (Senate Select Committee on Superannuation 1992, p. 9). Prior to World War 2, the initiative for such a policy came from non-Labor parties. Labor's interest in a national superannuation scheme manifested itself during the Second World War when the Curtin and Chifley Labor governments established the National Welfare Fund, but this failed to develop into a national superannuation scheme (Nielson and Harris 2008). When Labor came to power in the early 1970s, the party again supported a national superannuation scheme. The National Superannuation Committee of Inquiry, chaired by Keith Hancock, was set up in 1973 but the Whitlam government lost office before its recommendations for a national superannuation scheme could be implemented. However, the Hancock reports were influential in policy circles in drawing attention to the scope of the policy changes deemed necessary in the context of an ageing population

(National Superannuation Committee of Inquiry 1976; 1977).

When Labor returned to power in 1983, it still favoured a national superannuation scheme. A national scheme was part of the ALP platform and had been discussed intensively while in opposition, especially by the Caucus Welfare Committee. The ACTU adopted a policy for a national superannuation scheme in 1979 but it encouraged unions to pursue occupational superannuation until a national scheme was introduced (Pha 1992, p. 8). However, within a year of Labor gaining office, the national superannuation scheme had fallen off the public policy agenda. There were several factors that contributed to its demise.

First, powerful vested interests working against a national superannuation scheme were the life insurance and superannuation industry and employers as they controlled the existing, expanding superannuation investment funds. Employers had a strong interest in maintaining the status quo. They had long used superannuation as a means of attracting particular labour skills. Many company schemes were in the practice of using superannuation contributions and tax concessions as a source of cheap loans. Strong employer resistance contributed to the maintenance of a system of private-sector-controlled superannuation.

Second, key sections of the union movement also had a vested interest in superannuation that did not coincide with the development of a national superannuation scheme. The blue-collar union concept of superannuation was deferred pay. That is, superannuation was a substitute for current wages rather than a retirement benefit at the behest of employers. The changes necessary to implement a national superannuation scheme would have undermined the deferred pay gains of limited sections of the union movement and the hopes of further industry schemes.

Third, a national superannuation scheme also was inconsistent with 'economic rationalist' thinking which stressed a retirement incomes policy based on individual savings and the greater efficiency of the private sector in managing these savings. Treasury had consistently warned against such a policy on the grounds of the cost to the annual budget. By 1988 when the Social Security Review reported to the Hawke government with its issues paper *Towards a National Retirement Incomes Policy*, there was no agenda for a national superannuation scheme.

Fourth, Labor's interest in a national superannuation scheme was to some extent at odds with the culture of the welfare state as it had developed in Australia. Frances Castles describes it as a wage earners' welfare state and others have referred to the high level of 'occupational welfare' within the system (Castles 1985; Bryson 1992). In other words, Australia has a history of welfare protection of workers and their families through the wages system. In rejecting a national superannuation scheme and placing occupational superannuation at the centre of the industrial relations system, the ACTU, employers, the industry and government reinforced the existing culture of occupational welfare in a way that attempted to reflect the new economic conditions and philosophies of smaller government.

Fifth, the Accord Mark 2 (negotiated between the Accord partners in 1985) paved the way for Labor's unique policy of award superannuation, and in so doing further increased the remoteness of a national superannuation scheme. Political commentator Paul Kelly has argued that the superannuation element of the Accord Mark 2 deal was embraced by Hawke and Keating partly to kill off the push for a national superannuation scheme by the left faction of the Labor Party (Kelly 1992, p. 283). Financial journalist David Love in *Unfinished Business* (2008) ascribes a leading role to Paul Keating with his vision of radical financial change, his unique persuading skills within his party and the partnership he forged with Bill Kelty, leader of the ACTU, in prioritising occupational superannuation.

An important difference between a publicly administered national superannuation scheme and private sector occupational superannuation is that the former can be redistributive in its impact and often provides minimum benefits irrespective of labour market attachment. (A national scheme would also have socialised the losses of the current financial crisis which has dramatically extended the working life of many baby boomers.) However, women and low income groups did not have an effective voice in Labor's superannuation policy development, particularly in the formative years. For example, while women's units within the state itself had many policy successes, they had little involvement in superannuation in the early years of the Labor government. One area in which superannuation had received some attention was in relation to the sex discrimination legislation that state and federal levels of governments were

introducing or revising. However, just before the federal Labor government introduced its *Sex Discrimination Act 1984*, it succumbed
to pressure from the superannuation industry and introduced a late
change to its bill to exempt superannuation schemes.

Occupation superannuation within Labor's economic policy framework

As the concept of a national superannuation scheme gave way to a
more individualised occupational superannuation policy approach,
superannuation policy thinking came to reflect several emerging
economic policy goals under Labor. These were: an inducement
to trade unions to exercise wage restraint under the Accord; the
provision of an earnings-related source of retirement income for
individuals; and a means of increasing national savings. In addition,
there was the potential for another agenda, namely, ear-marking
superannuation savings for socially determined investments.

Each of these agendas was dominated by the tri-partite groups:
the Labor government, the ACTU and large businesses (large
employers and the superannuation and life offices specifically), as
well as key economic policy departments, economists and government policy review groups. Women have had limited representation in the policy process, particularly in relation to the Accord and
national savings agendas. Women and their concerns were most
visible in the government's Social Security Review consultation on
retirement incomes of 1986–88. This consultation allowed welfare
groups some access to the policy process.

Superannuation as part of a wages policy agenda

Under the Hawke government, the role of occupational superannuation in wages policy was new in the context of Australian industrial relations. The demise of a national superannuation scheme
from the Accord's Mark 1 initial reform agenda opened the way
for occupational superannuation to play a role in wages policy and
the economic restructuring of the Australian economy. In the first
few versions of the Accord, wage restraint was an important tool of
macroeconomic management, whereas in later Accords wages policy
in the form of award restructuring was central to labour market
microeconomic reform.

The basis for a substantial expansion of occupational superannu-

ation through the industrial award system arose from the search for a
method of distributing national productivity increases in forms other
than wage increases. At the 1983 National Wage Case, the ACTU
argued in its submission that there was also a need for a process
for sharing in national productivity gains (AIRC 1983). However,
it was not until the Accord was re-negotiated (Accord Mark 2) in
September 1985 that occupational superannuation became a crucial
arm of the Hawke government's wages policy. The agreement was
that the government would support the ACTU position at the 1986
National Wage Case for new or improved occupational superannuation to the value of 3 per cent of income for all awards. The 3 per
cent superannuation payment was to represent the employees' share
of productivity increases in Australian industry and was to be in lieu
of a 2 per cent national wage increase.

However, the National Wage Case decision of 1986 fell short of
providing award superannuation for all Australian workers. The
Australian Conciliation and Arbitration Commission decided against
the Accord agreement. Instead, it increased the market element in
the process by setting in place a collective bargaining procedure for
a phased-in introduction of award superannuation. The result of
the commission's decision was to reduce the speed and spread of
award superannuation coverage. The supporting policy element –
the national safety net scheme – never materialised. Furthermore,
the government's operational standards for occupational superannuation schemes fell short of making occupational superannuation a
universal and adequate source of retirement income support (Sharp
and Broomhill 1988, pp. 153–154).

While the introduction of award superannuation fell short of the
ACTU's original goal of providing superannuation to all employees,
it spread superannuation coverage throughout the workforce in
an unprecedented manner. Moreover, building superannuation
into wages policy provided a mechanism for extending national
productivity gains to labour in an economic climate and discourse
that mitigated against wage rises. Such wage restraint was seen by
the government as an important macroeconomic instrument. On
the other hand, the wages policy agenda of the ACTU differed to
that of the government. It sought to gain a share of national productivity increases for wage earners and was prepared to accept this in
a non-wage form. Award superannuation also offered the ACTU

the mechanism to create new industry-wide union-based superannuation funds, and, in doing so, challenge employers' control of superannuation. The spread of award superannuation throughout the workforce initially met these ACTU objectives, while at the same time providing a vehicle for mainstreaming superannuation as an industrial issue. However, this early fusion of the wages policy agendas of the government and the ACTU did not last. This was reflected in part in the subsequent (or re-negotiated) Accords.

The agenda of reforming the Australian retirement income support system

Labor's occupational superannuation policies did have the long-term aim of providing Australians with a better retirement income. There were two perceived economic problems that prompted a retirement income reform agenda. One was the rising proportion of the aged in the Australian population and the increasing cost to government of funding the age pension. The second issue was the rising expectations of the aged concerning an adequate standard of living. In the federal government's view, privatising (or greater self-provision for) aged income support provided the solution to this and other policy agendas. Treasurer Paul Keating argued during the Second Reading of the Superannuation Guarantee Bill 1992:

> The increased self-provision for retirement will permit a higher standard of living in retirement than if we continued to rely on the age pension alone. The increased self-provision will also enable future Commonwealth governments to improve the retirement conditions for those Australians who were unable to fund adequately their own retirement incomes.
>
> Lastly, self-provision will increase the flexibility in the Commonwealth's Budget in future years, especially as our population ages, and will increase national savings overall, thus reducing our reliance on the saving of foreigners to fund our development. (Senate Select Committee on Superannuation 1992, p. 9)

A retirement income agenda of greater self-provision, or reduced welfare spending, was revealed early by the Hawke Labor government. Soon after it was elected, Labor, like its Liberal government predecessor, signaled its concern with the age pension, for which the means test had been liberalised increasingly during the 1950s, 60s and early 70s. An income test was re-applied to the over-70s in 1983 as almost 100 per cent of this age group received the age pension at that time. Shortly afterwards in 1984 an assets test, designed primarily to reduce avoidance of the income test, was announced.

After these initial policy changes, the momentum for reform along the lines of increased self-provision was strengthened through the mechanism of award superannuation. However, these policy directions were reinforced by the perception of a 'demographic imperative' whereby the costs of providing retirement income support and other expenditures on the aged could not be sustained by the state in the face of the rising proportion of the aged in the population. In the early 1990s, the argument of a demographic imperative was re-visited and provided a key rationale for the introduction of compulsory superannuation retirement income reform.

The agenda of increasing national savings

Initially, for the Hawke government, the role of superannuation in promoting savings was largely seen in terms of its general contribution to Labor's broader agenda of micro and macro economic reform. However, a distinct change in emphasis emerged in the debate leading up to the introduction of compulsory superannuation (the Superannuation Guarantee Charge or SGC) in July 1992. As part of the justification for the policy shift away from award superannuation to mandated superannuation, both the government and the ACTU argued that superannuation would make a significant contribution to national savings.

The creation of a national savings agenda for superannuation played a crucial role in Labor's response to the intractability of Australia's current account deficit, high levels of foreign debt and reliance on foreign investment. Increasingly, analyses of these problems were pointing to Australia's low level of national savings as being a major cause. New economic analyses provided quantitative support to the idea that the introduction of mandated superannuation in 1992 would raise the overall level of national savings. The capacity of superannuation policy to increase aggregate savings, however, is a matter of considerable debate.

Industry policy: a new agenda for superannuation?

Under the Labor government, superannuation funds became one of the fastest growing sectors in the Australian economy. This growth, essentially a windfall for the superannuation industry, was a direct result of the Labor government's wages, taxation and retirement incomes policies.

Public debate concerning the use of superannuation funds was initiated by the release of the joint union–government document *Australia Reconstructed* which came out of the trade mission to Western Europe (ACTU/TDC 1987). The report raised the issue of a levy on superannuation funds to finance industry develop-ment. Later, in 1991, the notion of 'patient' or development capital funding was part of Minister John Button's industry policy state-ment (*Australian Financial Review*, 21 March 1991). However, the superannuation industry has always strongly resisted the notion of investment controls.

The introduction of the Superannuation Guarantee Charge marked the emergence of an industry policy agenda consistent with a non-interventionist approach to investment controls. The Keating Labor government identified the SGC as the main means for raising national savings. In doing so, the government argued that Australia's capacity to develop its domestic industries would be enhanced with the increased availability of investible funds, noting that 85 per cent of superannuation assets are invested in Australia (Dawkins 1992, p. 48). Unlike their Scandinavian counterparts, and contrary to the initial fears of employers, Australian unions have not paid much attention to issues such as socialised investment (Shaw 1986, p. 208).

The legacy

This chapter has explored key political-economic forces that led to the establishment of an employer-mandated occupational superan-nuation policy in Australia in the first two terms of the Hawke Labor government. While it rightfully could be claimed as a policy revolution at the time, it remains an incomplete revolution after eleven years of the Coalition government. Moreover, the privatised, occupational nature of superannuation has been a mechanism (albeit not the only one) for extending gender, class and race disparities to the aged population.

Underpinning the SGC legislation was Labor's timetable that by 2000, 15 per cent of the wages of workers would be compulsorily contributed to superannuation (Love 2008, p. 93). The Coalition government of 1996–2007 maintained the contribution at 9 per cent. As a result, the SGC has not fulfilled Labor's policy agendas. It does not provide an adequate level of independent retirement for most of the population. It has fallen short of its contribution to national savings, which has limited its role in insulating Australia from the current financial crisis. And it no longer serves a crucial role in wages policy with the shift to a radically deregulated wages policy under the Coalition government. Moreover, the direction of the Coalition's superannuation policy has provided extremely generous taxation concessions to high-income groups to foster voluntary superannuation contributions, leaving the mandated (SGC) component vulnerable to further withering as its expansion would add to the superannuation taxation concessions or total revenue foregone.

The unequal distributional impact of occupational superannuation remains despite the introduction of several changes to increase access and portability. Labor's policy of linking retirement income to working life patterns and incomes has disadvantaged women who have, on average, only half the superannuation savings of men (Sharp and Austen 2007). Many Aboriginal people, with their lower life expectancies, simply never get to retire with any of the superannuation they might accumulate.

The Rudd Labor government elected in 2007, while facing a dramatically new policy environment, has the option of completing the superannuation revolution. In the first instance, the government needs to substantially reduce the inefficiencies and inequities of an increasingly privatised retirement incomes (and health) system which combines with a family tax and support system that penalises women's labour supply (Apps, Rees and Wood 2007). Second, retirement incomes policy should systematically value women's contributions to unpaid care work (Smith 2007). Thirdly, the government needs to put in place a regulatory framework that provides greater certainty to individuals about their retirement income, including minimising the risk of individuals losing their retirement savings. Finally, a proper balance of public support (expenditures and taxation) between the different components of the retirement income system including the age pension, the SGC, voluntary superannuation and other forms of retirement savings (such as home ownership in the case of many women) needs to be established that fulfils the principles of adequate, equitable and sustainable retirement income support for men and women.

References

AIRC 1983, *National Wage Case, September 1983*, Australian Conciliation and Arbitration Commission, Commonwealth Government Printer, Melbourne

Australian Council of Trade Unions and Trade Development Council 1987, *Australia Reconstructed: ACTU/TDC Mission to Western Europe*, ACTU/TDC, Canberra

Apps, P. Rees, R. and Wood, M. 2007, 'Population ageing, taxation, pensions and health costs', *Australian Journal of Labour Economics*, vol. 10, no. 2, pp. 79–98

Broomhill, R. 2008, 'Paul Keating's "banana republic" statement and the end of the "golden age"' in eds M. Crotty and D.A. Roberts, *Turning Points in Australian History*, University of New South Wales Press, Sydney

Bryson, L. 1992, *Welfare and the State: Who Benefits?*, Macmillan, London

Campbell, K. 1981, *Final Report of the Committee of Inquiry into the Australian Financial System*, Australian Government Printing Service, Canberra

Castles, F. 1985, *The Working Class and Welfare: Reflections on the Political Development of the Welfare State in Australia and New Zealand, 1890–1980*, Allen and Unwin, Wellington

Dawkins, J. 1992, *Security in Retirement: Planning for Tomorrow Today*, Statement by the Treasurer, Australian Government Printing Service, Canberra

Hancock, K. 1983, 'Income security: the economics of retirement provision' in ed. R. Mendelsohn, *Australian Social Welfare Finance*, Allen and Unwin, Sydney

Kelly, P. 1992, *The End of Certainty: The Story of the 1980s*, Allen and Unwin, Sydney

Klumpes, P. 1992, 'Financial deregulation and the superannuation boom: a crisis in Australian financial services' in eds K. Davis and I. Harper, *Superannuation and the Australian Financial System*, Allen and Unwin, Sydney

Love, D. 2008, *Unfinished Business: Paul Keating's Interrupted Revolution*, Scribe Publications, Melbourne

McCallum, J. and Shaver, S. 1986, 'Industry superannuation: the great leap forward?', *Impact*, October, pp. 6–8

National Superannuation Committee of Inquiry 1976, *Part One: A National Scheme for Australia*, Australian Government Printing Service, Canberra

National Superannuation Committee of Inquiry 1977, *Part Two: Occupational Superannuation in Australia*, Australian Government Printing Service, Canberra

Nielson, L. and Harris, B. 2008, *Background Note: Chronology of Superannuation and Retirement Income in Australia*, Parliamentary Library, Canberra, http://www.aph.gov.au/library/pubs/BN/2007-08/Chron_Superannuation.htm, accessed 31 March 2008

Pha, A. 1992, *How Super is Super?*, Socialist Party of Australia, Sydney

Senate Select Committee on Superannuation 1992, *Second Report of the Senate Select Committee on Superannuation: Super Guarantee Bills*, Parliament of the Commonwealth of Australia, Canberra

Sharp, R. and Austen, S. 2007, 'The 2006 federal Budget: a gender analysis of the superannuation taxation concessions', *Australian Journal of Labour Economics*, vol. 10, no. 2, pp. 61–78.

Sharp, R. and Broomhill, R. 1988, *Short-Changed: Women and Economic Policies*, Allen and Unwin, Sydney

Shaw, D. 1986, 'Trade union and worker participation in the control of superannuation funds' in eds E. Davis and R. Lansbury, *Democracy and Control in the Workplace*, Longman Cheshire, Melbourne

Smith, J. 2007, 'Time use among new mothers, the economic value of unpaid care work and the gender aspects of superannuation tax concessions', *Australian Journal of Labour Economics*, vol. 10, no. 2, pp. 99–114

Stilwell, F. 1986, *The Accord and Beyond*, Pluto, Sydney

Whitwell, G. 1986, *The Treasury Line*, Allen and Unwin, Sydney

Chapter 16

Leading the unions: sexual politics and international alliances

Suzanne Franzway

Introduction

Bob Hawke played a strong and influential role in the Australian and international labour movements. An important aspect of his leadership of the trade union movement and then of the Australian federal government is that it coincided with a period of expansive women's political activism across most public institutions and movements. The so-called second wave of the women's movement was a time of political creativity and debates, conflicts and alliances that expanded into the trade unions. Any evaluation of the Hawke legacy must take account of his considerable influence on these movements.

This chapter examines the immediate and the longer term impact that Hawke's leadership had on the sexual politics of the broad union movement. The chapter commences by discussing the period during which Hawke became president of the Australian Council of Trade Unions (ACTU) in 1969 and led the peak union body until his election to federal Parliament in 1980. It was partly through Hawke's efforts that the ACTU achieved its most positive national and international influence since its creation in 1927. The chapter goes on to focus on the central period of his leadership of the Australian government when union women were gaining strategic and discursive grounds in the trade union movement both locally and internationally.

Leading the unions: Hawke the ACTU president, 1969–1980

Bob Hawke took up leadership positions in the Australian trade union movement during the 1960s, a period that is now remembered as one of great social change in both public and private life. The rapid increase in women's labour force participation was a significant part of the change. But it must also be remembered that there was a great deal of resistance to change, particularly around the question of gender equality. Women workers were increasingly joining unions, but they were finding that the union movement and the industrial relations system, which governed the pay and conditions of Australian workers, remained largely unaffected by their presence or their needs. Women's pay was not equal with men's and their opportunities for leadership roles in their workplaces or their unions were minimal. There were no women trade union leaders (although a small number of women had become union leaders during World War 2).

Australian trade unions had widespread reputations as 'boys' clubs' dominated by men's leadership and political agendas and by a culture of blue-collar masculinity (Muir 1997; Pocock 1997). Bray and Rouillard also write that the 'limitations of the Australian Labour movement's industrial and political strategies were especially evident when it came to advancing the interests of women' (1996, p. 210). The ACTU was no different at the time: its office bearers were all men, and its industrial and political agendas reflected men's interests.

Zelda D'Aprano (1995) provides a graphic illustration of male dominance of industrial and public life in her description of the Conciliation and Arbitration Commission hearing of the 1969 Equal Pay for Equal Work case. The sausage industry was being used as a test case and women from the sausage factories were brought into the court to support the claim.

> The door opened at the rear of the court and in walked the judges. All male judges … All the seats in front were occupied by men, the 'fors' and 'againsts'. The evidence given by Bob Hawke, the ACTU advocate of the time, was irrefutable. The women sat there day by day as if mute, while the men presented evidence for and against our worth. It was humiliating to have to sit there and not say anything about our own worth. I found the need to sit there silent almost beyond my control and was incensed with the entire set up. (D'Aprano 1995, p. 166)

It is in this context that Bob Hawke began his career in the Australian labour movement. In stark contrast to typical union practice, which demands a certain kind of apprenticeship, Bob Hawke won the ACTU presidency in 1969 without having ever stood for election by a union rank and file. As Pullan observed, 'he had never been a union organiser, shop steward, or secretary ... [but] he had captured the most powerful union job in the country. He was thirty-nine and the future belonged to him' (1980, p. 87). He had, however, played significant roles within the ACTU almost from the beginning of his career. As a newly recruited officer Hawke headed the ACTU team to the Conciliation and Arbitration Commission, and his initial success within the ACTU came in his first year as the Research Officer, at the 1959 Basic Wages Enquiry.

According to Hagan (1977), Hawke's presence at this enquiry was significant for several reasons. Most important was that 'his skills [as a professional economist] helped him undertake a devastating cross-examination of two witnesses that the employer had brought as experts, one of whom was induced to withdraw the substance of his argument, and the other shown to have given unreliable testimony' (1977, p. 294). Hawke succeeded in persuading the judges to award a 15 shillings increase.

By 1969, when Hawke became ACTU president, women were increasing their efforts to win equality across all fields with the rise of the women's movement. For significant groups of feminists, women's right to work and right to economic security were, and still are, central to women's equality. As Zelda D'Aprano's experience demonstrates, such rights are not won unless women themselves can participate in the politics of economic and social justice. Growing numbers of women were becoming aware that trade unions and the broad labour movement were important and useful vehicles for gaining women's equality, although I note that women have been active in the trade union movement since its inception. Second wave feminists saw that women needed to play leadership roles in decision making in the trade union movement so that women's needs and issues would not be ignored or excluded from union political and industrial agendas.

Feminists in and outside the trade union movement found that making feminist politics involves challenging prevailing gender relations, gendered discourses and gendered power. It involves challenging the sexual politics according to which not only are men seen as the norm, but also men's power as men is invisible. Because of this invisibility questions about how men achieve and maintain their dominance (including of trade unions) rarely arise (Franzway 2001). A small but critical mass of feminists active within and around the labour movement began to confront these sexual politics using the prevailing discourses of the women's movement, the civil rights/ human rights movement and, later, the global justice movement to forge a dynamic politics of union feminisms.

Union feminists drew on historical strategies such as separate women's committees, forums, conferences and courses, and on more recent technologies to create discursive alliances and political networks within and across labour movements and social movements. The commitment of union feminists to the 'greedy institution' of the trade union movement has called on their time, energy and passion, which has persisted through difficult and demanding periods (Franzway 2001). Their activism continues in today's context of intensified globalisation, where union feminists mobilise resources and discourses to address women's rights and campaign for pay equity and rights of LGBT (lesbian, gay, bisexual and transgender) workers, and against sweatshops and unfair trade agreements.

In the early phase of the second wave, equal pay had become the touchstone issue for women workers and unionists. At his first official function as president-elect, Hawke presented the argument for equal pay to a thousand members of the NSW VIEW Clubs (Voices, Interests and Education of Women). 'There is no argument of justice, economics or equality that can say a woman should get less than her male counterpart and I pledge to you that the ACTU will keep trying to remove this discrimination' (Pullan 1980, p. 114). Following the 1969 Equal Pay Case, the ACTU condemned the decision, which although 'conced[ing] the principle of equal pay for work of equal value ... limited its application so that women engaged in work not usually done by males could not benefit from it' (Hagan 1977, p. 84).

The 1969 judgement was extended in 1972 by 'deciding that the application of the principle of equal pay for work of equal value meant that award rates of pay should be fixed by consideration of the work performed irrespective of the sex of the worker' (Hagan 1977, p. 84). Interestingly, Pullan also offered a critique of Hawke's position on equal pay that seems counterintuitive to his arguments above. He argued that, although Hawke 'formally uttered words about equality for women, [he] did nothing to practice them within the ACTU and never raised his voice against sexist bigotry' (Pullan 1980, pp. 114–115). Nevertheless, during this period of Hawke's leadership, the women's claims for equal pay and for broader recognition of working women's concerns made tangible gains.

During the 1970s, the ACTU broadened its industrial agenda by campaigning for maternity leave, home nursing, child care, job training and the abolition of discrimination in employment. At the same time, a parallel organisation, the Australian Council of Salaried and Professional Associations (ACSPA)[1] won a Commonwealth grant under the Whitlam government's International Women's Year program in 1975 to establish a Working Women's Centre. It later moved to the ACTU as a site of advocacy for women workers, becoming a model for similar centres to be established in South Australia (1979) and later again, with federal government funding, NSW, Tasmania, Queensland, and the Northern Territory. Several of these centres have survived the years of the Howard government.

Under Hawke's leadership, the ACTU Working Women's Centre played a significant role in developing a Working Women's Charter, which was endorsed by the ACTU executive in 1977 (Owen and Shaw 1979). At this point women still occupied only a few formal positions in the ACTU and its affiliates and were not well-placed to ensure that the unions worked to implement the charter in their own organisations or in the workplace.

The centres are small, but I have a high regard for the valuable work they do. I have seen this work at close hand, having been a member of the South Australian management committee since 1992 and chair for a critical period (1994–2004). All the centres have contributed to understanding and advocacy of emerging workplace issues, such as outwork conditions, sexual harassment, domestic violence and paid maternity leave. It is extraordinary to reflect that, in spite of these lengthy efforts, Australia continues to have one of the worst records of paid maternity leave in the OECD. The recent decision by the Rudd Labor government to support paid maternity leave still leaves women waiting until 2011 before it is introduced.

Women and unions during the Hawke government era, 1983–1991

If the 1960s saw the rise of new social movements, the 1980s in Australia saw great efforts to win rights and equality for women in and around the state. As Marion Sawer observes, women were quick to insist that the ALP had won government through the support of women voters who expected the new Hawke government to meet its commitments to women's equality (Sawer 1990, p. 69). The *Sex Discrimination Act 1984* and the *Affirmative Action (Equal Opportunity for Women) Act 1986* were legislative moves towards women's equality. In 1985, Hawke outlined the process for developing a national agenda for women. Following wide consultations throughout 1986, the prime minister launched the Commonwealth government's plan of action for advancing the status of women towards the year 2000, published as the report *Setting the Agenda* in 1987.

> From the very wide consultations on the development of a national agenda for women there is, without any question, overwhelming evidence that Australian women want to dismantle the barriers to their opportunities for equal participation in all forms of economic and community activity in this country, especially in employment, education and recreation. So the fundamental principle underlying the government's policy of equal opportunity for women is for all Australian women to have a fair go, a say and a choice. That, simply put, is our principle. We have stuck to it and we have legislated for it. (Hawke 1987, p. 2444)

Hester Eisenstein (1986) described affirmative action as a kind of feminist judo, with feminists throwing with the weight of the state. It was a strategy that feminists outside the state also employed with some success. Women in the trade unions took it up as a means to increase the number of women in union leadership. In the ACTU, Jennie George, then president of the Australian Teachers' Federation was the first woman elected to its Executive in 1983. She became vice-president in 1987 and went on to become the first woman president of the ACTU in 1995. In congratulating her Bob Hawke said: 'It is pleasing to me that this important position is held by a principled person from the Left, and, for the first time, by a woman' (cited in Norrington 1998, p. 242).

During the 1980s, union women also drew on other strategies that were characteristic of the broad women's movement. Traditional union meeting procedures were rejected as too male and bureaucratic and meetings were opened up to outsiders including femocrats (feminist bureaucrats), students and community groups as well as union women from across the union factions. I had the good fortune to be present at such a meeting of a large group of women at a suburban restaurant when the idea for the Anna Stewart Memorial project was first mooted.

Anna Stewart herself had been a union official in Victoria who pioneered maternity leave campaigns in the early 1980s. She appeared to be a successful and highly competent active union feminist. Union women around the country were shocked when she committed suicide. It seemed that she had not felt able to call on her union sisters for support to help sustain both her family life and her union activism. The small national network of union feminists reverberated with discussion about how to overcome the isolation so many felt. Although they were strongly committed unionists, the women argued that the labour movement's blindness to women's concerns combined with the boundaries imposed on them by union structures and membership demarcation disputes was a great hindrance to mobilising union potential for women.

The women determined to honour Anna Stewart and tackle union sexual politics by developing a program for union women involving practical training and networking opportunities. Union training has long been sought after by union women, and it was also something that Bob Hawke endorsed. He was a member of the Australian Council for Union Training from 1975 to 80 and helped to establish the Clyde Cameron College for union training (1977–1996). By utilising their networks (which included the few women in key positions in the peak bodies and individual unions) the women won sufficient resources to allow 20 to 30 women to take leave from their jobs for the course.

Established in 1984 in several states, the project aims to increase women's union activism as well as the labour movement's recognition and understanding of women members. It has continued at the same rate each year since. Many of the women gained sufficient confidence and experience with union organising and industrial work to become elected officials in their own state and national union branches. Some have moved into government, including Gail Gago, who has become a minister in the Rann Labor government in South Australia.

A second result of the dismay over Anna Stewart's death was the formation of the Women's Trade Union Network, designed to provide tangible forms of support for union women. In the process of setting up the network, the women paid a great deal of attention to the development of its formal structure and constitution, something that seemed to me to be characteristic of union activists. In spite of their early rejection of traditional union structures the union women, who were well aware of the workings of power in organisations, saw some value in formal structures. The network became a forum for debates and collective campaigns about women's issues in the public domain. At first, little explicit attention was paid to so-called private matters of sexuality, care or domestic labour. Changing this became an important goal for union feminists who worked to extend the immediate concerns of union business.

International alliances

Consistent with his role as president of the national peak union body and with his own focus on the value of international alliances, Bob Hawke worked with international labour movements. In his speech at the H.V. Evatt Inaugural Memorial Lecture (Adelaide University, Bonython Hall) in 1976, Bob Hawke summed up his view on 'Australia's place in the world':

> There is a very real role for Australia to play in the quest for a new economic order and a responsibility for us to carry it out. We are a rich country in a poor region … The aspiration for economic change on the part of our neighbours is just and we for our part can play a leading role in exploring the bases for reconciliation between the countries of the Third World and those of the west. (Hawke and Badger 1976, p. 9)

It was also under Hawke's leadership that the first meeting of the Australia and New Zealand Trade Unions Co-ordinating Council (ANZTUCC) was held. Pullan (1980, p. 116) notes that on 28 March 1972 the leaders of the ACTU and the New Zealand Federation of Labour urged the governments of Australia and NZ, and the International Confederation of Free Trade Unions (ICFTU) in Brussels, to put pressure on the French government to stop nuclear testing in the Pacific.

Labour movements have always had international connections, organisations and concerns. During the twentieth century, the International Labour Organization (ILO) was established as a tripartite body of states, employers and unions. Its original role was to draft universal conventions regarding labour standards, monitor compliance, conduct research, publish information, and facilitate cooperation between labour, government and employers. The ILO develops conventions to establish international standards, endorsed by the member states. In 1951 it adopted the Equal Remuneration Convention (no. 100), 'the first multilateral treaty that focused exclusively on women's rights and directed states to take positive action to equalize the status of women and men' (Berkovitch 1999, p. 119). A second convention that is foundational to workers' rights is the Discrimination (Employment and Occupation) Convention, 1958 (no. 111), which Australia endorsed in 1973 under the Whitlam Labor government.

Unlike the recent Howard government's hostility towards international standards and conventions, Bob Hawke supported internationalisation, including international standards and conventions for workers. He was a member of the ILO Governing Body (1972–80) during his time as ACTU president and worked to build Australia's links with the international trade union movement. He shared this approach with union feminists for whom ILO conventions and campaigns have become important benchmarks for demands and campaigns, such as the Global Campaign for Decent Work, Decent Life for Women. This campaign focuses on upgrading the conditions of labour for women by strengthening women's recruitment, representation and participation in unions. The international peak trade union bodies have agreed to focus their activities on the sectors of work where women workers are most vulnerable such as Export Processing Zones, domestic work, part-time workers, women migrant workers and work in the informal economy.

Australian unions occupy a rather small space among international labour movements, but it is striking that Bob Hawke has been followed by other Australians into the international arena. One of his successors to the ACTU presidency, Sharan Burrow, became the first woman president of the International Confederation of

Free Trade Unions (ICFTU) and the founding president of the
International Trade Union Confederation (ITUC). She has won
high regard for her persistent advocacy for women workers and
women's issues worldwide.

Conclusion

Bob Hawke's political leadership was characterised by consensus
and his skill in bringing disputes to a close is well known. As president of the ACTU and as prime minister, his approach was clearly
influential, and no doubt contributed to the national political culture
at a time that coincided with the rise of the women's movement.
This may help explain Australian feminism's relatively confident
stance towards the trade union movement and the state, in contrast
for example to the USA, where feminists have been quite wary of
working with either.

In reflecting on the position of women in public life, including
in the trade union movement at the beginning of Bob Hawke's own
public life, it is clear that great gains have been made. Men are no
longer the only leaders of unions, or indeed of most other public
institutions. The principle of equal pay is well established, although
the practice is much more complicated and women still average less
pay than men, however the calculations are made.

Such success depends to a large degree on women's skills in
negotiating consensus with men in relevant organisations, but
also in negotiating among themselves since women were no more
likely to agree on philosophy, politics or strategy than were their
male comrades. The Working Women's Centres stand as striking
examples of such skills. Winning resources from a mix of state and
union funding, the centres negotiate, advocate and adapt in order
to support working women, but are frequently put to the test to
maintain their own survival by Labor as well as Liberal state and
federal governments seeking to cut their funding. Not all centres
have survived, since the union and feminist alliances on which they
rely are hard won when differences of class, feminist standpoint and
strategy must be accommodated, debated and reframed.

The strong movement of women into the trade union movement in Australia is aligned with the political legacy of Bob Hawke
and his leadership at national and international levels of the labour
movement. A different leader across this period would have shaped

the outcome for women and for the labour movement in quite different ways.

Acknowledgements

Thanks to Virginia Mapedzahama for research support.

Notes

1 ACSPA acted as a peak body for white-collar and professional workers, who were not eligible to participate in the Australian industrial relations system at this time.

References

Berkovitch, N. 1999, *From Motherhood to Citizenship: Women's Rights and International Organizations*, Johns Hopkins University Press, Baltimore

Bray, M. and Rouillard, J. 1996, 'Union structure and strategy in Australia and Canada', *Labour History*, vol. 71, pp. 198–238

D'Aprano, Z. 1995, *Zelda*, Spinifex Press, Melbourne

Eisenstein, H. 1986, 'Feminist judo: throwing with the weight of the state', *Australian Left Review*, no. 96, pp. 20–22

Franzway, S. 2001, *Sexual Politics and Greedy Institutions: Union Women, Commitments and Conflicts in Public and in Private*, Pluto Press Australia, Sydney

Hagan, J. 1977, *The ACTU: A Short History*, AH and AW Reed, Sydney

Hawke, R. and Badger, G.M. 1976, *Bob Hawke on Foreign Policy*, Adelaide University Union Press, Adelaide

Hawke, R.J.L. 1987, 'National agenda for women: the Commonwealth government's plan of action for advancing the status of women towards the year 2000: a statement by the Prime Minister' in Australia, House of Representatives, *Debates*, 1 May, p. 2444

Hurst, J. 1979, *Hawke: The Definitive Biography*, Angus and Robertson, Sydney

Muir, K. 1997, 'Difference or deficiency: gender, representation and meaning in unions' in ed. B. Pocock, *Strife: Sex and Politics in Labour Unions*, Allen & Unwin, Sydney

Norrington, B. 1998, *Jennie George*, Allen & Unwin, Sydney

Owen, M. and Shaw, S. 1979, *Working Women*, Working Women's Centre, Melbourne

Pocock, B. 1997, 'Gender, strife and unions' in ed. B. Pocock, *Strife, Sex and Politics in Labour Unions*, Allen & Unwin, Sydney

Pullan, R. 1980, *Bob Hawke: A Portrait*, Methuen, Sydney

Sawer, M. 1990, *Sisters in Suits: Women and Public Policy in Australia*, Allen & Unwin, Sydney

Chapter 17

The constant mediator: a tribute

Elizabeth Ho

> Let us do what we can in our own way, however small, to tilt the world
> towards reason. (Hawke 2006)

Bob Hawke often refers to the influence his father, Clem Hawke, a Congregational Minister, had on his life and, in particular, his sharing of Clem's belief in the 'brotherhood of man'. The full quotation expresses Clem's faith: 'If you believe in the Fatherhood of God, you must necessarily believe in the Brotherhood of Man'. Hawke was too distressed by his experience of Indian poverty in 1952 to maintain a formal faith in Christianity, but always held to the last part of his father's observation (Hawke 1994).

This belief strongly influenced Hawke to champion causes that have variously overcome conflicts or prejudices, built understandings, or contributed to the common good in some tangible way, whether on the national or global stage. During his period as prime minister, one of the greatest expressions of that drive was his galvanising of the Commonwealth Heads of Government to place economic sanctions on the racist regime of South Africa during the late 1980s. This led to the end of apartheid and the release of Nelson Mandela in 1990. Mandela always acknowledged Hawke for his anti-apartheid leadership and after his release he visited Australia to convey his thanks to Hawke personally. That meeting is described in Hawke's memoirs (Hawke 1994). Their longstanding mutual regard led to Mandela later becoming the international patron of the Bob Hawke Prime Ministerial Centre.

The ethical notions of human connection and mutual obligation embraced during his childhood and adolescence may also explain Hawke's capacity to be supremely comfortable in dealing with people of every background and culture, unlike some other world leaders. His commitment to the Asian region stands as a primary example of his dual focus on global economic advancement and the less tangible path of intercultural understanding, the latter being yet another expression of his father's creed.

Bob Hawke's emphasis was on achieving practical results, reflecting his innate pragmatism and energy, and it is not surprising that bringing stakeholders to the table remained a strong theme in his post-prime ministerial life. For example, while others focused on China's poor human rights record in the lead up to the bid for the 2008 Olympics, Hawke held firmly to principles of inclusion and supported the bid. As the record shows, he has always favoured keeping communication channels open in order to preserve the opportunity to influence directions in the long term.

His continuing connections with Asia run deep, and Hawke, with other past leaders in Asia, engineered the Boao Forum in 2001. This is described as 'the most prestigious and premier forum for leaders in government, business and academia in Asia and other continents to share visions on the most pressing issues in this dynamic region and the world at large' (Boao Forum for Asia n.d.). The chief purposes of the forum are to support regional economic integration and to assist Asian countries with development goals. Not surprisingly, there is a great emphasis on cooperation. The fact that the forum is widely supported by Asian leaders is testimony to the power of those who established it, including Hawke. It connects back to his successful drive to form APEC (Asia-Pacific Economic Cooperation) during his prime ministership, arguably one of his most significant and lasting international achievements.

In civil life at home, Hawke has been very active as a speaker and a commentator on public policy issues, including race relations.

In 1997 the University of South Australia established the Bob Hawke Prime Ministerial Centre, honouring Hawke as the only South Australian to have achieved that office and espousing the values of strengthening democracy, valuing diversity and building the future.[1] In the following year, Hawke delivered the first annual Hawke Lecture entitled 'A confident Australia'. This address showed that he was still very much driven to project the worth of a cohesive national psyche to his fellow Australians. He summarised his own sense of pride that when he had left office Australia was confident about itself as a nation, even if some were 'doing it tough'. By that time he felt that this sense of confidence was being seriously undermined by scaremongering about Indigenous land rights and Australians of Asian background.

In his lecture, he noted:

> It does no justice ... to wage campaigns calculated to have non-Aboriginal Australians believe that their homes everywhere are under threat from some open-ended land grab by Aborigines. One of the sadder spectacles in recent political history has been the television image of the Prime Minister dolefully displaying maps of Australia insinuating and supporting such divisive nonsense. This is not leadership, it is scaremongering. It is not the politics of confidence but the politics of fear. (Hawke 1998)

His assessment that some members of the Howard government were tolerating new independent MP Pauline Hanson's views towards Asians led him to state:

> Australia will never be a confident nation – nor will it deserve to be a respected one – if we tolerate within this country any lapse into our past with discrimination based on race being accepted as a legitimate attitude or basis of policy. (Hawke 1998)

Hawke observed that Prime Minister Howard needed to repudiate Hanson's views in much stronger terms if Australian cohesion were to be preserved. One senses in this first Hawke Lecture a deep foreboding that many years of effort to place Australia firmly in the Asian region would be unravelled, and it was a fear shared by many others at the time.

In 2001, Hawke spoke at the 'Visions for a Nation' official forum held during the Australian Centenary of Federation and once again took up the crucial matter of achieving fairness in Australian society and beyond:

> The overwhelmingly important issue for the new Australian federation of the twenty-first century will be to strengthen a tolerant society at home which will not countenance discrimination in any form on the basis of race, colour, creed or gender: and, on that solid basis, and

from considerations of morality and enlightened self-interest, to invest
more of our time, energy and resources together with other developed
nations – in providing help and hope to those billions on Earth who
still exist in poverty and despair. (Hawke 2001)

In June 2003, when launching *Continental Drift: Australia's Search
for a Regional Identity* by former diplomat Rawdon Dalrymple,
he spoke very directly about the poor handling of Asian relations
through a myopic Australian alignment with United States foreign
policy, noting:

The benefits that to some extent we still enjoy from that enlightened
generation of relations with Asia are at risk, including very particularly
optimum opportunities for trade with the region. Only a change of
government, in my judgement, will enable Australia to have that full,
constructive relationship with Asia which can enhance both our economic prosperity and our security. (Hawke 2003)

That change of government came in December 2007, and by the
end of July 2008 Hawke had already officially met with Chinese
Vice Premier Zhang Dejiang, with the reported agenda being the
strengthening of Sino-Australian relations (Xinhau News Agency
2008).

Hawke's abiding interest in dialogue, reconciliation and
mediation has had other expressions, especially in the aftermath
of the al-Qaeda terrorist attack on New York in September 2001.
Although he is widely reported to be a supporter of Israel, his
prescriptions for peace in the Middle East, his concerns for the
welfare of the Palestinian people, and his balanced position of
eschewing extremism and aiming for a stable future for all involved,
have received less media attention. Once again, his father's sense of
embracing the world rather than pulling back from it is embedded
in the rhetoric. For example, when delivering the Australian
Universities' International Alumni Conference Address in Hong
Kong, he stated:

there should be a concentrated attempt to identify and then, in a
manner appropriate to this particular circumstance, provide support
to the many individuals and groups throughout the Islamic world to
whom the tactic of terror is repugnant. This should be done in the
context of a demonstrated commitment to meeting the legitimate aspi-

rations of peoples in that part of the world, including, particularly, a resolution of the Israel/Palestinian dispute which entails the establishment of a viable Palestinian economy. (Hawke 2004)

Hawke's assessment of the world scene was enhanced by his deep knowledge of, and regular visits to, the Middle East, Pakistan and other Muslim nations. He was troubled by evidence of bigoted attitudes towards Australian Muslims inflamed by the Howard government's security and refugee policies, not to mention the invasion of Iraq without United Nations sanction.

In 2006, at an International Alert Forum attended by 800 citizens, he was moved to call for an entirely new approach to the Palestinian plight:

> What is required now is the equivalent of the Marshall Plan. The United States should take the lead, with the support of Europe, the moderate Arab states and Israel in making an unequivocal commitment to a massive supply of capital, technical and educational expertise and equipment dedicated to the creation of an education system and an economic structure that will give the reality of hope to the Palestinian people.
>
> Nothing could do more to change the anti-American mind-set of so much of the Muslim world if America were to take the lead in such an initiative. The financial and technical capacity of the United States and others to meet the requirements of this initiative is not in question. What is required is the will and the imagination. It is easy enough to list the difficulties that may lie in the path of carrying through with the initiative, but that is the counsel of despair and hopelessness. If genuinely embraced, I believe this concept can mark the beginning of a sea-change in the poisonous atmosphere of hatreds and misconceptions that threaten the very stability and existence of the world as we know it. (Hawke 2006)

Always a believer in the worth of learning, his concerns further led him to call for the establishment of an international research centre that would openly address the global divide between Muslim and non-Muslim worlds. In 2007 he approached the University of South Australia to consider creating this new centre and secured an undertaking from the university's leadership to do so. The critical objectives of this global institution include proposing ways of diffusing tensions and ameliorating relationships at the political, civil and social level both in Australia and internationally.

His request coincided with the university being endowed with its first UNESCO Chair in Transnational Diasporas and Reconciliation Studies, and the two initiatives were launched simultaneously on 14 October 2008. The launch also brought news of major support by the Australian and South Australian governments, with Deputy Prime Minister Julia Gillard and SA Premier Mike Rann pledging funds to hasten the centre's establishment. The Deputy Prime Minister noted at the time that the new centre would be able to facilitate 'the development of effective policy solutions that can be considered and utilised by governments' (Gillard 2008).

Endorsements were also received from Nelson Mandela, Imam Umer Ahmed Ilyasi, Secretary General of the All India Organization of Imams of Mosques, and, closer to home, Prime Minister Rudd, with the importance of peace and building bridges uppermost in their reflections.

When writing about the proposed International Centre for Muslim and non-Muslim Understanding, Hawke observed:

> One of the blessings of my life has been the opportunity to bring together disparate people to create common understanding in situations of dispute and confrontation. It is now my great wish to help play a part in finding solutions to one of the world's most difficult and dangerous problems – the basic lack of understanding and increasingly hostile tensions between the Muslim and non-Muslim worlds. The University of South Australia has accepted this challenge and will establish this centre to offer a new focus on the triggers for prejudice that present barriers to dialogue … In our hope for a better world it's time to bring our intellectual resources together and, with empathy and goodwill, do something to achieve that end. (University of South Australia 2009)

At the launch of the international centre, he gave an address attacking all forms of fanaticism and prejudice and expressed his profound concern for innocent Muslims who had been unfairly affected by community responses to terrorism. He was appointed patron on the same day and is working to establish credibility for this centre on the international stage (Hawke 2008).

In the year he turned 50, Hawke made his contribution to a great Australian tradition by delivering the Boyer Lectures on the topic 'The resolution of conflict' (Hawke 1979). Thirty years on and now turning 80, it seems Hawke will not cease from mental fight to resolve differences and overcome bigotry. The sword against complacency will not sleep in his hand.

Note

1 The centre presents expert lectures, forums and briefings on twenty-first century ideas and problems. Its community engagement effort is further complemented by the Hawke Library, holding Bob Hawke's personal papers, and the research program of the Hawke Research Institute at the University of South Australia.

References

Boao Forum for Asia, n.d., 'Profile', Boao Forum for Asia website, http://www. boaoforum.org/html/adoutjs-en.asp, accessed 25 March 2009

Gillard, J., 2008, *$7 million for new International Research Centre at UniSA*, media release, Canberra, 14 October, http://www.deewr.gov.au/Ministers/ Gillard/Media/Releases/Pages/Article_081107_142756.aspx, accessed 25 March 2009

Hawke, B. 1979, 'The resolution of conflict', The Boyer Lectures, Australian Broadcasting Commission, Sydney

Hawke, B. 1994, *The Hawke Memoirs*, Heinemann, Melbourne

Hawke, B. 1998, 'A confident Australia', Hawke Lecture, Adelaide, 12 May, http://www.unisa.edu.au/hawkecentre/ahl/1998ahl-hawke.asp, accessed 25 March 2009

Hawke, B. 2001, 'Visions for a nation', National Centenary of Federation Forum Address, Adelaide, 20 October, http://www.unisa.edu.au/ hawkecentre/events/2001events/hawke.asp, accessed 7 April 2009

Hawke, B. 2003, speech at the launch of *Continental Drift: Australia's Search for a Regional Identity* by R. Dalrymple, Research Institute for Asia and the Pacific, University of Sydney, 10 June, http://www.accci.com.au/hawke. htm, accessed 25 March 2009

Hawke, B. 2004, keynote address to Australian Universities' International Alumni Conference, Hong Kong, 2 December, http://www.library.unisa. edu.au/BHPML/speeches/post/2004_dec_hk.asp, accessed 25 March 2009

Hawke, B. 2006, 'Keeping the peace: avoiding the cost of conflict in humanitarian aid', address to the International Alert Forum, co-presented by World Vision, AusAID and the Hawke Centre, Adelaide, 3 October, http://www.unisa.edu.au/hawkecentre/events/2006events/WV_peace_ Hawke.asp, accessed 7 April 2009

Hawke, B. 2008, speech at the launch of the International Centre for Muslim and non-Muslim Understanding and the establishment of the UNESCO

Chair in Transnational Diasporas and Reconciliation Studies, Adelaide, 14 October, http://www.library.unisa.edu.au/BHPML/speeches/post/2008_Oct_SpeechByBobHawketoIntCentreforMuslimNonMuslim Understanding.pdf, accessed 25 March 2009

University of South Australia 2009, *International Centre for Muslim and non-Muslim Understanding*, outline booklet, University of South Australia, Adelaide (available from the Hawke Centre)

Xinhau News Agency 2008, 'Vice premier: China attaches great importance to ties with Australia', Xinhua, 24 July, http://news.xinhuanet.com/english/2008-07/24/content_8764264.htm, accessed 25 March 2009

Contributors

Pal Ahluwalia

Professor Ahluwalia has always had a deep interest in the complexities of identity formation, yet his own upbringing and professional career reflects a myriad of cultural influences. He was born in Kenya, schooled in Canada, received a Bachelors degree and a Master of Arts from the University of Saskatchewan, and then completed his PhD at Flinders University in Adelaide. He was subsequently at Adelaide University for 14 years, finishing as Professor of the Politics Department, then Visiting Professor with the University of California, and Professor at Goldsmiths College, University of London, where he was also Director of the Centre for Postcolonial Studies.

Prior to commencing his current position as Pro Vice Chancellor of the Division of Education, Arts and Social Sciences, Professor Ahluwalia was Research SA Chair and Professor of Post-colonial Studies in the Hawke Research Institute and Director of the Centre for Post-colonial Studies, all at the University of South Australia. At the same time he was a Professor in the Department of Ethnic Studies at the University of California. His main research interests lie in the areas of African studies, social and cultural theory, in particular, postcolonial theory and the processes of diaspora, exile and migration.

Gerry Bloustien

Associate Professor Geraldine Bloustien has been a Research Fellow (2003–04) and Deputy Director (2006–08) of the Hawke Research Institute at the University of South Australia, where she is now a core researcher. She has published extensively and internationally on the issues of social justice and social inclusion, cultural identities, youth cultures and the innovative methodology of auto-video ethnography. Her previous professional roles being in education and in various media industries, Associate Professor Bloustien has made several award-winning documentaries focusing on young people at risk and the power of media technology to provide a voice to those in our society usually denied such opportunities. Her most recent research projects extend this potential of media to include new digital technologies and social networking sites to investigate and educate about social inequality and injustice in areas of health, unemployment and cultural marginalisation in Australia, Europe and Asia. Her publications include *Girl Making: A Cross-Cultural Ethnography of Growing Up Female* (2003), *Sonic Synergies: Music, Technology, Community, Identity* (2008) and *Playing for Life: Global Youth, Local Music* (2009, in press).

Marie Brennan

Marie Brennan is a Professor of Education at the University of South Australia, where she recently finished a five-year term as Dean of Education and Head of School. Her previous academic jobs were at the University of Canberra, and Central Queensland and Deakin universities. Prior to being an academic, Marie worked for almost twenty years in the Victorian Education Department in a range of positions. She is active nationally in promoting the education sector, as well as conducting research, supervising doctoral students and providing leadership in the School of Education. Her research interests cover all sectors of education, with a particular focus on injustice.

Peter Buckskin

Professor Peter Buckskin is the Dean and Head of School of the David Unaipon College of Indigenous Education and Research (DUCIER) within the Division of Education, Arts and Social Sciences, University of South Australia. He has been a teacher and professional bureaucrat for thirty years, with a burning passion for the pursuit of educational excellence for Aboriginal students. He worked as a classroom teacher in Western Australia and South Australia, Chair of the South Australian Aboriginal Education Consultative Committee, Ministerial Adviser, Superintendent of Schools, and a Senior Executive at both state and federal level. For over a decade he worked as an officer in the Commonwealth's Senior Executive Service, where he occupied a number of strategic positions in the portfolios of Aboriginal Affairs, Employment, Education and Training. In recognition of his contribution to Aboriginal education he has received numerous awards and honours. In the 2001 Australia Day Honours he was awarded the Commonwealth Public Service Medal (PSM) in recognition of his outstanding public service in pursuing equality in education for Australia's Indigenous peoples. In 2007 he was admitted to the rank of Fellow of the Australian College of Education in recognition of his excellent contribution to education.

Barbara Comber

Barbara Comber is a key researcher in the Centre for Studies in Literacy, Policy and Learning Cultures in the Hawke Research Institute at the University of South Australia. Her particular interests include literacy education and social justice, teachers' work and identities, place and space, and practitioner inquiry. She has worked collaboratively with teachers in high poverty locations focusing on innovative and critical curriculum and pedagogies that address contemporary social challenges. She has recently published two books: *Literacies in Place: Teaching Environmental Communication* (Comber, Nixon and Reid 2007) and *Turn-Around Pedagogies: Literacy Interventions for At-Risk Students* (Comber and Kamler 2005).

Rosemary Crowley

Rosemary was the first South Australian ALP woman in the federal parliament. She was elected to the Senate in May 1983 and served until her retirement in June 2002. She was Minister for Family Services from 1993 to 1996 and was Minister Assisting the Prime Minister for the Status of Women in 1993.

After obtaining an MBBS (Bachelor of Medicine/Bachelor of Surgery) at the University of Melbourne, she became a medical practitioner. Rosemary has always been involved in community health, child care, parent education and women's health and had a distinguished career in the political arena. She demonstrates a dedication to the principles of social justice and democracy.

She is currently a Visiting Research Fellow with the Hawke Research Institute.

Ian Davey

Emeritus Professor Ian Davey is a social historian, with special interests in demography, childhood, schooling and education. He was the Pro Vice Chancellor and Vice President, Research and International at the University of South Australia from his appointment in 1994 to December 2003 and Pro Vice Chancellor and Vice President, Research and Innovation from 2004 to his retirement in 2006. Professor Davey is the author of over fifty publications on aspects of the social history of childhood and education and has held Australian Research Council grants on the historical demography of fertility. In 1987 he was president of the Australian and New Zealand History of Education Society. He has served as a member of a number of key research groups of the Australian Vice Chancellors' Committee: Standing Committee on Research (1997–98) and Deputy and Pro Vice Chancellors' Research Committee (1988–90, 1994–2006, chair in 1997). He was also the AVCC representative on the Ministerial Working Party on the Research Quality Framework in 2006.

Ron Donato

Dr Ronald Donato is a lecturer in economics in the School of Commerce at the University of South Australia. He has a PhD in Health Economics from Monash University and has researched and consulted in the area for over a decade. His work is published in a number of international journals and research volumes. Ron teaches health economics in masters programs and has conducted training workshops for healthcare professionals from developing countries under the auspices of the World Bank. Ron's research is primarily in the area of economics of healthcare reform, with a particular focus on managed competition. Recent research has investigated the application of diagnostic-based risk-adjustment methodology in the Australian context, the political economy of reform and the economics of contracting in health care.

Suzanne Franzway

Suzanne Franzway is Associate Professor in Gender Studies and Sociology, and is a core researcher in the Hawke Research Institute and an executive member of the Research Centre for Gender Studies at the University of South Australia. Her current research projects include epistemologies of workplace change: transforming gender relations in engineering (ARC Discovery with a multi-disciplinary research team), international labour movements and activism, and the impact of domestic violence on women's work. She is a founding member of the UNESCO Women's Studies and Gender Research Network and is deputy chair of the Working Women's Centre, South Australia. Her books include *Sexual Politics and Greedy Institutions: Union Women, Commitment and Conflict in Public and in Private* (2001), *Staking a Claim: Feminism, Bureaucracy and the State* (1989), and *New Feminist Politics: Transnational Alliances between Women and Labor* (forthcoming). She is co-editor of *Making Globalization Work for Women: Women's Social Rights and Trade Leadership* (under contract).

Elizabeth Ho

Elizabeth Ho has been Director of the Bob Hawke Prime Ministerial Centre at the University of South Australia since 1999, a centre devoted to informing the community about key concerns for the twenty-first century. She has held various senior posts in library, cultural and education sectors and has contributed to professional literature in those fields, particularly heritage topics. In April 2008 she was selected as one of 1000 Australians to participate in the Prime Minister's 2020 Summit and was a member of the governance stream. In May 2006 she was appointed by the Premier as a South Australian Business Ambassador and in October 2006 was appointed a National Fellow of the Institute for Public Administration Australia for outstanding contribution to public sector administration in education and libraries. She is Deputy Chair of the Migrant Resource Centre of South Australia, devoted to the settlement of refugees, and serves on the Catherine Helen Spence Memorial Scholarship Committee reporting to the SA Minister of Education. She co-authored *My Food* (1995) with celebrated international chef Cheong Liew, and continues to co-write regular food columns for the *Adelaide Review.*

Brian Howe

Brian Howe AO is a professorial fellow at the Centre for Public

Policy at Melbourne University where he has researched and taught social policy over the last ten years. He has written a book called *Weighing up Australian Values on Transition and Risk in Modern Australia* in which he explored the possible relevance of German social scientist Günther Schmid's work on 'transitional labour markets' to Australian public policy. He is currently the chair of Housing Choices Australia, a housing company focused on increasing the supply of affordable rental housing in Australia.

Brian was a member of federal parliament from 1977 to 1996 and held several ministerial positions in the Hawke and Keating governments. He was deputy prime minister of Australia from 1991 to 1995.

Carol Johnson

Carol Johnson is a Professor of Politics at the University of Adelaide. Her main teaching and research interests are in Australian politics, the politics of gender and sexuality, and analyses of ideology and discourse. She has published numerous articles and book chapters on the ALP and Labor governments, including comparative analyses of the ALP and British Labour and studies of Labor's ideology in the 1998, 2001, 2004 and 2007 election campaigns. She is the author of two books that deal with Labor governments: *The Labor Legacy: Curtin, Chifley, Whitlam, Hawke* (1989) and *Governing Change: From Keating to Howard* (2000). A revised edition of *Governing Change* was published by Network Books, in its Australian Scholarly Classics Series, in 2007. Carol is also a regular contributor to Online Opinion, where she has written on topics ranging from Kevin Rudd's Christianity to Labor's policies on climate change. Carol is a former president of the Australian Political Studies Association (the peak body of Australian political scientists) and was elected a Fellow of the Australian Academy of the Social Sciences in 2005.

Alison Mackinnon

Alison Mackinnon AM was the Foundation Director of the Hawke Research Institute at the University of South Australia from 1997 to December 2005. Appointed Professor of History and Gender Studies in 1997, she is now an Emeritus Professor. She has an honorary doctorate from Umeå University, Sweden (2000) for her international contribution to educational research and is a Fellow of the Academy of the Social Sciences in Australia. She has written widely on women's education, the impact of women's education on their family formation and professional lives, and women's history. She is the author of several books including *Love and Freedom: Professional Women and the Reshaping of Personal Life*, which won a NSW Premier's literary award in 1997.

Alan Mayne

Alan Mayne holds a Research SA Chair and is Professor of Social History and Public Policy in the Hawke Research Institute, University of South Australia. His research focuses on social life and social policy in Australia, Britain, North America and South Asia. His research interests and publications range across Australian immigration and settlement policy, cultural heritage interpretation and cultural tourism, historical archaeology, 'slums' and urban 'renewal' in late nineteenth- and early twentieth-century Britain, the United States and Australia, urban social policy in contemporary India, and community formation and resilience in regional Australia.

Greg McCarthy

Associate Professor Greg McCarthy is the Head of School of Social Sciences at the University of Adelaide. He has written extensively on politics and culture, with an emphasis on the relationship between cultural representation and sovereignty. He has also related the politics of culture to public policy, in such diverse fields as Royal Commissions, university administration and banking institutions. He has also written on the politics of race, nation and identity for major journals in the UK, America and Australia.

Barbara Pocock

Professor Barbara Pocock studies work in Australia. Barbara is Director of the Centre for Work + Life, part of the Hawke Research Institute at the University of South Australia. The centre was established in 2006. Barbara has been researching work, employment and industrial relations since 1981. She joined the University of South Australia in January 2006, after fourteen years at the University of

Adelaide. Barbara has worked in many jobs – in shearing sheds, advising politicians, the public service, on farms, in unions, teaching and researching in universities, for governments and as a mother. Barbara was initially trained as an economist, completed her doctorate in gender studies, and has taught and researched labour studies and social science since the mid 1980s. Her research has included work, industrial relations, trade unionism, pay and pay equity, vocational education and inequality in the labour market. She was awarded a Queen Elizabeth II Fellowship (2003–2007) to study the intersections between work, family and community.

Alan Reid

Alan Reid is Professor of Education at the University of South Australia. He is involved in a range of national and state professional organisations. Professor Reid's research interests include educational policy, curriculum change, social justice and education, citizenship education, and the history and politics of public education. He has published widely in these areas and gives many talks and papers to professional groups, nationally and internationally.

Alan is also involved in policy development at the state and national levels. For example, in 2004–05 he was appointed by the Minister of Education to be a member of a three-person panel that reviewed the South Australian Certificate of Education (SACE); and he was engaged by the South Australian Education Department to lead the development of a system-wide culture of research and inquiry. In 2002–03 he was the DEST National Research Fellow based in Canberra. Prior to that he was Dean of Education at the University of South Australia for three years. In 2004, the Australian College of Educators awarded Alan the inaugural MacKillop Medal in recognition of his distinguished services to education; and in 2009 he was awarded the Alby Jones Medal in recognition of his contributions to education.

Martin Shanahan

Martin Shanahan is Dean of Research in the Division of Business and an associate professor in the School of Commerce at the University of South Australia. He is co-editor of the *Australian Economic History Review* and a co-recipient of an Australian Carrick

Award for his contribution to the scholarship of learning in economics. His research interests include economic history, especially in the fields of wealth distribution and globalisation; the history of water use in Australia; factor markets; and the history of cartels. He has also published on economic education, the price of irrigation water and the economic cost of child abuse. He is deputy director of the Centre for Regulation and Market Analysis.

Rhonda Sharp

Rhonda Sharp is a Professor of Economics at the Hawke Research Institute as well as a member, and a past director, of the Research Centre for Gender Studies which is a key concentration in the Hawke Research Institute, University of South Australia. Her research and scholarship have straddled the interrelated areas of economics, political economy, gender studies and public policy. Her superannuation research included her doctoral thesis, *Occupational Superannuation and the Labor Government, 1983–1996*, and she was a member of the South Australian government's task force on restructuring the SA public sector's superannuation schemes. She has undertaken research and policy work on gender and economic issues with governments and community groups in the United Kingdom, Norway, South Africa, Indonesia, Timor Leste, Sri Lanka, Italy, the Basque Country, Sweden, Barbados, Samoa and the Republic of the Marshall Islands. She has been commissioned for research and consultancy by international agencies including the Commonwealth Secretariat, the United Nations Development Programme, UNIFEM, Asian Development Bank, Swedish International Development Agency and AusAid. Her scholarship on gender and economic issues has led to invitations to present papers to international and national academic and community audiences.

Joan Staples

Joan Staples is a Visiting Fellow in the Faculty of Law at the University of NSW. Her research and publications centre on democratic issues associated with civil society organisations and their relationships with government; on the Hawke government; and on various aspects of climate change. Her academic work is informed by her previous career with non-government organisations.

Joan has worked in policy and advocacy for national civil society organisations in the areas of environment, international development, Indigenous affairs, social services and consumer affairs. She was the Australian Conservation Foundation national lobbyist for the first five years of the Hawke government. She has been a ministerial appointee to the National Women's Consultative Council and the National Consumer Affairs Advisory Council, a Board Member of the Australian Federation of Consumer Organisations, the Tasmanian Council of Social Services, the Australian Council for Overseas Aid (now ACFID) and Deputy Chair of CHOICE (the Australian Consumers' Association).

Ianto Ware

Dr Ianto Ware completed a PhD on new media and participatory culture in 2008 and runs the Format media, arts and activism festival in Adelaide. His research interests include subcultural media practice, activism and the arts, as well as academic workforce regeneration. He currently works for the Hawke Research Institute at the University of South Australia.

Appendix:

Chronology of prime ministers of Australia and election dates, 1972–2007

9 December 1929	Bob Hawke born in Bordertown, South Australia
1963	Bob Hawke contested the federal seat of Corio in Victoria, but failed to enter parliament this time.
1969	Bob Hawke elected president of the Australian Council of Trade Unions
2 December 1972	**Gough Whitlam** (ALP) elected prime minister
18 May 1974	**Gough Whitlam** (ALP) re-elected
21 March 1975	Malcolm Fraser became leader of the opposition.
11 November 1975	Gough Whitlam dismissed as prime minister by Governor-General John Kerr. **Malcolm Fraser** (Lib) appointed as caretaker prime minister.
13 December 1975	**Malcolm Fraser** (Lib) elected
10 December 1977	**Malcolm Fraser** (Lib) re-elected
July 1978	Gough Whitlam retired from parliament and Bill Hayden became leader of the opposition.
18 October 1980	**Malcolm Fraser** (Lib) re-elected as prime minister. Bob Hawke elected to federal parliament in seat of Wills (Victoria).
8 February 1983	Bob Hawke replaced Bill Hayden as leader of the parliamentary Labor Party
5 March 1983	**Bob Hawke** (ALP) elected prime minister in a landslide victory. Paul Keating became treasurer and Andrew Peacock leader of the opposition.
1 December 1984	**Bob Hawke** (ALP) re-elected with a greatly reduced majority.

5 September 1985	John Howard became leader of the opposition.
11 July 1987	**Bob Hawke** (ALP) re-elected with an increased majority.
May 1989	Andrew Peacock became leader of the opposition again.
24 March 1990	**Bob Hawke** (ALP) re-elected with a reduced majority. John Hewson became leader of the opposition.
20 December 1991	**Paul Keating** defeated Bob Hawke in a leadership ballot and became prime minister.
20 February 1992	Bob Hawke resigned from parliament.
13 March 1993	**Paul Keating** (ALP) elected prime minister.
23 May 1994	Alexander Downer became leader of the opposition.
30 January 1995	John Howard became leader of the opposition again.
2 March 1996	**John Howard** (Lib) elected prime minister. Kim Beazley became leader of the opposition.
3 October 1998	**John Howard** (Lib) re-elected.
10 November 2001	**John Howard** (Lib) re-elected. Simon Crean became leader of the opposition
2 December 2003	Mark Latham became leader of the opposition.
9 October 2004	**John Howard** (Lib) re-elected.
28 January 2005	Kim Beazley became leader of the opposition again.
4 December 2006	Kevin Rudd became leader of the opposition.
24 November 2007	**Kevin Rudd** (ALP) elected prime minister. Brendan Nelson became leader of the opposition.
16 September 2008	Malcolm Turnbull became leader of the opposition.

Index

Aboriginal affairs, xiv, 21–22, 49, 83–93, 108
  Aboriginal women, 22, 49
Aboriginal and Torres Straight Islander
  Commission, 22, 50, 83, 87–89, 93, 100
Accord, the
  see Prices and Incomes Accord
affirmative action, 10, 46–48, 50, 72, 108, 114,
  116, 217
ageing population, 53, 199, 201, 206
Antarctica, xi, 28, 153
apartheid, ix, 28, 223
Asia, 15, 19–20, 72–74, 99, 102–104, 224, 226
Asia-Pacific Economic Cooperation, 27–28,
  224
Australia 2020 Summit, 11, 189
Australian Conciliation and Arbitration
  Commission, 205, 213–214
Australian Conservation Foundation, xv, 152,
  154–158, 161–162
Australian Council of Trade Unions, ix, xvi,
  52, 107, 188, 199, 202–207, 213, 217, 219–220
  see also Hawke in the ACTU
Australian Democrats, 89, 114, 158–159
Australian Education Council, 60, 64, 67
Australian Institute of Multicultural Affairs,
  98–99
Australian Labor Party, x–ix, xii, 6–7, 23,
  30–31, 33, 39, 46, 57, 65, 125, 152, 155–162,
  202
    factions, 37, 203
    legitimacy, xii, 31–36, 38
    see also Hawke, Keating, Rudd
    government, Whitlam government
Australian Medical Association, 128–129
Australian Research Council, 75–76
Australian Vice-Chancellors' Committee, 76

banking, 169, 173
  deregulation, 11, 59
Beazley, Kim, 6–7

Bishop, Julie, 80
Blainey, Geoffrey, 99, 102–103, 105, 107
Blair, Tony, xii, 3, 5–7, 11–12, 16–17, 40
Blewett, Neal, 130
Boao Forum, 224
Bob Hawke Prime Ministerial Centre, x,
  223–224
Bradley Review of Higher Education, 71,
  80–81
Brown, Gordon, 16–17
Brown, John, 117
Burke, Brian, 21
Burrow, Sharan, 52, 220
Bush, George Snr, 23–24, 40
Bush, George W., 4
Button, John, 208

Cabinet government, 34–37
Calwell, Arthur, 30
Carr, Bob, 30
Cambodia, 28
Chifley government, 5, 6, 12, 31, 126, 201
child care, 7, 52–53, 216
China, 19–21, 224, 226
climate change, xi, xv, 10, 28, 54, 152,
  161–162, 194
Cohen, Barry, 155–156
Cold War, 32
Commonwealth Scientific and Industrial
  Research Organisation, 76, 161
consensus, xii, 3–5, 8, 11–12, 34, 37, 40, 47–48,
  52, 61, 65, 87, 106, 126, 129, 135, 175, 180,
  221
Cooperative Research Centres, 76–77
Council of Australian Governments, xv, 143,
  147–150
Crean, Simon, 30, 38, 107–108
Crowley, Rosemary, xiii, 46, 112–121
Curtin government, 5, 6, 12, 31, 180–181, 201

Dawkins, John, xiii, 58–59, 64–67, 70–71, 74–77, 84, 87, 89
Defence of Government Schools, 61
Dunstan, Don, 20
dismissal of the Whitlam government, 31–32, 112
domestic violence, 22, 54, 216

economic crises, 3, 11, 38, 52–53, 66, 68, 87, 99, 128, 141, 149, 170, 181, 187–189, 203
economic reform, x–xii, xv–xvi, 17, 39, 59, 72, 87, 97, 141, 150, 155, 167–177, 188
education
    Aboriginal education, xiv, 60, 65, 72, 84–87, 89–93
    and equity, xiii–xiv, 26, 49, 57–62, 65–66, 68, 71, 73
    and the economy, 20, 58–59, 63, 65–67, 70, 73, 75
    curriculum, 63–65
    funding, 61–62, 68
    girls' education, 49, 60, 65, 71–72
    higher education, xiii, 70–81
    school retention, xiv, 26, 49, 59
    vocational education, 60, 64, 75, 81
elections
    1972, 32, 40
    1974, 32
    1983, x, 4, 18, 34, 57, 153–155
    1984, 34, 155
    1987, 34, 58, 66, 99, 129, 153, 157
    1990, 34, 105, 129–130, 153, 158–159
    1993, 105, 112, 129–130, 160
    1996, xv, 175
    2007, 11, 39, 163
employment, xvi, 51, 183–184, 186, 189, 194
    and women, 10, 184–185, 187, 192, 194–195, 213–216, 220–221
    casual, 185–187, 195
    job creation, 191–192, 194
environment policy, xi, xv, 10, 28, 152–163
equal opportunity, xi, xiii, 12, 46, 48, 50, 176–177, 217
    see also affirmative action, sex discrimination, women's policies and rights
exchange rate, 169, 174, 201

federal–state relations, 57, 60, 63–65, 67–68, 91, 131–132, 134, 141, 143, 146–150
FitzGerald report, 99–103, 105

foreign policy
    see international relations
France, 28, 220
Franklin Dam, xi, 10, 153–154, 157
Fraser government, 8, 18, 57–58, 61, 63, 112–113, 128, 141, 154, 168
Fraser, Malcolm, 19, 34, 37, 98, 103
Freudenberg, Graham, xii–xiii, 30–41

Gago, Gail, 219
George, Jennie, 217
Germany, xii, 6
Gillard, Julia, 52, 130–131, 228
globalisation, 27, 59, 67, 74, 167, 215
Gobbo, James, 100, 106–108
Goward, Pru, 49–50
Grassby, Al, 98
Green Party, 153, 160–162
Greiner, Nick, 102–103

Hand, Gerry, 88
Hanson, Pauline, 22, 225
Hawke, Bob
    and emotion, 4, 9, 15
    and sport, 118–120
    and the ALP, 31
    biography, viii–ix, 19, 214, 223–224
    in the ACTU, ix, 16, 18, 26, 106, 112, 116, 199, 213–216, 220
    on Aboriginal affairs, 22, 225
    on Asia, 19–20, 224, 226
    on consensus, 8, 9, 18, 129
    on education, 26–27, 57
    on equality, 10, 47–48, 83, 102, 106, 119, 215, 217
    on immigration, 104, 106
    on international relations, 19–20, 23–25, 27–28, 219–220, 224, 227
    on multiculturalism, 23, 97, 105–106
    on racism, 225
    on reconciliation, 4, 8, 9, 17–19
    on the economy, 5, 8, 17
    popularity, 15, 181
    the negotiator, ix, xii, xvi, 4, 35, 48
Hawke Research Institute, x–xi
Hayden, Bill, ix, 40, 46
health insurance, private, 125, 127, 130–134
health policy, xi, 125–136
Henderson inquiry, 98, 140, 144
higher education, xiii, 70–81

balkanisation, 71, 78

Bradley Review of Higher Education,
    71, 80–81

    research quality assessment, 79–80

    unified national system, 71, 75, 78, 81

Higher Education Contribution Scheme, 71,
    77, 79

Hewson, John, 188, 200

Holding, Clive, 86

housing policy, xv, 140–150

Howard government, x–xi, 3, 8–12, 38–39,
    49, 53, 58, 62, 66–67, 78, 93, 109, 120, 126,
    130, 149, 185–186, 189–191, 193, 208–209,
    227

Howard, John, 12, 22, 103–106, 130, 175, 190,
    200, 225

human rights, 54, 91, 115, 215

immigration, 23, 96–104, 106

industrial relations, xvi, 3, 5, 38, 51, 188–191,
    195, 203, 213

industry policy, 11, 208

inflation, 6, 18, 38, 58, 168–170, 172, 174, 189

interest rates, 168–169, 172–174

International Centre for Muslim and Non-
    Muslim Understanding, 228

International Labour Organization, xvi, 220

international relations, ix, xi, 23–25, 27–28,
    78, 219–220, 224

    enterprise bargaining, 78, 190

international students, 15, 19–20, 71–74, 79

Iraq wars, 23–24, 227

Israel, 24–25, 226–227

Karmel report, 57, 84

Keating, Paul, 6, 8, 21, 34, 87, 143, 153, 157,
    162, 190, 198, 201, 203, 206

Kelly, Ros, 160

Kelty, Bill, 38, 188, 203

Kemp, David, 79

Kennett, Jeff, 103

Kerr, John, 32

Keynesianism, 6–7, 12, 39, 198

Kyoto Protocol, 10

land rights, 21, 83, 109, 225

Liberal Party, 7–8, 32–33, 39, 103–104,
    125–127, 130, 188

    see also Howard government, Fraser
        government

Mabo, 21, 109

    see also land rights

Mandela, Nelson, 223, 228

maternity leave

    see parental leave

Medicare, xiv–xv, 48, 125–126, 128–136

Menzies government, 32, 57

Middle East, 24–25, 226–227

mining, 28, 153, 157, 160, 162

multiculturalism, xiv, 9, 22–23, 96–109

Muslim–non-Muslim relations, 24–25,
    226–228

National Aboriginal and Torres Strait
    Islander Education Policy, 89–90, 93

National Aboriginal Education Committee,
    83–89, 92

National Agenda for a Multicultural
    Australia, xiv, 96–97, 102, 106, 109

National Economic Summit, 11, 17–18,
    37–38, 40, 189

National Housing Strategy, 143–147

National Party, 103–104

Nelson, Brendan, 79–80

neo-liberalism, 6–8, 10–12, 16, 27, 50, 52, 67,
    74, 159–160, 163, 198–200, 202–203

nuclear testing, 220

Obama, Barack, 4, 9, 24, 28

Office of Aboriginal Women, 49

Office of Multicultural Affairs, 100–101,
    106, 108

Office of the Status of Women, 45, 50, 72

Olsen, John, 103

Palestine, 24–25, 226–227

parental leave, 51–54, 216, 218

parliamentary process, xiii, 113–115

Peacock, Andrew, 104–105

Plibersek, Tanya, 53

poverty, 58, 66, 140, 142–144, 149, 223, 226

Powell, Colin, 24

Prices and Incomes Accord, xvi, 18, 47–48,
    61, 128, 135, 170, 188–189, 191, 198, 201,
    203–205

privatisation, 7, 11, 39, 172, 175, 186

racism, 22, 99, 103–104, 225, 228

Rann, Mike, 219, 228

Reagan, Ronald, 39, 74, 200

reconciliation, 4–5, 8, 12, 18–19, 24–25
Richardson, Graham, xv, 120, 152, 154–156, 158–161
Rudd government, 35–36
  challenges for, xi, 51–52, 54, 62, 67–68, 93, 136, 150, 163, 188, 209
  lessons from Hawke era, viii, x–xi, 45
  policies, 11–12, 80–81, 92, 130–132, 149, 191, 193–194, 216
Rudd, Kevin, 11, 228
Ruddock, Philip, 104–105, 109
Ryan, Susan, xiii, 46–47, 51, 58, 61, 65, 70–74, 84, 86–87, 89, 114–117

Sawer, Marion, 50, 53–54, 217
Schools Commission, 60, 62–63, 65, 85
sex discrimination, 46, 49, 72, 108, 113–117, 121, 203–204, 217, 220
Shergold, Peter, 100, 102, 106–107
Sinclair, Ian, 103–104
social democracy, 6, 8, 10–12, 16–17
South Africa, ix, 28, 223
Soviet Union, ix, 39
Special Broadcasting Service, 98–99, 109
sport, 117–120
Staples, Peter, 142
Stone, John, 104
Summers, Anne, xiii, 45, 47, 49
superannuation, 53, 170, 198–210

taxation, xvi, 77, 126, 130, 145, 170–171, 175–176, 188, 193–194, 200, 202, 208–209
terrorism, 24–25, 226, 228
Thatcher, Margaret, 39–40, 74, 200
'Third Way', xii, 3, 6, 10, 13, 17
trade, 27, 104, 157, 169, 175, 180, 188, 194, 207–208, 215, 226

unemployment, 18, 39, 58, 66, 99, 168, 170, 172–174, 180–182, 184, 187–189, 191–195

unions, ix, 3, 7, 12, 17, 38–39, 52, 61, 128, 135, 172, 175, 181, 186, 188, 190, 194–195, 199–200, 202, 204, 208, 212–222
  women in, xvi, 52, 213–221
United Kingdom, xii, 22, 168
United Nations, 23–24, 227
United States, 11, 20, 22, 24–25, 32, 168, 227
Unsworth, Barrie, 30

Vanstone, Amanda, 78
Vietnam War, xii, 32

wage restraint, 12, 38, 129, 170, 189–190, 199, 204–205
welfare policy, 7, 52, 98, 142, 147, 149, 174, 200, 203, 206
White Australia Policy, 15, 20, 23, 97, 105
Whitlam, Gough, 30, 32–34, 36, 40–41, 84
Whitlam government, 5–6, 18, 32, 38, 57, 59–63, 66, 71, 84, 93, 98, 113, 126–127, 141, 168, 176, 192, 199, 201, 220
  dismissal of, 31–32, 112
Wilderness Society, The, 153–158, 162
women and sport, 117–120
Women's Budget Statements, 50, 120
Women's Electoral Lobby, 47
women's movement, xiii, 47, 51, 214–219
women's policies and rights, xi, 12, 45–55, 204, 209, 217
Women's Statistics Unit, 50
Women's Trade Union Network, 219
WorkChoices, 3, 12, 53, 190–191, 195
Working Women's Centres, 216, 221
Wran, Neville, 30, 37, 40–41, 71, 77

Zhang Dejiang, 226
Zhao Ziyang, 19
Zubrzycki, Jerzy, 98